# CONTENTS

**Targeting English Homework**
**Year 3**


ISBN: 978 1 925726 60 2

Published by Pascal Press
PO Box 250
Glebe NSW 2037
www.pascalpress.com.au
contact@pascalpress.com.au

Author: Norah Colvin
Publisher: Lynn Dickinson
Editor: Marie Theodore
Cover Design: Janice Bowles
Typesetter: Stacey Grainger
Images & Illustrations: Dreamstime (unless otherwise indicated)

**Acknowledgements**
Thank you to the publishers, authors and illustrators who generously granted permission for their work to be reproduced in this book.

# Introduction

**Targeting English Homework** aims to build and reinforce English skills. This book supports the ACARA V9 Australian Curriculum for Year 3 and helps children to revise and consolidate what has been taught in the classroom. ACARA codes are shown on each unit, and a chart explaining their content descriptions is on pages v and vi. The inside front and back covers show the topics in each unit.

## The structure of this book

This book has 32 carefully graded double-page units which are divided into three sections:

- ★ Reading and Comprehension – includes a wide variety of literary and cross-curriculum texts
- ★ Grammar and Punctuation
- ★ Phonic & Word Knowledge.

Each unit also includes a Reading Review segment for children to record and rate their home reading books.

**What I'm reading**

Title: ____________________

It's: ☐ a paper book/magazine/comic

☐ an audiobook

☐ online

It's: ☐ imaginative ☐ informative

Rating ☆☆☆☆☆

## Reviews

The last unit in each term features a Review where children are encouraged to consider their opinion of a popular TV show, movie, computer game or book. They are asked in-depth questions about the subject over 4 pages. As responses will vary widely, there are no answers provided for these units (8, 16, 24 and 32). These Reviews are a great way to foster critical thinking skills and encourage reflection.

## Assessment

Term Reviews follow Units 1–8, 9–16, 17–24 and 25–32 to test work covered during the term and allow parents and carers to monitor their child's progress. Children are encouraged to mark each unit as it is completed and to colour in the traffic lights at the end of each segment. These results are then transferred to the Marking Grid. Parents and carers can see at a glance if their child is excelling or struggling!

- **Green** = Excellent — 2 or fewer questions incorrect
- **Orange** = Passing — 50% or more questions answered correctly
- **Red** = Struggling — fewer than 50% correct and needs help

SCORE /18 0-6 8-14 16-18 *Score 2 points for each correct answer!*

# How to Use This Book

The activities in this book are specifically designed to be used at home with minimal resources and support. Helpful explanations of key concepts and skills are provided throughout the book to help understand the tasks. Useful examples of how to do the activities are provided.

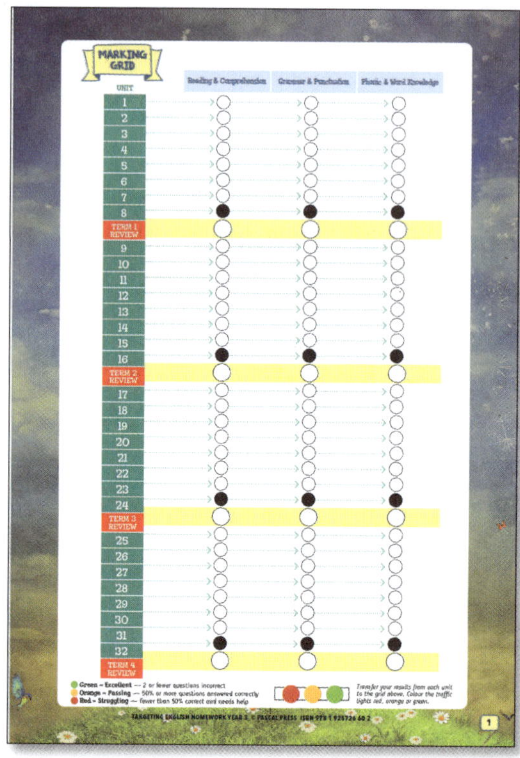


Regular practice of key concepts and skills will support the work your child does in school and will enable you to monitor their progress throughout the year. It is recommended that children complete 8 units per school term (one a week) and then the Term Review. Every unit has a Traffic Light scoreboard at the end of each section.

*Score 2 points for each correct answer!*

You or your child should mark each completed unit and then colour the traffic light that corresponds to the number of correct questions. This process will enable you to see at a glance how your child is progressing and to identify weak spots. The results should be recorded at the end of each term on the Marking Grid on page 1. The Term Review results are important for tracking progress and identifying any improvements in performance. If you find that certain questions are repeatedly causing difficulties and errors, then there is a good reason to discuss this with your child's teacher and arrange for extra instruction in that problem area.

## Home Reading Journal

Each unit provides space for your child to log, review and rate a book they have read during the week. These details can then be transferred to the handy Reading Journal Summary on page 146, which can be photocopied and shared with their teacher or kept as a record.

## Answers

The answer section on pages 147–162 can be removed, stapled together and kept somewhere safe. Use it to check answers when your child has completed each unit. Encourage your child to colour in the Traffic Light boxes when the answers have been calculated.


TARGETING ENGLISH HOMEWORK YEAR 3 © PASCAL PRESS ISBN 978 1 925726 60 2

## Australian Curriculum Correlations Year 3 English

| CODE | CODE DESCRIPTION | Reading & Comprehension UNITS | Grammar & Punctuation UNITS | Phonic & Word Knowledge UNITS |
|---|---|---|---|---|
| **LANGUAGE** | | | | |
| AC9E3LA02 | Understand how the language of evaluation and emotion, such as modal verbs, can be varied to be more or less forceful | | 4, 12, 17, 18, 19, 20, 25, 28 | |
| AC9E3LA06 | Understand that a clause is a unit of grammar usually containing a subject and a verb that need to agree | | 1, 2, 7, 10, 12, 13, 14, 15, 19, 20, 21, 22, 28, 29, 31 | |
| AC9E3LA07 | Understand how verbs represent different processes for doing, feeling, thinking, saying and relating | | 2, 3, 6, 9, 10, 13, 14, 15, 18, 22, 23, 25, 26, 29, 31 | |
| AC9E3LA08 | Understand that verbs are anchored in time through tense | | 3, 6, 30 | 2, 6, 15, 20, 29 |
| AC9E3LA09 | Identify how images extend the meaning of a text | 19, 25 | | |
| AC9E3LA10 | Extend topic-specific and technical vocabulary and know that words can have different meanings in different contexts | | 4, 5, 6, 10, 13, 18, 19, 21, 28, 29, 30 | 21, 22 |
| AC9E3LA11 | Understand that apostrophes signal missing letters in contractions, and apostrophes are used to show singular and plural possession | | | 9 |
| **LITERATURE** | | | | |
| AC9E3LE01 | Discuss characters, events and settings in different contexts in literature by First Nations Australian, and wide-ranging Australian and world authors and illustrators | 15, 19, 25 | | |
| AC9E3LE02 | Discuss connections between personal experiences and character experiences in literary texts and share personal preferences | 1, 3, 4, 8, 9, 14, 15, 16, 17, 18, 24, 25, 27, 28, 32 | | |
| AC9E3LE03 | Discuss how an author uses language and illustrations to portray characters and settings in texts, and explore how the settings and events influence the mood of the narrative | 8, 16, 24, 32 | 7, 11, 17, 23, 27 | |
| AC9E3LE04 | Discuss the effects of some literary devices used to enhance meaning and shape the reader's reaction, including rhythm and onomatopoeia in poetry and prose | | 11, 27 | |
| **LITERACY** | | | | |
| AC9E3LY03 | Identify the audience and purpose of imaginative, informative and persuasive texts through their use of language features and/or images | 1, 2, 3, 4, 5, 6, 7, 8, 9, 10, 11, 12, 13, 14, 15, 16, 17, 18, 19, 20, 21, 22, 23, 24, 25, 26, 27, 28, 29, 30, 31, 32 | | |
| AC9E3LY04 | Read a range of texts using phonic, semantic and grammatical knowledge to read accurately and fluently, re-reading and self-correcting when required | 1, 2, 3, 4, 5, 6, 7, 9, 10, 11, 12, 13, 14, 15, 17, 18, 19, 20, 21, 22, 23, 25, 26, 27, 28, 29, 30, 31 | | |
| AC9E3LY05 | Use comprehension strategies when listening and viewing to build literal and inferred meaning, and begin to evaluate texts by drawing on a growing knowledge of context, text structures and language features | 1, 2, 3, 4, 5, 6, 7, 8, 9, 10, 11, 12, 13, 14, 15, 16, 17, 18, 19, 20, 21, 22, 23, 24, 25, 26, 27, 28, 29, 30, 31, 32 | | |
| AC9E3LY06 | Plan, create, edit and publish imaginative, informative and persuasive written and multimodal texts, using visual features, appropriate form and layout, with ideas grouped in simple paragraphs, mostly correct tense, topic-specific vocabulary and correct spelling of most high-frequency and phonetically regular words | | 2, 14, 20, 31 | 1, 2, 3, 7, 11, 12, 13, 14, 15, 17, 18, 20, 21, 23, 26, 27, 31 |
| AC9E3LY08 | Write words using joined letters that are clearly formed and consistent in size | | | |
| AC9E3LY09 | Understand how to apply knowledge of phoneme–grapheme (sound–letter) relationships, syllables, and blending and segmenting to fluently read and write multisyllabic words with more complex letter patterns | | | 1, 2, 3, 4, 5, 6, 7, 9, 10, 11, 12, 13, 14, 15, 17, 18, 20, 23, 25, 26, 27, 29, 30 |
| AC9E3LY10 | Understand how to apply knowledge of common base words, prefixes, suffixes and generalisations for adding a suffix to a base word to read and comprehend new multimorphemic words | | 2, 20, 21 | 2, 6, 13, 14, 15, 17, 18, 19, 20, 22, 25, 26, 28, 29, 31 |
| AC9E3LY11 | Use phoneme–grapheme (sound–letter) relationships and less common letter patterns to spell words | | | 2, 4, 9, 11, 12, 13, 14, 15, 17, 18, 23, 30 |
| AC9E3LY12 | Recognise and know how to write most high-frequency words including some homophones | | | 1, 2, 4, 9, 12, 15, 17, 18, 19, 21, 22, 23 |

| Australian Curriculum Correlations Year 3 English | | Reading & Comprehension | Grammar & Punctuation | Phonic & Word Knowledge |
|---|---|---|---|---|
| **CODE** | **CODE DESCRIPTION** | **UNITS** | **UNITS** | **UNITS** |
| **CROSS CURRICULAR COMPREHENSION TEXTS** | | | | |
| **HEALTH & PHYSICAL EDUCATION** | | | | |
| AC9HP4P08 | Describe and apply protective behaviours and help-seeking strategies in a range of online and offline situations | 18 | | |
| AC9HP4P10 | Investigate and apply behaviours that contribute to their own and others' health, safety, relationships and wellbeing | 18, 20 | | |
| **HASS INQUIRY AND SKILLS** | | | | |
| AC9HS3S02 | Locate, collect and record information and data from a range of sources, including annotated timelines and maps | 6 | | |
| **HISTORY** | | | | |
| AC9HS3K01 | Causes and effects of changes to the local community, and how people who may be from diverse backgrounds have contributed to these changes | 6, 12, 14, 30 | | |
| **GEOGRAPHY** | | | | |
| AC9HS3K03 | The representation of contemporary Australia as states and territories, and as the Countries/Places of First Nations Australians prior to colonisation, and the locations of Australia's neighbouring regions and countries | 6 | | |
| **CIVICS AND CITIZENSHIP** | | | | |
| AC9HS3K06 | Who makes rules, why rules are important in the school and/or the local community, and the consequences of rules not being followed | 12, 18 | | |
| **SCIENCE** | | | | |
| AC9S3U01 | Compare characteristics of living and non-living things and examine the differences between the life cycles of plants and animals | 6, 12, 13, 21 | | |
| AC9S3U02 | Compare the observable properties of soils, rocks and minerals and investigate why they are important Earth resources | 22, 29, 30 | | |
| AC9S3U04 | Investigate the observable properties of solids and liquids and how adding or removing heat energy leads to a change of state | 10, 26 | | |

AC Australian CURRICULUM



TARGETING ENGLISH HOMEWORK YEAR 3 © PASCAL PRESS ISBN 978 1 925726 60 2

# MARKING GRID

| UNIT | Reading & Comprehension | Grammar & Punctuation | Phonic & Word Knowledge |
|---|---|---|---|
| 1 | | | |
| 2 | | | |
| 3 | | | |
| 4 | | | |
| 5 | | | |
| 6 | | | |
| 7 | | | |
| 8 | | | |
| TERM 1 REVIEW | | | |
| 9 | | | |
| 10 | | | |
| 11 | | | |
| 12 | | | |
| 13 | | | |
| 14 | | | |
| 15 | | | |
| 16 | | | |
| TERM 2 REVIEW | | | |
| 17 | | | |
| 18 | | | |
| 19 | | | |
| 20 | | | |
| 21 | | | |
| 22 | | | |
| 23 | | | |
| 24 | | | |
| TERM 3 REVIEW | | | |
| 25 | | | |
| 26 | | | |
| 27 | | | |
| 28 | | | |
| 29 | | | |
| 30 | | | |
| 31 | | | |
| 32 | | | |
| TERM 4 REVIEW | | | |

**Green** = **Excellent** — 2 or fewer questions incorrect
**Orange** = **Passing** — 50% or more questions answered correctly
**Red** = **Struggling** — fewer than 50% correct and needs help

*Transfer your results from each unit to the grid above. Colour the traffic lights red, orange or green.*

# Reading & Comprehension

AC9E3LY03, AC9E3LY04, AC9E3LY05, AC9E3LE02

## Imaginative text – Anecdote



### Chocolate Crackles

One day, Grandpa texted me. He said he'd like to come for afternoon tea. When Mum went out to get him, I looked in the cupboards. Chocolate crackles were Grandpa's favourites. Mum and I had made them many times before, so I knew what to do. I got out all the ingredients and mixed them together. Then, I put them in the freezer to help them set more quickly.

Grandpa was very happy to see my chocolate crackles. He took two and stuffed them both into his mouth. Suddenly, his eyes began to roll. His belly began to gurgle, and his cheeks puffed up. Then, a whole lot of white froth started coming out of his mouth.

Mum screamed and said, "What did you put in the chocolate crackles?"

I said, "Just the usual."

She ran to the kitchen. "Oh no!" she said. "You put in baking powder. You should have used icing sugar."

I was worried that Grandpa would be really sick. Or worse. But Mum said he'd be okay in a little while. And he was, but he didn't eat any more of my chocolate crackles. Neither did we.

Source: Adapted from *Chocolate Crackles*, Sparklers, Blake Education.

**Shade the bubble next to the correct answer. Write the answer on the line where appropriate.**

1. **When did Grandpa visit?**
   - ◯ morning tea time
   - ◯ lunchtime
   - ◯ afternoon tea time

2. **Why did the writer make chocolate crackles? (Choose any that apply.)**
   - ◯ Chocolate crackles were Grandpa's favourites.
   - ◯ All the ingredients were in the cupboard.
   - ◯ They wanted to see Grandpa froth at the mouth.
   - ◯ They knew what to do.
   - ◯ They wanted to make Grandpa happy.



TARGETING ENGLISH HOMEWORK YEAR 3 © PASCAL PRESS ISBN 978 1 925726 60 2

# Reading & Comprehension



3. **Why did they put the chocolate crackles in the freezer?**
   - ◯ to hide them
   - ◯ to help them set
   - ◯ to cook them

4. **How did Grandpa feel when he saw the chocolate crackles?**
   - ◯ happy
   - ◯ disappointed
   - ◯ worried

5. **How many chocolate crackles did Grandpa eat?**
   - ◯ all of them
   - ◯ two
   - ◯ seven

6. **What did not happen when Grandpa ate the chocolate crackles?**
   - ◯ He started to laugh.
   - ◯ His cheeks puffed up.
   - ◯ His eyes started to roll.
   - ◯ His belly gurgled.
   - ◯ White froth came out of his mouth.

7. **What was the wrong ingredient they put in the chocolate crackles?**
   - ◯ flour
   - ◯ icing sugar
   - ◯ baking powder

8. **What should they have put in the chocolate crackles?**
   - ◯ flour
   - ◯ icing sugar
   - ◯ baking powder

9. **Why didn't they eat more of the chocolate crackles?**
   - ◯ They weren't hungry.
   - ◯ They didn't want to froth at the mouth.
   - ◯ They had to have lunch first.

10. **What do you think?**

What do you think they did with the rest of the chocolate crackles?

______________________________

______________________________

______________________________

______________________________

Why?

______________________________

______________________________

______________________________

______________________________

## What I'm reading

Title: ______________________________

It's: ☐ a paper book/magazine/comic
☐ an audiobook
☐ online

It's: ☐ imaginative ☐ informative

Rating ☆ ☆ ☆ ☆ ☆

Score 2 points for each correct answer!

SCORE /20 0-8 10-16 18-20

UNIT 1

# Grammar & Punctuation

AC9E3LA06

## Sentences

A sentence is a group of words that states a complete thought. It makes sense on its own.

**Circle the two sentences.**

1. One day, Grandpa texted me.
2. for afternoon tea
3. in the freezer
4. Mum screamed.

**Add words to change the two non-sentences into sentences.**

5. ______________________________
6. ______________________________

A statement is a sentence that tells us about everyday things, facts and ideas. A statement begins with a capital letter and ends with a full stop (.).

A question is a sentence that asks for information. It begins with a capital letter and ends with a question mark (?).

**Circle the two questions. Underline the two statements.**

7. What is your name?
8. Where do you live?
9. The shop is across the road from my house.
10. We go to the beach on Sundays.

**Write statements to answer the two questions.**

11. ______________________________
12. ______________________________

**Write questions for the two statements.**

13. ______________________________
14. ______________________________

**Reread *Chocolate Crackles*. Underline any questions you find. Write one on this line.**

15. ______________________________

**Punctuate these sentences correctly with capital letters, full stops or question marks.**

16. why did the elephant cross the road
17. the mouse ran between the elephant's legs

**Draw lines to match these riddle questions with the statements that answer them.**

| | |
|---|---|
| 18. What time was it when the elephant sat on the fence? | They are afraid of the worldwide web. |
| 19. What gives milk and has a horn but is not a cow? | It was time to get a new fence. |
| 20. Why don't flies ever land on computers? | He had no body to go with. |
| 21. Why didn't the skeleton go to the party? | A milk truck has a horn and gives milk. |

Score 2 points for each correct answer! SCORE /42    

0-18 20-36 38-42

TERM 1



TARGETING ENGLISH HOMEWORK YEAR 3 © PASCAL PRESS ISBN 978 1 925726 60 2

# Phonic & Word Knowledge

AC9E3LY06, AC9E3LY09, AC9E3LY12



## Short vowel sounds – a, e, i, o, u

**Say each word. Circle the words that do not have the same short vowel sound.**

| | | | | | |
|---|---|---|---|---|---|
| 1 **ran** | day | crack | grand | made | had |
| 2 **set** | text | tea | went | when | cheeks |
| 3 **in** | him | sick | mix | white | like |
| 4 **lot** | got | both | role | froth | of |
| 5 **mum** | but | you | use | puff | up |

## Long vowel sounds – a, e, i, o, u

**Write the words you circled in the examples above. Write three words that have the same long vowel sound.**

6 ______________________

7 ______________________

8 ______________________

9 ______________________

10 ______________________

## Digraph 'wh'

When two letters together spell one sound, they are called a digraph.

The digraph wh usually spells the w sound. The 'h' is silent.

*Example:* **Wh**ite froth came out of Grandpa's mouth.

Sometimes the digraph wh spells the h sound. The 'w' is silent.

*Example:* **Wh**o ate two chocolate crackles?

**Read these wh words. Colour the words with the w sound green.**

**Colour the words with the h sound yellow.**

| | |
|---|---|
| 11 whole | 17 which |
| 12 while | 18 whose |
| 13 whale | 19 wheel |
| 14 who | 20 whom |
| 15 what | 21 when |
| 16 white | 22 whether |

## Plurals

To make a word plural (more than one), you usually just add –s.

*Example:* crackle, crackles  favourite, favourites

**Write these words as plurals.**

23 table ______________________

24 book ______________________

25 pencil ______________________

26 time ______________________

27 ingredient ______________________

28 eye ______________________

**Choose a singular or plural word from the previous question to complete these sentences.**

29 The cook put all the ______________ back in the cupboard.

30 Tan's left ______________ was very sore.

31 The children put all their ______________ into their pencil cases.

32 I play soccer four ______________ a week.

Score 2 points for each correct answer! SCORE /64  0-30  32-58  60-64

## Informative text – Procedure



# Baked Potatoes

Baked potatoes make a delicious and healthy lunch or snack!

**Ingredients**

- 4 large potatoes
- 2 rashers bacon
- 1 small onion
- 2 tablespoons butter
- 2 tablespoons milk
- Salt and pepper
- 1 tablespoon chopped chives
- Extra butter

**Utensils**

- Fork
- Chopping board
- Knife
- Frying pan
- Tablespoon
- Measuring spoons
- Mixing spoon
- Mixing bowl
- Potato masher
- Baking tray

**Method**

(Ask an adult for help with the chopping and cooking, if needed.)

1. Turn on the oven to heat it to 180 °C.
2. Wash the potatoes until they are clean. Prick them once with a fork.
3. Put the potatoes on a rack in the oven. Cook them for 1¼ hours.
4. Chop the onion and bacon finely. Fry them gently until cooked. Drain.
5. Take the potatoes from the oven. Slice them in half lengthwise. *Caution*: They will be hot!
6. Scoop out the cooked potato, leaving the skins whole. Put the potato in a bowl.
7. Add the butter and milk to the potato. Mash it well. Stir in the salt and pepper, chives and the cooked onion and bacon mixture.
8. Pile the potato mixture back into the potato skins.
9. Put dots of butter on top of the potato.
10. Place the potatoes on a baking tray and bake them in the oven for 15 minutes.

# Reading & Comprehension

TERM 1

**Shade the bubble next to the correct answer.**

1. **What is an ingredient?**
   - ◯ an item of food
   - ◯ a tool to use
   - ◯ a way to do things

2. **What is a utensil?**
   - ◯ an item of food
   - ◯ a tool to use
   - ◯ a way to do things

3. **What is a method?**
   - ◯ an item of food
   - ◯ a tool to use
   - ◯ a way to do things

4. **How many potatoes do you need?**
   - ◯ 1
   - ◯ 2
   - ◯ 4

5. **How many people do you think this recipe will serve?**
   - ◯ 1
   - ◯ 2
   - ◯ 4
   - ◯ more

6. **How hot does the oven need to be?**
   - ◯ 100 °C
   - ◯ 180 °C
   - ◯ 280 °C

7. **What is the first thing you do to the potatoes?**
   - ◯ cook them
   - ◯ wash them
   - ◯ cut them in half

8. **Why might adult help be required? (Choose any that apply.)**
   - ◯ so children don't hurt themselves with sharp knives
   - ◯ so children don't burn themselves
   - ◯ so children share the potatoes with the adults
   - ◯ to make sure the potatoes are clean

9. **How long are the whole potatoes cooked?**
   - ◯ 15 minutes
   - ◯ 1 hour
   - ◯ 1¼ hours
   - ◯ 1½ hours

10. **How long are the potato halves cooked?**
    - ◯ 15 minutes
    - ◯ 1 hour
    - ◯ 1¼ hours
    - ◯ 1½ hours

11. **Separate the ingredients from the utensils.**
    - Circle the ingredients.
    - Underline the utensils.
    - Cross out items that don't belong.

| | |
|---|---|
| pan | table |
| bacon | light |
| cork | bowl |
| better | tray |
| onion | knife |
| milk | pencil |
| chives | masher |
| board | potato |
| fork | silk |
| tablespoon | butter |

## What I'm reading

Title: ______________________

It's: ☐ a paper book/magazine/comic
☐ an audiobook
☐ online

It's: ☐ imaginative ☐ informative

Rating ☆☆☆☆☆

*Score 2 points for each correct answer!* SCORE /22

# Grammar & Punctuation

AC9E3LA06, AC9E3LA07, AC9E3LY06, AC9E3LY10



## Sentences

Remember! A sentence is a group of words that states a complete thought. It makes sense on its own.

A statement tells us about something. It begins with a capital letter and ends with a full stop (.).

A question asks for information. It begins with a capital letter and ends with a question mark (?).

**Punctuate these sentences correctly with capital letters, full stops or question marks.**

1. do you like baked potatoes
2. do you like onions and bacon on baked potatoes
3. we had baked potatoes for lunch on Sunday
4. sometimes we add corn instead of bacon to our baked potatoes

## Exclamations

An exclamation is a sentence that shows surprise, fear, happiness or excitement. Exclamations begin with a capital letter and end with an exclamation mark (!).

**Circle the two exclamations.**

5. Baked potatoes make a delicious and healthy lunch or snack!
6. I would rather have an omelette.
7. You can add corn instead of bacon.
8. Caution: They will be hot!

## Commands

A command is a sentence that tells you to do something. It begins with a capital letter and ends with a full stop (.) or an exclamation mark (!). Commands begin with a doing word or verb.

*Examples:* **Chop** the onion and bacon. **Eat** them while they are hot!

The instructions, or method, in a procedure tell you what to do. They are a series of commands that begin with verbs.

**Reread the method for making baked potatoes. Circle the doing words that begin each command. Write them on these lines.**

9. ______________________

______________________

______________________

**Add words to these doing words to write commands. Use a full stop or exclamation mark at the end.**

10. Run ______________________
11. Put ______________________
12. Take ______________________
13. Close ______________________

**Punctuate this paragraph with full stops, question marks or exclamation marks. (*Hint:* The capital letters will help you find the sentence beginnings.)**

14. What will we have for lunch today I know Let's make baked potatoes They are my favourite Do you like baked potatoes too Which would you prefer

*Score 2 points for each correct answer!* SCORE /28

0-12

14-22

24-28



TARGETING ENGLISH HOMEWORK YEAR 3 © PASCAL PRESS ISBN 978 1 925726 60 2

# Phonic & Word Knowledge

AC9E3LA08, AC9E3LY06, AC9E3LY09, AC9E3LY10, AC9E3LY11, AC9E3LY12

TERM 1

## Short vowel sounds – a, e, i, o, u

**Say each word. Circle the words that do not have the same short vowel sound.**

| | | | | | |
|---|---|---|---|---|---|
| (1) **add** | pan | rack | bake | snack | place |
| (2) **well** | them | be | heat | help | when |
| (3) **milk** | mix | if | knife | slice | prick |
| (4) **hot** | bowl | on | top | coal | dots |
| (5) **cut** | plus | you | use | but | up |

**Choose words from the lists in questions 1–5 to complete these sentences.**

(6) Be careful to not cut yourself when you are using a __________.

(7) You might need an adult to __________ with the cutting.

(8) Three __________ four makes seven.

(9) I went over to Jack's __________ to play.

(10) You turn on the oven first so it will be __________.

## Adding -ed and -ing

A command tells you what to do.
*Example:* Wash the potatoes.

When you are following the command, you add -ing.
*Example:* I am wash**ing** the potatoes.

When you have done the action, you add -ed.
*Example:* I wash**ed** the potatoes.

**Add endings to these commands to tell what you are doing and what you did. The first one is done for you.**

| | Command | Doing now (present tense) | Did (past tense) |
|---|---|---|---|
| | Wash the potatoes. | I am washing the potatoes. | I washed the potatoes. |
| (11) | Turn on the oven. | | |
| (12) | Mix in the onion. | | |
| (13) | Mash the potato. | | |
| (14) | Add the milk. | | |
| (15) | Scoop out the potato. | | |

## High-frequency words

High frequency words occur frequently in text. It is good to memorise them so that you recognise them by sight.

**Word search. Circle these high-frequency words in the grid.**

until they them are with once
put for half from

**Words go left to right or top to bottom.**

| | | | | | | | |
|---|---|---|---|---|---|---|---|
| U | N | T | I | L | I | W | L |
| I | K | H | A | R | E | I | E |
| T | H | E | M | P | U | T | T |
| F | O | Y | E | H | A | H | T |
| O | N | C | E | A | B | A | K |
| R | E | D | P | L | O | T | A |
| T | O | E | S | F | R | O | M |

(16) When you have found all the words, the remaining letters (from left to right and top to bottom) will spell out a sentence. Write it here.

______________________________

______________________________

______________________________

______________________________

*Score 2 points for each correct answer!* SCORE /32 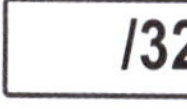 0-14  16-26  28-32

AC9E3LY03, AC9E3LY04, AC9E3LY05, AC9E3LE02

## Imaginative text – Narrative



### Batbat

Toby was staying at his Gran's house. He was sleeping on his own in the back room. It felt like he was miles away from everybody else. He had never slept in such a big room before or such a big bed.

He looked towards the doorway. A small crack of light was coming in from the hall. The light turned everything in the room into strange, large shapes.

Gran had tucked him in so tightly that he couldn't move. He had to wriggle to get his arms free. On the chair beside the bed, there was a shape he hadn't seen in a long time.

It was Batbat, the teddy Gran had made for him when he was little. Batbat was no ordinary teddy. For a start, he didn't look anything like a bear. He had long limbs and big paws. His body was thin and striped. His ears were floppy like a rabbit's, and he had a face like a bat's.

Toby reached out and grabbed Batbat. He brought him in under the covers. With Batbat by his side, he didn't feel so alone. He settled in and tried to wish himself to sleep.

It was no good.

Source: Adapted from *The Heebie Jeebie*, Gigglers, pages 12–16, Blake Education.



TARGETING ENGLISH HOMEWORK YEAR 3 © PASCAL PRESS ISBN 978 1 925726 60 2

# Reading & Comprehension



**Shade the bubble next to the correct answer. Write the answer on the line where appropriate.**

1. **Where was Toby staying?**
   - ◯ at school camp
   - ◯ at his Gran's house
   - ◯ at home

2. **Where was Toby sleeping?**
   - ◯ in the back room
   - ◯ on the verandah
   - ◯ in his Gran's room

3. **How do you think Toby felt about sleeping there?**
   - ◯ excited
   - ◯ alone
   - ◯ grown-up

4. **Where was the light coming from?**
   - ◯ Gran's room
   - ◯ the hall
   - ◯ the kitchen

5. **Why couldn't Toby move?**
   - ◯ He was scared.
   - ◯ His legs hurt.
   - ◯ His Gran tucked him in too tight.

6. **What was on the chair beside Toby?**
   - ◯ his favourite toy
   - ◯ an old toy
   - ◯ his Gran

7. **What was Batbat?**
   - ◯ a rabbit
   - ◯ a teddy
   - ◯ a bat

8. **Which of these words and phrases describe Batbat? (Choose any that apply.)**
   - ◯ ordinary
   - ◯ old
   - ◯ long, floppy ears
   - ◯ short legs and big paws
   - ◯ striped body

9. **What did Toby wish for?**
   - ◯ to fall asleep
   - ◯ his Gran would come
   - ◯ a new bear

10. **What do you think?**

    Why do you think Toby couldn't fall asleep?

    ______________________________

    ______________________________

    What do you do if **you** can't fall asleep?

    ______________________________

    ______________________________

    What do you think Toby should do?

    ______________________________

    ______________________________

## What I'm reading

Title: ______________________________

It's: ☐ a paper book/magazine/comic
☐ an audiobook
☐ online

It's: ☐ imaginative ☐ informative

Rating ☆ ☆ ☆ ☆ ☆

Score 2 points for each correct answer!

SCORE /20 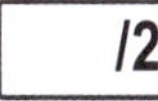 0-8 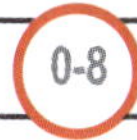 10-14  16-20 

UNIT 3

# Grammar & Punctuation

AC9E3LA07, AC9E3LA08

TERM 1

## Verbs

Every sentence has a verb. Verbs tell us what is happening in a sentence.

*Example:* Toby **looked** towards the doorway.

**Circle the verbs in these sentences.**

1. Toby slept in the back room.
2. The light shone under the door.
3. Toby wriggled his arms.
4. Toby saw Batbat on the chair.
5. Toby got Batbat into bed with him.

## Verb groups

A verb group has more than one verb. It is made up of a main verb and a helper verb.

*Example:* Toby **was staying** at his Gran's house.

(was = helper verb, staying = main verb)

The helper verb is called an auxiliary verb.

**Underline the verb groups in these sentences.**

6. Toby was sleeping on his own in the back room.
7. A small crack of light was coming in from the hall.
8. Gran had tucked him into bed.
9. Gran had made Batbat for Toby.
10. Batbat didn't look like a bear.

## Helper verbs – Time

Some helper verbs tell us about time – whether things are happening in the present, the past or the future.

*Examples:*

| | |
|---|---|
| Toby **is staying** at his Gran's house. | (present) |
| Toby **was staying** at his Gran's house. | (past) |
| Toby **will stay** at his Gran's house. | (future) |

**Underline the verb groups in these sentences. Circle whether they are happening in the present, past or future.**

11. Toby was wriggling to get his arms free.
    present past future
12. Toby will keep Batbat in bed with him.
    present past future
13. Gran is sleeping in another part of the house.
    present past future

## Simple past and past continuous tense

Simple past tense tells us about something that happened at a definite time.

*Example:* Gran **tucked** Toby into bed.

Past continuous tense tells us about something that happened for a time in the past.

*Example:* Toby **was staying** at his Gran's house.

**Read these sentences. Write S for simple past tense and C for past continuous tense.**

14. _____ Toby looked at the strange, large shapes in the room.
15. _____ Toby was looking at the strange, large shapes in the room.

*Score 2 points for each correct answer!*

SCORE /30   

0-12 14-24 26-30



TARGETING ENGLISH HOMEWORK YEAR 3 © PASCAL PRESS ISBN 978 1 925726 60 2

AC9E3LY06, AC9E3LY09

## Digraphs

When two letters together spell one sound, they are called a digraph.

These digraphs can spell the sound at the beginning of words and at the end:

- sh **sh**ape wi**sh**
- th **th**in wi**th**
- ch **ch**air su**ch**

The digraph ng spells the sound at the end of lo**ng**. It does not appear at the beginning of words.

**Which of these digraphs form words with the word endings? Draw lines to match. Write the words on the lines below.**

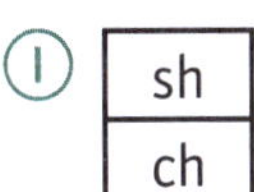

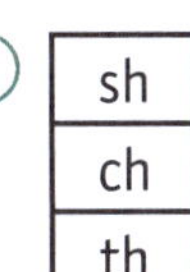

| | | | | | | | |
|---|---|---|---|---|---|---|---|
| 1 | sh / ch / th | op | 2 | sh / ch / th | in | 3 | sh / ch / th | at |

______________________

______________________

______________________

**Which of these digraphs form words with the word beginnings? Draw lines to match. Write the words on the lines below.**

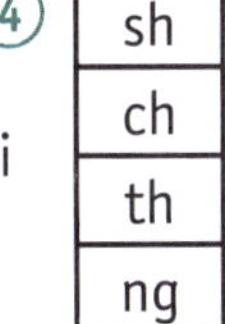

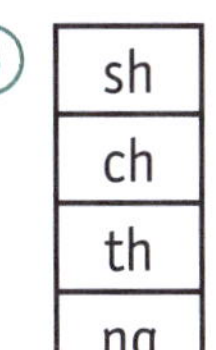

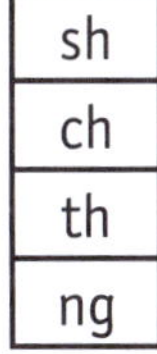

| | | | | | | | | |
|---|---|---|---|---|---|---|---|---|
| 4 | wi | sh / ch / th / ng | 5 | su | sh / ch / th / ng | 6 | ga | sh / ch / th / ng |

______________________

______________________

______________________

## Two-letter and three-letter consonant blends

In digraphs, the letters spell just one sound.

In a blend, each of the letters represents its own sound. Each letter is sounded separately and then blended.

*Examples:*

**sl**eeping — We pronounce **s** + **l** and blend them in the word **sl**eeping.
Toby was **sl**eeping in the back room.

**str**ange — We pronounce **s** + **t** + **r** and blend them in the word **str**ange.
The light turned everything into **str**ange shapes.

**Read these words. Write D if the letters in bold are a digraph. Write B if they are a blend.**

7. **st**aying ________
8. **sl**ept ________
9. **sm**all ________
10. **sh**apes ________
11. **th**in ________
12. **ch**air ________
13. **str**iped ________
14. **fl**oppy ________

## Compound words

A compound word is two words joined together to make one word.

*Example:* door + **way** = door**way**

**Make compound words by joining way to these words.**

15. hall ______________
16. motor ______________
17. air ______________
18. cause ______________
19. clear ______________
20. stair ______________

*Score 2 points for each correct answer!*

SCORE /40

AC9E3LY03, AC9E3LY04, AC9E3LY05, AC9E3LE02

## Persuasive text – Book review

TERM 1

### Whodunnit, Eddie Woo? Time Out! (Book #1)

Authors: Eddie Woo and Jess Black
Pan Macmillan, 2022
ISBN: 9781760982997

*Time Out!* is the first book in the *Whodunnit, Eddie Woo?* series.

It is a fun adventure story for young readers who love to solve mysteries.

Eddie Woo, the main character, loves maths, adventure and solving mysteries. His best friends, Rusty and DT, do too. They work together as a team of super-sleuths.

In *Time Out!*, Eddie and his friends search for lost treasure. It all begins with a clue that Eddie finds hidden in an old piano at school. Each clue leads to another clue with another mystery to solve and another exciting adventure.

Soon they discover that others are looking for the treasure too. The super-sleuths must find it first, but the others try to stop them. The team uses their wits to stay out of danger. They face their fears and go on.

In the end, the super sleuths win. They solve the mystery, and they earn their place in history.

*Time Out!* is a great book for bookworms and math nerds alike!

I give it 5 stars. It is suitable for readers over 7 years.



TARGETING ENGLISH HOMEWORK YEAR 3 © PASCAL PRESS ISBN 978 1 925726 60 2

# Reading & Comprehension

TERM 1

Write your answers on the lines provided.

1. What is the title of the book?

2. Who wrote the book?

3. Who published the book? When?

4. What is the International Standard Book Number (ISBN)?

5. Who is the main character?

6. What do you know about the main character?

7. Who are some other characters in the book?

8. Write three words to describe the type of story.

9. Did the reviewer enjoy the book? How do you know?

10. What do you think?

Do you think you would like to read this book? Explain your reasons.

## What I'm reading

Title

It's: ☐ a paper book/magazine/comic
☐ an audiobook
☐ online

It's: ☐ imaginative ☐ informative

Rating ☆ ☆ ☆ ☆ ☆

Score 2 points for each correct answer!

SCORE /20 0-8 10-14 16-20

# Grammar & Punctuation

AC9E3LA02, AC9E3LA10

## Nouns and proper nouns

Nouns are the names of things.

Remember! Common nouns are words used to name people, animals, places and things.

*Examples:* book, story, publisher, mystery, maths, people

Proper nouns are the names of particular people, places, objects and events. Proper nouns begin with a capital letter.

*Examples:* Pan Macmillan, Eddie Woo, Jess Black, Australia, Olympics Games

**Are these words common nouns or proper nouns? Write CN next to the common nouns. Write PN next to the proper nouns.**

1. Sydney Harbour _____
2. land _____
3. Anthony Albanese _____
4. March _____
5. Uluru _____
6. road _____
7. pencil _____
8. Australia Day _____
9. marching band _____
10. elephant _____

**Read these paragraphs. Underline the common nouns. Circle the proper nouns.**

11. Eddie Woo is a maths teacher. He lives in Sydney, Australia. He likes to help people learn maths. He posts a lot of maths lessons on YouTube. He writes a lot of books about mathematics too.

In the book, *Time Out*, Eddie Woo is the main character. His best friends are Rusty and DT. The character in the book is not the real Eddie Woo. But just like the real Eddie Woo, he likes maths and likes to solve problems too.

**Write one proper noun for each of these words.**

12. person ____________________
13. place ____________________
14. object ____________________
15. event ____________________

## Emotive words

In a book review, emotive words are used to convince the reader to feel the same way about the book as the writer does. The words will be positive if the writer enjoyed the book or negative if they did not enjoy it.

*Examples:* great, best, funny, worst, awful

**Reread the review of *Time Out* by Eddie Woo and Jess Black. Circle the emotive words that try to convince you the book is good. Write them here.**

16. ____________________

____________________

____________________

____________________

____________________

____________________

____________________

17. **Read these emotive words. Use green to circle the positive words. Use red to circle the negative words.**

| | |
|---|---|
| funny | scary |
| strange | horrible |
| boring | great |
| exciting | best |
| fantastic | worst |
| unbelievable | wonderful |
| dreadful | |

Score 2 points for each correct answer! SCORE /34   

TARGETING ENGLISH HOMEWORK YEAR 3 © PASCAL PRESS ISBN 978 1 925726 60 2

# Phonic & Word Knowledge

AC9E3LY09, AC9E3LY11, AC9E3LY12

TERM 1

## Vowel sound 'oo'

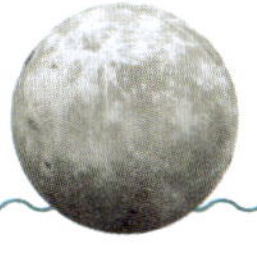

There are different ways of spelling the vowel sound oo as in Woo and moon.

*Examples:* clue, do, suitable, super, sleuth

**Read the words. Draw lines to match them to the pictures. Underline the part of the word that spells the oo sound.**

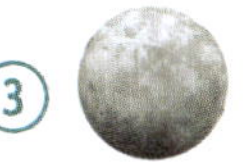

| Picture | Word | Picture | Word |
|---|---|---|---|
| 1 | moon | 6 | flute |
| 2 | screw | 7 | sleuth |
| 3 | glue | 8 | school |
| 4 | fruit | 9 | boot |
| 5 | stew | 10 | suit |

**Choose oo words from the box to complete the sentences.**

soon clue too two suitable do sleuth to

11. We will be going ________ the beach on the weekend.
12. Eddie Woo found a ________ for a mystery to solve.
13. Bare feet are not ________ for playing soccer.
14. I brought ________ apples, one for me and one for a friend.
15. It is getting dark. It will be night-time ________.

## Vowel sound 'er'

There are different ways of spelling the vowel sound er as in fern.

*Examples:* first, work, search, earn, nerd

**Look at the pictures and read the words. Underline the parts that spell the er sound.**

16. worm 17. bird 18. surf 19. nurse 20. pearl

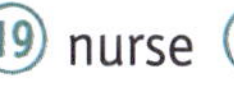

21. shirt 22. church 23. skirt 24. fern 25. Earth

## Consonants – The letter c

We usually think of the letter c representing the hard 'ck' sound, as in cat.

It can also represent the soft c sound, as in cent.

It combines with the letter 'h' to make the digraph ch, as in chips.

Sometimes the digraph ch represents the hard 'ck' sound, as in character.

**Read these words. Underline the letter c or ch. Write C if you hear the hard 'ck' sound (cat), S if you hear the soft 'c' sound (cent), and CH if you hear 'ch' (chips).**

26. ice _____
27. character _____
28. place _____
29. chicken _____
30. school _____
31. discover _____
32. city _____
33. clue _____
34. search _____

*Score 2 points for each correct answer!* SCORE /68

0-32 34-62 64-68

## Informative text – Table

## Billy's Takeaway Menu

OPEN LUNCH & DINNER

# BILLY'S TAKEAWAY

7 DAYS 10 am — 8 pm

Fast Food • Fish & Chips

| Seafood | | Burgers | |
|---|---|---|---|
| Cod (battered, crumbed, grilled) | $8.50 | Plain Burger (BBQ sauce) | $8.50 |
| Calamari Rings | $0.90 | Burger with the Lot (BBQ sauce) | $10.50 |
| Prawn Cutlets | $2.20 | Chicken Burger (mayo) | $9.50 |
| Crab Claw | $2.50 | Steak Burger (BBQ sauce) | $9.50 |
| Scallops | $4.00 | Fish Burger (mayo) | $9.00 |
| Fish Sticks | $2.50 | Vegan Burger (mayo) | $9.50 |

| Sides | | Drinks | |
|---|---|---|---|
| Hot Chips | Small $2.50 Large $5.00 | Soft Drinks | $3.80 |
| Potato Scallop | $1.20 | Juice (orange, apple, pineapple) | $5.00 |
| Garden Salad | $5.00 | Bottled Water | $4.60 |
| Gravy | Small $1.50 Large $2.50 | Milkshakes (van, choc, straw) | $6.50 |

All menu items available for delivery or pick-up.

Order by phone, online or instore.

Allow 25–40 minutes for delivery.

Allow 20 minutes for pick-up instore.



TARGETING ENGLISH HOMEWORK YEAR 3 © PASCAL PRESS ISBN 978 1 925726 60 2

## Reading & Comprehension

TERM 1

**Shade the bubble next to the correct answer. Write the answer on the line where appropriate.**

1. **Where would you see a menu like this?**
   - ◯ in a café
   - ◯ in an expensive restaurant
   - ◯ in a takeaway store

2. **Can you sit in the store to eat the food you buy?**
   - ◯ Yes
   - ◯ No
   - ◯ Maybe

3. **Explain your reason for answer 2.**

   ______________________________

   ______________________________

   ______________________________

   ______________________________

4. **What is the main food that the store sells?**
   - ◯ fast food
   - ◯ dairy food
   - ◯ fruit and vegetables

5. **How many different types of seafood can you buy at the store?**
   - ◯ four
   - ◯ five
   - ◯ six

6. **Which burger is the most expensive?**
   - ◯ vegan burger
   - ◯ burger with the lot
   - ◯ chicken burger

7. **Explain why it might be the most expensive.**

   ______________________________

   ______________________________

   ______________________________

   ______________________________

8. **How can you place your order? (Choose any that apply.)**
   - ◯ by phone
   - ◯ online
   - ◯ in-store

9. **How do you think the orders may be delivered? (Choose any that apply.)**
   - ◯ by car
   - ◯ by bicycle
   - ◯ by parachute
   - ◯ by foot
   - ◯ by drone

10. **What do you think?**

    Why do you think you need to allow more time for your order to be delivered than if you pick it up instore?

    ______________________________

    ______________________________

    ______________________________

    ______________________________

### What I'm reading

Title: ______________________________

It's: ☐ a paper book/magazine/comic
☐ an audiobook
☐ online

It's: ☐ imaginative ☐ informative

Rating ☆ ☆ ☆ ☆ ☆

*Score 2 points for each correct answer!*

SCORE  /20  0-8  10-14  16-20

# Grammar & Punctuation



AC9E3LA10

## Lists and commas

Items on a list, like a menu, may be written below each other.

On a formal list, like a menu or advertisement, they usually begin with a capital letter.

On an informal list, like a shopping list or a spelling list, they do not have a capital letter.

**Write the items for these lists below each other. Use capital letters if needed.**

1. At the car wash, we will: wash, polish, vacuum, wash the windows
2. Things to remember: feed the cat, walk the dog, water the plants, relax
3. Bring on Friday: swimmers, towel, bathing cap, sunscreen
4. Available instore: mobile phones, headphones, speakers, computers

**1** ANDY'S CAR WASH
We will:

______________
______________
______________
______________

**2** Things to remember

______________
______________
______________
______________

**3** Bring on Friday

______________
______________
______________
______________

**4** ON SALE NOW!

______________
______________
______________
______________

## Commas

Commas (,) are used to separate the items in a list that is written in a sentence. We do not put a comma before **and** and the last item.

*Example:* I must feed the cat, walk the dog, water the plants and then relax.

**Add the missing commas in these sentences.**

5. At school, we do maths reading writing HASS PE and art.
6. I play soccer after school on Monday Wednesday and Friday.
7. My friends Kristin Casey Jamie Trang and Tema came over to my house last night.
8. At the shop, I bought some bread milk apples bananas and ice-cream.
9. To make a cake, you need flour butter sugar eggs milk and salt.
10. This is the best book I've ever read. It's funny sad scary and spooky.

## Abbreviations

Abbreviations are a short way of writing words. They don't take up as much space, but they can be confusing if you don't know what they mean. Abbreviations do not have full stops.

*Example:* **Mon** is an abbreviation for Monday.
**am** is an abbreviation that means morning.

**Abbreviations are used on Billy's takeaway menu. Write the meaning beside each abbreviation.**

11. pm ____________
12. BBQ ____________
13. mayo ____________
14. van ____________
15. choc ____________
16. straw ____________

Score 2 points for each correct answer! SCORE /32

TARGETING ENGLISH HOMEWORK YEAR 3 © PASCAL PRESS ISBN 978 1 925726 60 2

AC9E3LY09



## Words with double letters

**All the words below in the word bank have double letters.**

| | | | |
|---|---|---|---|
| batter | glitter | scallop | bottle |
| butter | pepper | bubble | sudden |
| happen | soccer | letter | funny |
| swimmers | shopping | ribbon | middle |
| wriggle | traffic | | |

**Write two words from the word bank that have the same vowel sound before the double letters as each of these words.**

1. madder ______________ ______________
2. fitted ______________ ______________
3. hotter ______________ ______________
4. redder ______________ ______________
5. puddle ______________ ______________

**Choose words from the word bank to complete these sentences.**

6. I don't know what will ______________ after I finish my work.
7. We always take water in a ______________ when we play sport.
8. My baby brother likes popping the ______________ wrap.
9. We were late getting home because there was a lot of ______________.
10. I laugh a lot when my mum tells jokes because they are so ______________.

## Syllables

Syllables are chunks of sounds in words. We can tell how many chunks of sounds there are in a word by clapping the beats.

**Each word from the word bank has two syllables. How many syllables do each of these words have?**

11. chips ____ 12. chicken ____ 13. burger ____
14. fish ____ 15. scallop ____ 16. grilled ____

## The letter c

Remember! The letter c can be used to represent different sounds: the hard 'ck' sound, as in cat; the soft 'c' sound, as in cent; the digraph 'ch', as in chips.

**Read these words. Underline the letter c or the letters ch. Write C if you hear the hard 'ck' sound, S if you hear the soft 'c' sound, and CH if you hear 'ch'.**

17. scallops ___
18. cod ___
19. sticks ___
20. cutlets ___
21. chicken ___
22. crumbed ___
23. chop ___
24. chocolate ___
25. crab ___

*Score 2 points for each correct answer!* SCORE /50    

AC9E3LY03, AC9E3LY04, AC9E3LY05, AC9HS3S02, AC9HS3K01, AC9HS3K03, AC9S3U01

## Informative text – Report



# The Cane Toad

Cane toads are not native Australian animals. They were brought to Australia in 1935 from Hawaii. Farmers in North Queensland wanted the toads to eat the beetles that were eating their sugarcane crops. Sadly, the cane toad liked other food better.

The cane toad arrived in Australia to get rid of a pest. Now it is a pest. There were just 100 cane toads in Australia in 1935. In 2015, there were more than 200 million.

The cane toad harms Australia's small native animals in many ways. It eats their food. It even eats them. But there are no animals in Australia that eat cane toads. Sometimes birds or reptiles think cane toads look good to eat. But they are not. They are poisonous. If an animal eats a cane toad, it dies.

We need to stop the spread of cane toads. Cane toads like dark and damp places. They hide under logs and pot plants. They lay their eggs in water. Think about ways you can make your home a cane toad-free zone. But remember, they are living creatures so always treat them humanely.

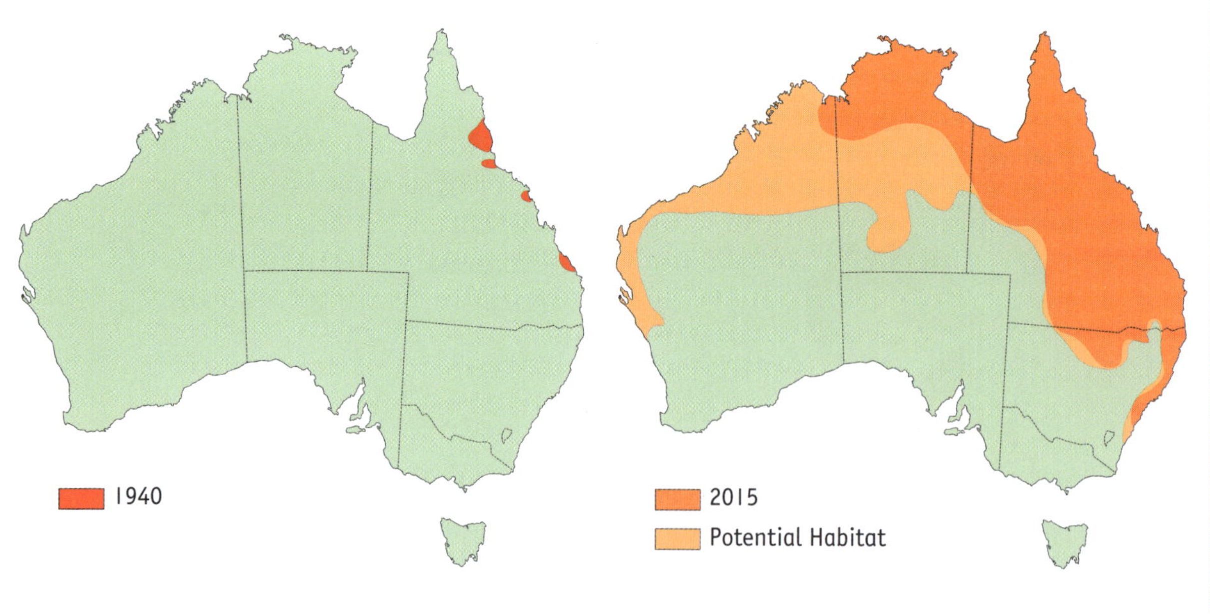


Source: Adapted from *Terry the Toad*, Rebecca Johnson, Pascal Press.



TARGETING ENGLISH HOMEWORK YEAR 3 © PASCAL PRESS ISBN 978 1 925726 60 2

# Reading & Comprehension

TERM 1

Shade the bubble next to the correct answer.

① Are cane toads native Australian animals?

- ◯ Yes
- ◯ No

② When were cane toads first brought to Australia?

- ◯ 1935
- ◯ 2000
- ◯ 2015

③ Where did cane toads come from?

- ◯ Australia
- ◯ New Zealand
- ◯ Hawaii
- ◯ Queensland

④ Why were cane toads brought to Australia?

- ◯ to eat sugar cane
- ◯ to eat the sugarcane beetles
- ◯ to kill native animals

⑤ Did the plan work?

- ◯ Yes
- ◯ No

⑥ Why?

- ◯ The cane toads didn't like the sugarcane beetles.
- ◯ The cane toads ate too much sugar cane.
- ◯ The cane toads went back to Hawaii.

⑦ In which parts of Australia did cane toads live in 1940? (Choose any that apply.)

- ◯ New South Wales
- ◯ Victoria
- ◯ Queensland
- ◯ Northern Territory
- ◯ Western Australia
- ◯ South Australia
- ◯ Tasmania

⑧ In which parts of Australia did cane toads live in 2015? (Choose any that apply.)

- ◯ New South Wales
- ◯ Victoria
- ◯ Queensland
- ◯ Northern Territory
- ◯ Western Australia
- ◯ South Australia
- ◯ Tasmania

⑨ Which is **not** a reason for stopping the spread of cane toads in Australia?

- ◯ They are ugly.
- ◯ They are poisonous to native Australian animals.
- ◯ They eat food that native Australian animals need to eat.
- ◯ They eat native Australian animals.

⑩ You are told to treat cane toads **humanely**. Choose a word that means the same.

- ◯ friendlily
- ◯ kindly
- ◯ meanly
- ◯ cruelly

## What I'm reading

Title: ______________________________

It's: ☐ a paper book/magazine/comic
☐ an audiobook
☐ online

It's: ☐ imaginative ☐ informative

Rating ☆ ☆ ☆ ☆ ☆

*Score 2 points for each correct answer!* SCORE /20

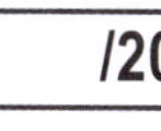

# Grammar & Punctuation



AC9E3LA07, AC9E3LA08, AC9E3LA10

## Noun groups

A noun group is a group of words built around a noun. Noun groups give more information about the main noun.

*Example:* small Australian animals

noun group — noun

**Underline the noun groups built around the noun in bold.**

1. Cane toads like dark and damp **places**.
2. Make your home a toad-free **zone**.
3. **Farmers** in North Queensland grow sugar cane.
4. Australia is a wide, brown **land**.
5. It is important to keep your pets away from poisonous cane **toads**.

## Subject, verb and object

Every sentence has a verb. Verbs tell us what is happening in a sentence. They tell us what the subject of a sentence is doing, thinking, saying and feeling.

*Example:* Cane toads **harm** small Australian animals.

**Cane toads** is the subject (who or what the sentence is about).

What do cane toads do? They **harm**.

Many subjects also have an object. The subject does the action to the object. The object usually follows the verb.

*Example:*

Cane toads **harm** small Australian animals.

subject — verb — object

Cane toads harm **(what?)** small Australian animals.

Subjects and objects can be single nouns, noun groups or pronouns.

**Underline the subject (noun, noun group or pronoun) in each sentence. Circle the verb. Then highlight the object. (Hint: Ask who or what after the verb to find the object.)**

6. Beetles were eating the sugar cane.
7. Cane toads eat small animals.
8. They like dark and damp places.
9. Farmers in North Queensland grow sugar cane.
10. Beware! Dogs and cats may chase cane toads.

## Relating verbs

Relating verbs help to link information in a sentence. They include verbs like am, is, are, were, was, have, has.

*Example:* The cane toad **is** a pest. Cane toads **have** poison glands.

**Read this paragraph. Circle the relating verbs. Can you find eight? Write them on the lines below.**

Australia is home to more than 200 native frogs. Most Australian frogs are not found anywhere else in the world. Australia has no native toads. The only toad in Australia is the cane toad. It is a pest. It eats Australian frogs. It eats their food too. Most Australian frogs are not poisonous, but the cane toad is poisonous. It has poison glands on its back and neck.

11. ______
12. ______
13. ______
14. ______
15. ______
16. ______
17. ______
18. ______

*Score 2 points for each correct answer!*

SCORE /36 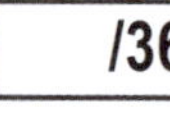   

TARGETING ENGLISH HOMEWORK YEAR 3 © PASCAL PRESS ISBN 978 1 925726 60 2

# Phonic & Word Knowledge

UNIT 6

AC9E3LA08, AC9E3LY09, AC9E3LY10

TERM 1

## Long vowel sounds – a, e, i, o, u

Long vowel sounds, in which the sound is the name of the letter, are often spelled with a split digraph. However, long e is not often spelled with a split digraph.

*Examples:* cane  hide  zone  cute

There are other ways of spelling these long vowel sounds.

**Read the words in the word bank. The sound of each long vowel is the name of a letter.**

| | | | | |
|---|---|---|---|---|
| cane | eat | hide | zone | cute |
| came | beetles | pie | home | huge |
| rain | need | find | toad | mule |
| place | treat | right | row | use |
| may | free | fly | dough | new |

**Write words from the word bank to complete these sentences.**

1. Cane toads like to ____________ in dark and damp places.
2. The farmers didn't like the ____________ eating their sugar cane.
3. Try to make your home a toad-free ____________.
4. Cane toads are not very ____________.
5. Cane toads first ____________ to Australia in 1935.

## Verb tense – Adding –ing and –ed

For most verbs, when we change tense between present and past, we simply add –ing or –ed to the base verb.

*Example:* harm  harm**ing**  harm**ed**

When the base verb ends with –e, we leave off the 'e' and add –ing or –ed.

*Example:* like  lik**ing**  lik**ed**

When the base verb has one vowel followed by one consonant, we double the consonant before adding –ing and –ed.

*Example:* stop  stop**ping**  stop**ped**

**Add endings to these base verbs to show present tense and past tense.**

| | Base verb | Doing now (present tense) | Did (past tense) |
|---|---|---|---|
| 6 | want | | |
| 7 | arrive | | |
| 8 | hop | | |
| 9 | jump | | |
| 10 | live | | |

## Irregular verbs

Some verbs are irregular and don't follow the usual pattern for past tense. Instead of adding –ed, the verb changes.

*Example:* Today I **think**. I am **thinking**. Yesterday I thought.

**Draw lines to match the base verb with its past tense verb.**

| | |
|---|---|
| 11 catch | brought |
| 12 make | hid |
| 13 bring | caught |
| 14 eat | laid |
| 15 hide | ate |
| 16 lay | made |

*Score 2 points for each correct answer!* SCORE /32   

# Reading & Comprehension

AC9E3LY03, AC9E3LY04, AC9E3LY05

## Imaginative text – Science fiction



### Ready to Go!

This story is an excerpt from *A Step in Time* in the Time Quest series by Del Merrick.

*The street is dark and empty. In a backyard shed, a light shines under the door. Inside, Sid Smekkles and his friend, Bee, are working on a machine on the floor of the shed. The clock on the wall says 2:00 am. A storm wind rattles the tin roof.*

"Well, Sid, almost done," says Bee, fitting a glass porthole into the front of the machine.

"Yes, at last," says Sid, rubbing his hands together happily.

The machine looks like a shiny, green egg on four short, steel legs. Inside is a control panel with a screen and rows of buttons and levers.

"Let's check it out," says Sid, stepping up into the machine.

"Control panel. Check!" calls Bee.

Sid presses buttons and pushes levers.

"Check!" he calls back.

"Tracking system. Check!" calls Bee.

Sid switches on the computer and data trails across the screen.

"Check!" he calls back.

"Wave communicator. Check!" calls Bee.

Sid speaks into his headset. His voice crackles from a box behind Bee.

"Check!" Bee laughs.

"Well, Bee, I think we've done it," Sid chuckles.

"Yes, Sid, I think we have. This is one mean machine!" says Bee.

"Quickly, Bee, let's test it out," Sid says.

Outside, the storm is loud and angry. Lightning flashes and thunder rumbles.

Rain begins to drum on the tin roof.

Source: Excerpt from *A Step in Time*, Time Quest Series, Blake Education.



TARGETING ENGLISH HOMEWORK YEAR 3 © PASCAL PRESS ISBN 978 1 925726 60 2

# Reading & Comprehension



Use these clues to complete the crossword.

**Across**

2. Last, Sid checked the wave ________.
5. The machine looked like an ________.
7. The shed was in a ________.
8. Sid and Bee were working in a ________.
9. Sid and Bee worked at ________ time.
10. It was dark and stormy ________ the shed.
12. Sid presses buttons and pushes ________.
13. Sid's last name is ________.

**Down**

1. The roof of the shed was made of ________.
2. Sid and Bee had to ________ everything.
3. Sid and Bee made a ________.
4. The storm was loud and ________.
6. There was a ________ at the front of the machine.
8. There was thunder and lightning in the ________.
11. The person working with Sid is called ________.

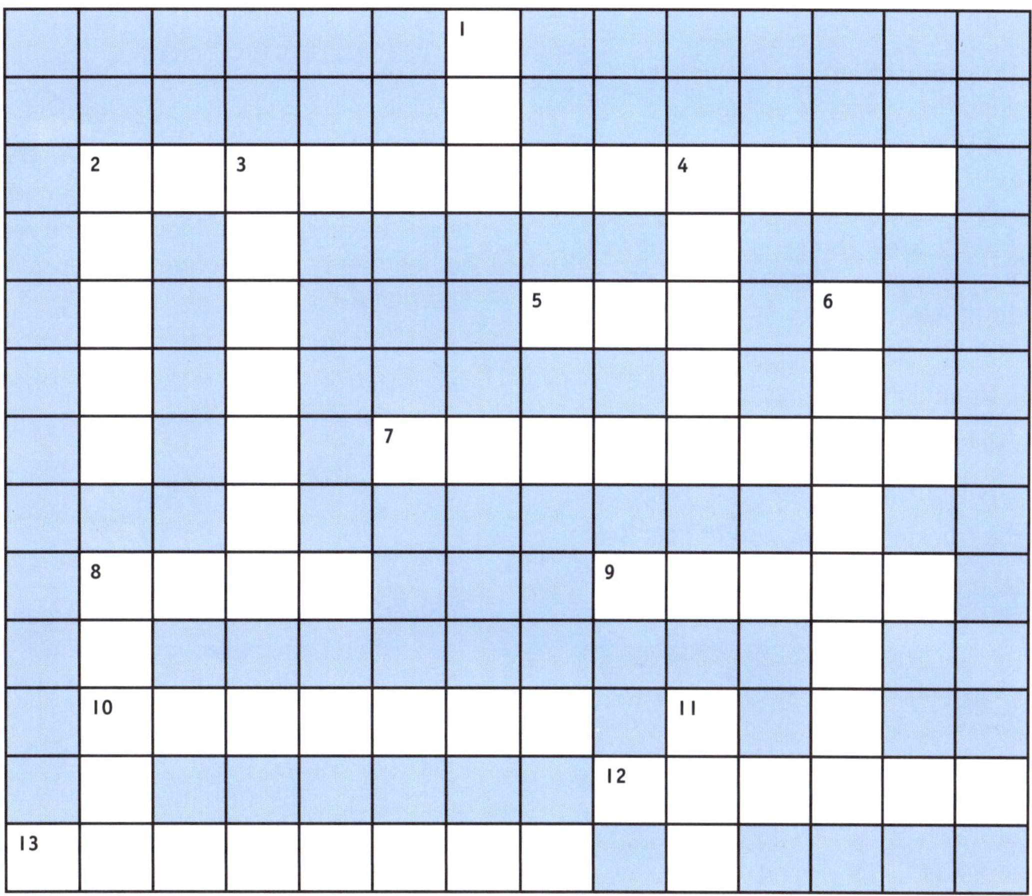

## What I'm reading

Title: ____________________

It's: ☐ a paper book/magazine/comic
☐ an audiobook
☐ online

It's: ☐ imaginative ☐ informative

Rating ☆☆☆☆☆

Score 2 points for each correct answer! SCORE /30 0-12 14-24 26-30

# Grammar & Punctuation



AC9E3LA06, AC9E3LE03

## Direct speech

Writers tell us what people say to each other by using speech marks ("…"). The speech marks go at the beginning and end of what was said. The first spoken word always has a capital letter. A comma marks off the spoken words from the rest of the sentence.

*Example:*

NOTE: If the sentence has a question mark (?) or an exclamation mark (!), do not use a comma.

**Read these sentences. Underline the words that the character says. Circle the speech marks. Highlight the comma, question mark or exclamation mark.**

1. "I think we've done it," says Sid.
2. "This is one mean machine!" says Bee.
3. "Wave communicator. Check!" calls Bee.
4. "Does the tracking system work?" asks Bee.
5. "Check the control panel first," says Bee.

**Read these sentences. The punctuation is missing. Underline the words that the character says. Add the speech marks and commas, question marks or exclamation marks where they are needed.**

6. Our machine is ready to go said Sid.
7. Where will you go asked Bee.
8. Tracking system. Check called Bee.
9. Should we make sure the door locks asked Bee.
10. I've already checked the door said Sid.

## Describing words

Adjectives are words used to describe people, places and things. They work with a noun to tell us more about it. They help the reader to build up a clear picture of what is being described.

*Examples:* Compare these two sentences.

The machine looks like an egg on legs.

The machine looks like a **shiny**, **green** egg on **four short**, **steel** legs.

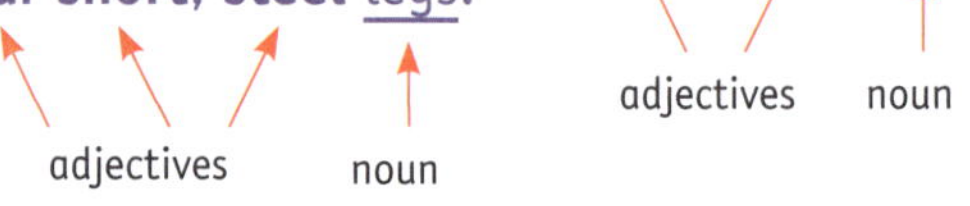


Adjectives can describe colour (green), size (short), shape (round), number (four), sound (loud), feelings (angry), qualities (mean).

**Circle the adjectives in these sentences.**

11. The street is dark and empty.
12. Bee fits a glass porthole into the machine.
13. Rain drums on the tin roof.
14. The wall clock says 2:00 am.
15. A light shines under the door of a backyard shed.
16. The control panel has a screen with rows of buttons and levers.

*Score 2 points for each correct answer!*

SCORE /32   

TARGETING ENGLISH HOMEWORK YEAR 3 © PASCAL PRESS ISBN 978 1 925726 60 2

## Consonant digraphs and blends

When two letters together spell one sound, they are called a digraph.

The digraph sh spells the one sound 'sh' as in **sh**ed and **sh**ine.

In a blend of two or three letters, each sound is pronounced separately.

*Examples:*

**str**eet — We pronounce **s** + **t** + **r** and blend them in the word **str**eet.
The **str**eet was dark and empty.

**fr**iend — We pronounce **f** + **r** and blend them in the word **fr**iend.
Sid Smekkles worked with his **fr**iend Bee.

**Read these words. Write D if the letters in bold are a digraph. Write B if they are a blend.**

1. **scr**een ______
2. **Sm**ekkles ______
3. **gl**ass ______
4. **sh**ort ______
5. ma**ch**ine ______
6. **sh**out ______
7. **fr**ont ______
8. **sh**iny ______
9. **sp**eak ______
10. **sw**itches ______
11. **st**orm ______
12. **str**eet ______
13. **ch**eck ______
14. **cl**ock ______

## Syllables

Syllables are chunks of sounds in words. We can tell how many chunks of sounds, or syllables, there are in a word by clapping the beats. Words may have 1, 2, 3 or even more syllables. We can also tell the number of syllables by counting the vowel sounds we hear. Each syllable has one vowel sound.

**Read these words. Clap the syllables. Write the number of syllables on the line.**

15. empty ______
16. shed ______
17. buttons ______
18. communicator ______
19. crackles ______
20. machine ______
21. happily ______
22. computer ______
23. green ______
24. lightning ______

Breaking words into syllables is easy when you know how.

Double consonants: If the word has double consonants, you break between the consonants.

*Example:* buttons = but + tons

Two or more consonants: As for double consonants, you break between the consonants.

*Example:* compute = com + pute

**Look at the words. Show how to break them into syllables.**

25. empty = ______ + ______
26. almost = ______ + ______
27. system = ______ + ______
28. control = ______ + ______
29. rubbing = ______ + ______
30. stepping = ______ + ______
31. angry = ______ + ______
32. lightning = ______ + ______
33. thunder = ______ + ______
34. rumbles = ______ + ______

*Score 2 points for each correct answer!* SCORE /68

# Review

TERM 1

AC9E3LE02, AC9E3LE03, AC9E3LY03, AC9E3LY05

## Book review: *Sass and Traz Save the Library*

### Sass and Traz Save the Library

Written by Michelle Worthington and illustrated by Naomi Greaves.

Daisy Lane Publishing

ISBN:978-0-6488193-5-6

Reviewed by Mia, 9, NSW.

I really enjoyed this book. I recommend it for 8-year-olds and 9-year-olds, especially if they are twins and like reading, like I do. It is a chapter book, but it has just 13 chapters, so it doesn't take long to read.

Sass and Traz are the main characters. They are twins, like me and my brother. They both love books, and they love going to the library on the weekends to hang out with Ms Burns, the librarian. They think she's cool.

One Saturday, when they get to the library, Ms Burns is very upset. Mayor Carter plans to tear the library down to build a carpark. Ms Burns says there is nothing they can do to stop it.

But the library doesn't want to be pulled down. Lots of book characters come to life. They help Sass and Traz, and Ms Burns save the library. There are pirates, and King Arthur and his knights. There are also a whole bunch of dinosaurs. Even Einstein turns up to help. My favourite part is when the dinosaurs chase Mayor Carter out of the library. He thought he was big and powerful, but he got scared away by the tiny dinosaurs.

If you love fun, action-packed adventure stories as much as I do, you'll love this book. It is very exciting!

I give it 5 stars. ☆☆☆☆☆

1. **Do you think you'd like to read *Sass and Traz Save the Library*?**

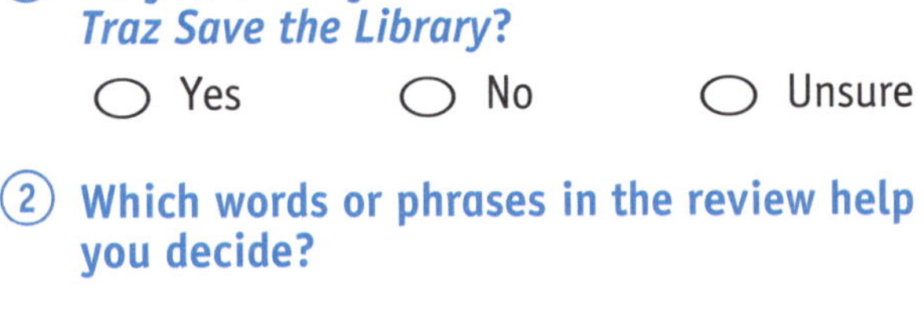

◯ Yes ◯ No ◯ Unsure

2. **Which words or phrases in the review help you decide?**

_______________

_______________

_______________

_______________

_______________

3. **List some books that you have read during the term.**

_______________

_______________

_______________

_______________

_______________

4. **Circle your favourite.**

# Review



Now you can write a review of your favourite book so that others can decide whether to read it or not.

① **About the book**

Title: ______________________

Author: ______________________

Illustrator: ______________________

Publisher: ______________________

ISBN: ______________________

② **Circle the word that best describes the type of story.**

| | |
|---|---|
| science fiction | fantasy |
| fairytale | realistic fiction |
| historical fiction | adventure |
| mystery | poetry |
| fable | humour |
| comic | picture book |

If the type of story is not listed, write it here: ______________________

## The characters

③ **Who is the main character (MC)?**

Name: ______________________

Age: ______________________

Country of birth: ______________________

Physical features: ______________________

Personality: ______________________

Likes: ______________________

Dislikes: ______________________

Goal (What does the character want to do or achieve?)

______________________

④ **Who are the supporting characters?**

Names: ______________________

Specialities (What are they good at?)

______________________

How do they support (help) the MC?

______________________

**Draw a picture of your character.**

⑤ **Who are the villains or baddies?**

Names: ______________________

Specialities (What are they good at?)

How do they try to foil (stop) the MC?

## The setting

⑥ **Where is the story set?**

Where and when does the story take place?

## The plot

⑦ **What happens in the beginning of the story?**

## Complication

⑧ **What happens that makes a problem for the characters?**

⑨ **How do they try to solve the problem?**

First: ______________________

Second: ______________________

Third: ______________________

⑩ **Is the problem solved?**

◯ Yes ◯ No ◯ Unsure



TARGETING ENGLISH HOMEWORK YEAR 3 © PASCAL PRESS ISBN 978 1 925726 60 2

## Conclusion

⑪ What happens at the end of the story?
How do things work out for the characters?

⑫ What is your favourite part of the story?

Why?

Draw your favourite part.

⑬ Who else would like to read this book?
Who do you recommend it for?

⑭ How many stars do you give it?

# Reading & Comprehension

## A Strange Noise

Toby was staying at his Gran's house. He was sleeping on his own in the back room. He noticed that the sheets smelled like lavender and mothballs. He hoped the sweet smell could calm his fears. The back room felt like the scariest place in the whole world. He closed his eyes and hoped the Jeepers Creepers that Olivia had spent hours telling him about didn't show up.

Then he heard a noise – a noise that made him stiffen with fright.

The scratching sound came from behind the curtains. Toby began to tremble. He held Batbat close and wrapped himself as tight as he could in the smell of lavender and mothballs.

Source: Adapted from *The Heebie Jeebie*, Gigglers, pages 17–18, Blake Education.

**Shade the bubble next to the correct answer. Write the answer on the line where appropriate.**

1. **Where was Toby staying?**
   - ◯ at school camp
   - ◯ at his Gran's house
   - ◯ at home

2. **What did the sheets smell like? (Choose any that apply.)**
   - ◯ mothballs
   - ◯ strawberries
   - ◯ lavender

3. **Do you think Toby liked the smell of the sheets?**
   - ◯ Yes
   - ◯ No
   - ◯ Unsure

4. **Write a word or phrase that supports your answer.**

   ______________________________

5. **How was Toby feeling?**
   - ◯ happy
   - ◯ proud
   - ◯ scared

6. **What was Toby afraid of?**
   - ◯ his Gran
   - ◯ Jeepers Creepers
   - ◯ Olivia

7. **What sort of noise did Toby hear?**
   - ◯ knocking
   - ◯ trembling
   - ◯ scratching

8. **Where was the noise coming from?**
   - ◯ outside
   - ◯ behind the curtains
   - ◯ under the bed

9. **What did Toby think was making the noise?**

   ______________________________

10. **What do you think was making the noise?**

    ______________________________

*Score 2 points for each correct answer!* SCORE /20

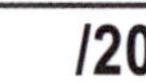

TARGETING ENGLISH HOMEWORK YEAR 3 © PASCAL PRESS ISBN 978 1 925726 60 2

# Grammar & Punctuation

TERM 1 REVIEW

Circle the **sentences**.

1. Then he heard a noise.
2. a scary noise
3. Jeepers Creepers!
4. The scratching sound came from behind the curtains.

Add words to change the two non-sentences into sentences.

5. ______________________________

6. ______________________________

Circle the two **questions**. Underline the two **statements**.

7. What is that noise?
8. Where is the noise coming from?
9. The room was at the back of the house.
10. Batbat was in bed with Toby.

Write statements to answer the two questions. Punctuate them correctly.

11. ______________________________

12. ______________________________

Rewrite these sentences to make them **commands**. Use a full stop or exclamation mark at the end.

13. Toby turned off the light.
14. Toby held Batbat tight.
15. Toby tried to be brave.
16. Toby stayed still and listened.

Circle the **verbs** or **verb groups** in these sentences. Circle whether they are happening in the present, past or future.

17. Toby is noticing the sweet smell of the sheets.
    present past future
18. The back room felt like the scariest place in the whole world.
    present past future
19. Olivia was telling Toby about Jeepers Creepers.
    present past future
20. The scratching sound is coming from behind the curtains.
    present past future
21. Toby will feel better when the noise stops.
    present past future

Are these words common nouns or proper nouns? Write **CN** next to the **common nouns**. Write **PN** next to the **proper nouns**. Make sure each proper noun begins with a capital letter.

22. toby _____
23. olivia _____
24. house _____
25. jeepers creepers _____
26. gran _____
27. batbat _____

Write one **proper noun** for each of these.

28. person ______________________________
29. object ______________________________
30. place ______________________________
31. event ______________________________

Add the missing **commas** in these sentences.

32. Toby looked under the bed behind the curtains on the chair and behind the door.
33. Toby liked sweet things like strawberries watermelon oranges and lavender.
34. Olivia told Toby stories about goblins dragons Jeepers Creepers and other monsters.

TERM 1

TERM 1

## Grammar & Punctuation

**Match pairs of emotive words with a similar meaning.**

| | |
|---|---|
| 35 scared | worried |
| 36 anxious | peaceful |
| 37 brave | happy |
| 38 calm | frightened |
| 39 content | courageous |

**Underline the noun groups built around the noun in bold.**

40 Toby liked the **smell** of lavender and mothballs.

41 He was sleeping on his own in the back **room**.

42 Batbat was Toby's toy **teddy** from long ago.

**Underline the subject in each sentence. Circle the verb. Then highlight the object.**

43 Olivia told monster stories.

44 Toby liked the sweet smell of lavender and mothballs.

45 Toby held Batbat tight.

**Circle the adjectives in these sentences.**

46 Toby was sleeping in the back room.

47 Toby hoped the sweet smell would calm his fears.

48 The scratching sound came from behind the curtains.

**Read and punctuate these sentences. Underline the words that are spoken. Add the speech marks and commas, question marks or exclamation marks where they are needed.**

49 I wish I didn't have to sleep here on my own said Toby.

50 Don't be such a baby said Olivia.

51 What do you think is making the noise asked Gran.

*Score 2 points for each correct answer!*

## Phonic & Word Knowledge

**Say each word. Circle the words that have a short vowel sound. Underline the words with a long vowel sound.**

| | | | | |
|---|---|---|---|---|
| 1 Batbat | stay | back | place | scratch |
| 2 sleep | sweet | sheets | smell | felt |
| 3 like | him | stiff | with | fright |
| 4 told | hope | on | moth | whole |
| 5 up | you | use | puff | but |

**Choose words from the lists in questions 1–5 to complete these sentences.**

6 Toby got a ____________ when he heard a noise.

7 Toby was happy he had Batbat ____________ him.

8 The back room seemed like the scariest place in the ____________ world.

9 Toby wished he could go to ____________.

10 Toby didn't want to be scared ____________ he was.

**Write these words as plurals.**

11 sheet ____________

12 bed ____________

13 mothball ____________

14 curtain ____________

15 moth ____________

16 noise ____________

**Write the digraphs to complete these words.**

17 _____eels

18  _____op

19  _____ed

20  _____umb



TARGETING ENGLISH HOMEWORK YEAR 3 © PASCAL PRESS ISBN 978 1 925726 60 2

# Phonic & Word Knowledge

Read these words. Write **D** if the letters in bold are a **digraph**. Write **B** if they are a **blend**.

(21) **scr**atch ______
(22) scrat**ch** ______
(23) **sm**ell ______
(24) **sh**eets ______
(25) **wr**ap ______
(26) **wh**ole ______
(27) mo**th**balls ______
(28) **tr**emble ______

Match pairs of words to form **compound words**. Write them on the lines below.

(29) moth fly
(30) grand way
(31) stair mother
(32) butter balls

______
______
______
______

Read the words. Draw lines to match them to the pictures. Underline the part of the word that spells the **vowel sound**.

(33) **moon**
(34) **fern**
(35) **glue**
(36) **nurse**
(37) **bird**
(38) **pearl**
(39) **fruit**
(40) **worm**

Read these words. Underline the letters **c** or **ch**. Write **C** if you hear the hard 'ck' sound (cat), **S** if you hear the soft 'c' sound (cent), and **CH** if you hear 'ch' (chips).

(41) piece _____
(42) curtains _____
(43) cheese _____
(44) ice _____
(45) match _____
(46) clue _____

Add endings to these base verbs to show **present tense** and **past tense**. Watch for irregular verbs.

| | Base verb (do) | Present tense (doing now) | Past tense (did) |
|---|---|---|---|
| (47) | stay | | |
| (48) | sleep | | |
| (49) | hope | | |
| (50) | notice | | |
| (51) | feel | | |
| (52) | shine | | |

Read these words. Clap the **syllables**. Write the number of syllables on the line.

(53) Toby ______
(54) calm ______
(55) lavender ______
(56) grandmother ______
(57) mothballs ______
(58) scariest ______
(59) hours ______
(60) tremble ______

*Score 2 points for each correct answer!*

  ISBN 978 1 925726 60 2

## Imaginative text – Narrative



### Hair-raising

The first thing Emma did when she woke up was sneeze. Very loudly.

Her schoolbag fell off the back of the door. Books spilled out. Her pencil case sprang open. Pencils and shavings scattered on the carpet. An orange rolled under her little sister's bed.

The mound of covers on the bed moved slowly like a tortoise. Alice poked her head out from under the blankets.

"What's going on?" she asked. She looked at everything spilled on the floor.

"Oh well," she said, "you won't need them today. It's the first day of the holidays."

Before Emma could respond, she sneezed again. This time Alice's hair flew up into a cone on the top of her head.

"Hey," said Alice. "What did you do?"

"Nothing," replied Emma. She looked at Alice. "Wow, Alice. What have you done to your hair?"

"I didn't do anything," Alice said tearfully. She looked at herself in the mirror. "You did it to me when you sneezed. I think you should be careful with your sneezing. You could hurt someone."

"Sneezing isn't something you can be careful with," replied Emma. "Sneezes just sort of sneak up on you. Then whoosh, they're out there."

Source: Adapted from *Sneeze Power*, Gigglers, pages 4–7, Blake Education.



TARGETING ENGLISH HOMEWORK YEAR 3 © PASCAL PRESS ISBN 978 1 925726 60 2

# Reading & Comprehension

Shade the bubble next to the correct answer. Write the answer on the line where appropriate.

1. Who is the main character in the story?
   - ◯ Emma
   - ◯ Alice
   - ◯ Sneezy

2. What is the problem in the story?
   - ◯ Alice is sleepy.
   - ◯ It is the school holidays.
   - ◯ Emma's sneezes

3. Emma and Alice are:
   - ◯ friends.
   - ◯ sisters.
   - ◯ cousins.

4. Who is older?
   - ◯ Emma
   - ◯ Alice

5. When does the story take place?
   - ◯ the first day of school
   - ◯ the first day of the holidays
   - ◯ Alice's birthday

6. Which of these things did **not** happen when Emma sneezed the first time?
   - ◯ Emma's schoolbag fell off the back of the door.
   - ◯ Alice's hair flew up into a cone on the top of her head.
   - ◯ Books spilled out of Emma's schoolbag.
   - ◯ An orange rolled under Alice's bed.

7. What happened to Alice when Emma sneezed the first time?
   - ◯ She turned into a tortoise.
   - ◯ She looked like a tortoise.
   - ◯ She moved slowly like a tortoise.
   - ◯ She fell out of bed.

8. What happened to Alice when Emma sneezed again?
   - ◯ She turned into an ice-cream cone.
   - ◯ Her hair made a cone shape on the top of her head.
   - ◯ Her hair fell off.
   - ◯ She disappeared.

9. How do you think Alice felt when she looked at herself in the mirror?
   - ◯ delighted
   - ◯ proud
   - ◯ shocked
   - ◯ sad

10. Why do you think Alice told Emma to be careful of her sneezes?

______________________________

______________________________

______________________________

______________________________

11. What do you think?

Emma says you can't be careful with sneezes. She says they just creep up on you. Do you agree? Why?

______________________________

______________________________

______________________________

______________________________

## What I'm reading

Title: ______________________________

It's: ☐ a paper book/magazine/comic
☐ an audiobook
☐ online

It's: ☐ imaginative ☐ informative

Rating ☆ ☆ ☆ ☆ ☆

Score 2 points for each correct answer!

SCORE /22 0-8 10-16 18-22

TERM 2

# Grammar & Punctuation



## Adverbial phrases

A phrase is a group of words without a verb. It often begins with a preposition.

Here are some prepositions:

above across after around
at below beneath between
by down during except for
from in like near of off
on out over past through
to under upon with

An adverbial phrase tells us how, when, where and why things happen.

*Examples:*

**how** Emma woke up **with the sneezes**.

**when** Emma sneezed **on the first day** of the holidays.

**where** An orange rolled **under her little sister's bed**.

**why** Alice gave Emma a bag **for her pencils**.

**Choose a preposition from the list above to complete each underlined adverbial phrase.**

1. Alice moved __________ a tortoise.
2. Everything came out of Emma's bag and spilled __________ the floor.
3. Alice's hair flew up into a cone on the top of her head __________ the morning.
4. Alice looked at herself __________ the mirror.
5. Emma looked __________ everything on the floor.
6. Alice looked for the orange __________ the bed.
7. The schoolbag fell __________ the hook.
8. The pencils rolled __________ the floor.

AC9E3LA07

## Direct speech and saying verbs

Remember! Writers tell us what people say to each other by using speech marks ("…"). The speech marks go at the beginning and end of what was said. The first spoken word always has a capital letter. A comma marks off the spoken words from the rest of the sentence.

*Example:*

"I didn't do anything," Alice said.

If the sentence is a question, a question mark (?) is used instead of a comma.

*Example:*

"What did you do?" asked Emma.

If it is an exclamation, an exclamation mark (!) is used instead of a comma.

*Example:*

"Look at my hair!" screamed Alice.

Saying verbs show which people are talking and how they say things.

*Examples:*

"What did you do to your hair?" Emma **asked**.

"I didn't do anything!" Alice **screamed**.

**Read these sentences. Underline the words that are spoken. Circle the saying verb. Highlight who is speaking. Write S for statement. Q for question. E for exclamation.**

9. _____ "Argh!" screamed Alice.
10. _____ "What's the matter?" asked Mum.
11. _____ "Look what Emma did to my hair!" replied Alice.
12. _____ "How did she do that?" enquired Mum.
13. _____ "I sneezed," admitted Emma. "That's all."
14. _____ "A sneeze can't do that," said Mum.
15. _____ "My sneeze did," stated Emma.

*Score 2 points for each correct answer!* SCORE /30 0-12 14-24 26-30


TARGETING ENGLISH HOMEWORK YEAR 3 © PASCAL PRESS ISBN 978 1 925726 60 2

AC9E3LA11, AC9E3LY09, AC9E3LY11, AC9E3LY12

## Apostrophes – Contractions and possession

Apostrophes are used in contractions. Contractions are two words shortened into one word. They are often used in speaking.

*Examples:*

"**What's** going on?" Alice asked. ("**What is** going on?" Alice asked.)

"I **didn't** do anything," Alice said. ("I **did not** do anything," Alice said.)

Apostrophes are also used to show possession, or ownership.

*Examples:*

Emma**'s** schoolbag sister**'s** bed Alice**'s** hair

Watch out! Don't confuse it's and its.

It's is a contraction. It means it is or it has.

*Examples:*

**It's** the first day of the holidays. (**It is** the first day of the holidays.)

**It's** been a long time since Christmas. (**It has** been a long time since Christmas.)

Its is a possessive pronoun. It is used to show possession.

*Example:*

The cat licked **its** paw. (its own paw, not 'it is' paw)

**Read these sentences. Circle the words with an apostrophe. Write C for contraction. Write P for possession.**

1. _____ Emma doesn't need her pencils because it is the first day of the holidays.
2. _____ Alice won't go outside with her hair like that.
3. _____ Emma's schoolbag fell off the back of the door.
4. _____ Alice's sister's sneezes are very strong.
5. _____ "You shouldn't sneeze like that," said Alice.
6. _____ "I can't help it," said Emma.
7. _____ No-one else's sneezes can do that!
8. _____ Only an elephant's sneeze would be that big.

**Draw lines to match these contractions with their meanings.**

| | |
|---|---|
| 9. he's | cannot |
| 10. doesn't | you have |
| 11. couldn't | could not |
| 12. can't | I would |
| 13. you've | he is |
| 14. I'd | does not |

**All these words are built from the word thing: nothing, something, anything, everything. Choose words built from thing to complete these sentences.**

15. _______________ fell out of Emma's bag and onto the floor.
16. _______________ was left in Emma's bag. It was empty.
17. Emma looked under the bed, but she couldn't reach _______________.
18. She needed _______________ long to reach them.

## Consonant blends

Remember! In a blend of two or three letters, each sound is pronounced separately.

*Example:*

**spr**ang We pronounce **s + p + r** and blend them in the word **spr**ang.

**Read these words. Underline the consonant digraph or blend. Write two more words that begin with the same digraph or blend.**

19. scatter ______________________________
20. sneeze ______________________________
21. blanket ______________________________
22. sprang ______________________________
23. floor ______________________________
24. slowly ______________________________

*Score 2 points for each correct answer!*

SCORE    

TERM 2

AC9E3LY03, AC9E3LY04, AC9E3LY05, AC9S3U04

## Informative text – Report



# Solids, Liquids and Gases

Look around where you are right now. Everything you see is made of matter. Matter is anything that has weight and takes up space. Molecules are the tiny parts or bits that make up all matter. There are millions of molecules in a tiny pinhead.

Your shoes, your desk, your hair and even the food in your tummy is made of matter (which is made up of these tiny molecules).

Matter can be broken into three main groups: Solids, Liquids and Gases.

| Solids | Liquids | Gases |
| --- | --- | --- |
| • Solids hold their shape. When you leave them alone, they stay in the same shape they were before. They only change shape if you do something to them, like cut them or melt them.<br>• Solids do not flow. | • Liquids take the shape of the container they are in.<br>• Liquids flow. Some liquids flow slowly, like honey, and others flow quickly, like water. | • Gases are invisible. Air is made of gases. You cannot see air, but you can see what air does. |

A **solid** has its own shape. A solid will not change unless you do something to it, like cut it or melt it.

A **liquid** does not have its own shape. A liquid can flow, drip, and splash. It will take the shape of what it is in.

A **gas** is invisible. Air is made of gases. You cannot see air, but you can see what air does.

Source: *Targeting Science*, Year 3, pages 92 & 94, Pascal Press.



TARGETING ENGLISH HOMEWORK YEAR 3 © PASCAL PRESS ISBN 978 1 925726 60 2

# Reading & Comprehension

Shade the bubble next to the correct answer.

1. Everything you see around you is made up of:
   - ◯ liquids.
   - ◯ matter.
   - ◯ gases.
   - ◯ solids.

2. How many groups can matter be broken into?
   - ◯ three
   - ◯ a million
   - ◯ infinity

3. Matter is anything that:
   - ◯ is about business.
   - ◯ is important.
   - ◯ has weight and takes up space.

4. Matter is made up of millions of tiny:
   - ◯ pinheads.
   - ◯ molecules.
   - ◯ weights.

5. Which type of matter holds its shape and does not flow?
   - ◯ solid
   - ◯ liquid
   - ◯ gas

6. Which type of matter flows and takes the shape of the containers it is in?
   - ◯ solid
   - ◯ liquid
   - ◯ gas

7. Which type of matter is invisible?
   - ◯ solid
   - ◯ liquid
   - ◯ gas

8. Which type of matter is this book?
   - ◯ solid
   - ◯ liquid
   - ◯ gas

9. Which type of matter is sunscreen?
   - ◯ solid
   - ◯ liquid
   - ◯ gas

10. Which type of matter is inside a balloon?
    - ◯ solid
    - ◯ liquid
    - ◯ gas

TERM 2

## What I'm reading

Title: ______________________________

It's: ☐ a paper book/magazine/comic
☐ an audiobook
☐ online

It's: ☐ imaginative ☐ informative

Rating ☆ ☆ ☆ ☆ ☆

Score 2 points for each correct answer!

SCORE /20 0-8 10-14 16-20

# Grammar & Punctuation

AC9E3LA06, AC9E3LA07, AC9E3LA10

TERM 2

## Sentences, relating verbs and topic words

A statement is a sentence that tells about everyday things, facts and ideas.

In an information report, most sentences are statements. They usually begin with the subject.

*Example:* **Matter** is anything that has weight and takes up space.

Relating verbs are used to link the information in a sentence. They include verbs like am, is, are, were, was, have, has.

*Example:* Matter **is** anything that has weight and takes up space.

Topic words are words that have special meaning for the topic in the report.

*Example:* **Matter** is anything that has **weight** and takes up **space**.

**Read these sentences. Underline the subject. Circle the verb. Highlight the topic words.**

1. Molecules are the tiny parts that make up all matter.
2. Your shoes are made up of matter.
3. A gas is invisible.
4. Millions of molecules are in a tiny pinhead.
5. Everything is made of matter.
6. Your hair is a solid.
7. The helium in a balloon is a gas.
8. Honey is my favourite liquid.

## Pronouns

Pronouns are words that are used to take the place of nouns. They may be used to avoid too much repetition.

*Example:* Liquids take the shape of the container **they** are in.

The pronoun they replaces the noun liquids.

Pronouns can be singular or plural.

*Examples of singular pronouns:*

I, me, you, he, she, it, him, her

*Examples of plural pronouns:*

we, us, them, they, you

**Read these sentences. Circle the pronoun. Underline the noun it refers to.**

9. When you leave solids alone, they stay in the same shape.
10. You cannot see air, but you can see what it does.
11. Chocolates will melt if they are left in the sun.
12. A solid will not change unless you do something to it.
13. Liquids may flow fast, or they may flow slowly.
14. People cannot see air, but they can see what it does.

## Subject–verb agreement

Nouns and pronouns can be singular or plural. Verbs can be singular or plural too.

A singular verb must always be used with a singular noun or pronoun.

*Example:* Your **desk is** made up of matter. (1 desk)

A plural verb must always be used with a plural noun or pronoun.

*Example:* Your **shoes are** made up of matter. (2 or more shoes)

**Choose the correct verb for each sentence.**

15. A solid ______________ in the same shape. (stays, stay)
16. Honey ______________ a liquid. (is, are)
17. Balloons ______________ filled with gas. (is, are)
18. Millions of molecules ______________ in a tiny pinhead. (is, are)

*Score 2 points for each correct answer!* SCORE /36

TARGETING ENGLISH HOMEWORK YEAR 3 © PASCAL PRESS ISBN 978 1 925726 60 2

# Phonic & Word Knowledge

UNIT 10

AC9E3LY09

## Syllables

Remember! Syllables are chunks of sounds in words. Every syllable has a vowel.

If the word has double consonants, or two or more consonants together, you break between the consonants. However, you don't break between a digraph or a blend.

*Example:* matter = mat + ter
contain = con + tain

**Look at the words. Show how to break them into syllables.**

1. tummy = ________ + ________
2. sunscreen = ________ + ________
3. cannot = ________ + ________
4. only = ________ + ________
5. quickly = ________ + ________
6. balloon = ________ + ________

## Vowels

Sometimes a syllable may start or end with a vowel. Usually, we break before the consonant if the vowel sound is long. Usually, we break after the consonant if the vowel sound is short.

*Examples:*

tiny = ti + ny (The first syllable has a long vowel sound.)

solid = sol + id (The first syllable has a short vowel sound.)

**Look at the words. Show how to break them into syllables.**

7. even = ________ + ________
8. slowly = ________ + ________
9. gases = ________ + ________
10. honey = ________ + ________
11. liquids = ________ + ________
12. broken = ________ + ________

## More than 2 syllables

We use the same rules when we break longer words into syllables. Breaking words into syllables helps us read longer, unfamiliar words. Find the vowels first to find the number of syllables. Then look at the consonants to see where to make the breaks. Some longer words contain different kinds of breaks.

*Examples:*

molecules = mol + e + cules

invisible = in + vis + a + ble

**Look at the words. Show how to break them into syllables.**

13. syllables = _____ + _____ + _____
14. anything = _____ + _____ + _____
15. everything = _____ + _____ + _____ + _____
16. container = _____ + _____ + _____
17. everywhere = _____ + _____ + _____ + _____
18. information = _____ + _____ + _____ + _____

**All these items are made up of matter. Complete the words using syllables from the box.**

| -tain -dow -der -rate -cil<br>-bage -tle -dle -pet |
|---|

19. bee______
20. can______
21. win______
22. pi______
23. pen______
24. cap______
25. cab______
26. spi______
27. car______

*Score 2 points for each correct answer!*

TERM 2

AC9E3LY03, AC9E3LY04, AC9E3LY05

## Imaginative text – Poem

TERM 2

### The Owl and the Pussy-Cat

by Edward Lear

The Owl and the Pussy-Cat went
to sea
In a beautiful pea-green boat:
They took some honey, and
plenty of money
Wrapped up in a five-pound note.
The Owl looked up to the stars
above,
And sang to a small guitar,
"O lovely Pussy, O Pussy, my
love,
What a beautiful Pussy you are,
You are,
You are!
What a beautiful Pussy you are!"

Pussy said to the Owl, "You
elegant fowl,
How charmingly sweet you sing!
Oh! let us be married; too long
we have tarried:
But what shall we do for a ring?"
They sailed away, for a year and a
day,
To the land where the bong-tree
grows;
And there in a wood a Piggy-wig
stood,
With a ring at the end of his nose,
His nose,
His nose,
With a ring at the end of his nose.

"Dear Pig, are you willing to sell for one shilling
Your ring?" Said the Piggy, "I will."
So they took it away, and were married next day
By the Turkey who lives on the hill.
They dined on mince and slices of quince,
Which they ate with a runcible spoon;
And hand in hand, on the edge of the sand,
They danced by the light of the moon,
The moon,
The moon,
They danced by the light of the moon.



TARGETING ENGLISH HOMEWORK YEAR 3 © PASCAL PRESS ISBN 978 1 925726 60 2

Write your answers on the lines provided.

1. Who are the main characters in the poem?

2. Where did they go?

3. What did they travel in?

4. What did they take with them?

5. How did the characters feel about each other?

6. What did they decide to do?

7. What did they need before they could get married?

8. Where did they go to get it?

9. Who did they get it from?

10. Who married them?

11. What do you think?
    Could this poem be about real events? Explain.

## What I'm reading

Title:

It's: ☐ a paper book/magazine/comic
☐ an audiobook
☐ online

It's: ☐ imaginative ☐ informative

Rating ☆ ☆ ☆ ☆ ☆

Score 2 points for each correct answer!

SCORE /22 0-8 10-16 18-22

# Grammar & Punctuation

AC9E3LE03, AC9E3LE04

TERM 2

## Adjectives

Remember! Adjectives are used to describe people, places and things.

*Example*:

The Owl and the Pussy-Cat went to sea in a beautiful pea-green **boat**.

adjectives　　noun

Adjectives can describe colour (green), size (short), shape (round), number (four), sound (loud), feelings (angry), qualities (mean).

The adjective beautiful describes a quality.

The adjective pea-green describes a colour.

**Circle the adjectives in these sentences. Write what the adjective is describing, e.g. colour, size, shape, number, sound, feelings or quality.**

1. The Owl and the Pussy-Cat took some money. (__________)
2. The Owl was an elegant fowl. (__________)
3. The Owl played a small guitar. (__________)
4. The Owl sang in a sweet voice. (__________)
5. The Pig sold the ring for one shilling. (__________)

**Read this sentence. Underline the adjective.**

6. They ate with a runcible spoon.

**What sort of spoon do you think it is? (There is no right or wrong answer. Edward Lear made the word up.)**

7. ________________________________________

## Adjectival phrases

An adjectival phrase is a group of words that does the work of an adjective. It tells you which person, place or thing is being spoken about. It usually follows the noun and begins with a preposition.

*Example*: There was a **pig** with a ring at the end of his nose.

noun

adjectival phrase

**Underline the adjectival phrase that describes the noun in bold.**

8. They danced by the **light** of the moon.
9. They went to see the **Turkey** on the hill.
10. They went to the **land** of bong-trees.

## Personification

Personification is when a writer makes an animal or object behave like a person. In the poem *The Owl and the Pussy-Cat*, all the animals behave like people. They do not behave like normal animals.

*Example:* The Owl and the Pussy-Cat went to sea in a boat.

Owls and cats do not usually become friends with each other. They do not usually go to sea. They would not be able to drive a boat. These are all things that people do.

**List three other examples of personification in the poem.**

11. ________________________________________
12. ________________________________________
13. ________________________________________

*Score 2 points for each correct answer!* SCORE 

TARGETING ENGLISH HOMEWORK YEAR 3 © PASCAL PRESS ISBN 978 1 925726 60 2

AC9E3LY06, AC9E3LY09, AC9E3LY11

## Rhyming words

**Use different colours to draw lines linking pairs of rhyming words.**

| | |
|---|---|
| 1 money | grows |
| 2 day | mince |
| 3 nose | honey |
| 4 ring | away |
| 5 quince | sing |
| 6 moon | above |
| 7 are | stood |
| 8 sand | spoon |
| 9 wood | land |
| 10 love | star |

## The digraph 'oo'

The digraph oo is used to spell two different sounds.

It spells the long vowel sound oo as in moon.

It also spells the short vowel ound oo as in book.

**Read these words. Write L if you hear the long oo sound. Write S if you hear the short oo sound.**

11 _____ wood
12 _____ spoon
13 _____ stood
14 _____ boot
15 _____ look
16 _____ pool

## The digraph 'ng'

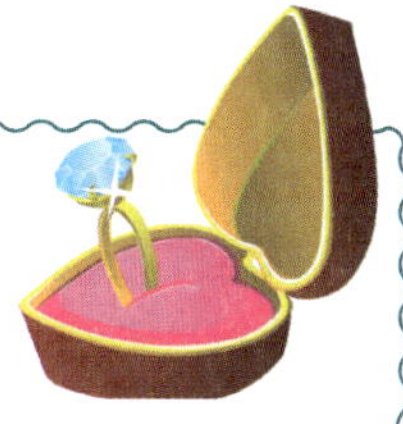

The digraph ng is used to spell the consonant sound you hear at the end of ring.

**Add ng to complete these words.**

17 si_____
18 bo_____-trees
19 wi_____s
20 fa_____s
21 lo_____
22 sa_____

**Use an ng word from the previous exercise to complete these sentences.**

23 The Owl and the Pussy-Cat went to the land where the __________ grow.

24 The Owl played a guitar and __________ a song.

25 The Owl and the Pussy-Cat were away for a __________ time.

26 Owls are birds so they have __________.

## Consonant sound 'z' spelt with 's'

The letter s usually spells the sound we hear in sweet, sing and sand.

And usually, we use the letter z to spell the sound we hear in zoo, zoom and zip.

But sometimes, the letter s spells the sound that z usually spells.

*Examples:*

nose grows

**Read these words. Write S if you hear the s sound. Write Z if you hear the z sound.**

27 _____ rose
28 _____ hands
29 _____ sea
30 _____ zoo

*Score 2 points for each correct answer!*

SCORE

TERM 2

AC9E3LY03, AC9E3LY04, AC9E3LY05, AC9HS3K06, AC9S3U01, AC9HS3K01

## Persuasive text – Discussion

TERM 2

### Get Rid of Cane Toads

Carl and Tan are discussing cane toads.

CARL: Dad and I went out collecting cane toads last night.

TAN: Why?

CARL: There were thousands in our front yard. We have to get rid of them.

TAN: Why?

CARL: Have you seen them? They're ugly.

TAN: You don't kill something just because it's ugly, do you?

CARL: There's lots of other reasons too. First, they're not native animals. They shouldn't even be here.

TAN: A lot of other animals and people, including me, weren't born here.

CARL: You're not bad for the environment. Cane toads are.

TAN: How?

CARL: They're poisonous. If our native animals eat them, they die. Nothing eats them, so there's more and more of them all the time. They keep spreading further and further. Also, they eat the food that our native animals want to eat. Then there's not enough food for them.

TAN: But it's mean to kill animals. They have a right to live, just like you and me.

CARL: If we don't get rid of the cane toads, they'll get rid of all our small wildlife. Dad says it's important to protect our native species. I think so too. Anyway, we always kill them humanely.

TAN: Were there really thousands in your front yard?



TARGETING ENGLISH HOMEWORK YEAR 3 © PASCAL PRESS ISBN 978 1 925726 60 2

# Reading & Comprehension

Shade the bubble next to the correct answer. Write the answer on the line where appropriate.

1. What are Carl and Tan discussing?
   - ◯ poisonous animals
   - ◯ cane toads
   - ◯ Australian animals

2. What did Carl do last night?
   - ◯ collected cane toads
   - ◯ played a game
   - ◯ visited Tan

3. How many cane toads did Carl say were in his front yard?
   - ◯ hundreds
   - ◯ thousands
   - ◯ millions

4. Which was **not** a reason for getting rid of cane toads?
   - ◯ They are ugly.
   - ◯ They are bad for the environment.
   - ◯ They kill native animals.

5. What does Tan think about killing cane toads?
   - ◯ It's okay.
   - ◯ It's mean.
   - ◯ It's kind.

6. What does **native to Australia** mean?
   - ◯ have always lived in Australia, weren't brought here
   - ◯ were born here
   - ◯ live on farms in Australia
   - ◯ live in zoos in Australia

7. Are cane toads native to Australia?
   - ◯ Yes
   - ◯ No
   - ◯ Unsure

8. Was Tan born in Australia?
   - ◯ Yes
   - ◯ No
   - ◯ Unsure

9. What does humanely mean?
   - ◯ kindly
   - ◯ cruelly
   - ◯ meanly

10. What do you think?

    Tan asked, "Were there really thousands in your front yard?"

    What do you think Carl replied?

    ______________________________
    ______________________________
    ______________________________
    ______________________________
    ______________________________
    ______________________________
    ______________________________
    ______________________________

TERM 2

## What I'm reading

Title: ______________________

It's: ☐ a paper book/magazine/comic
☐ an audiobook
☐ online

It's: ☐ imaginative ☐ informative

Rating ☆ ☆ ☆ ☆ ☆

Score 2 points for each correct answer!

SCORE 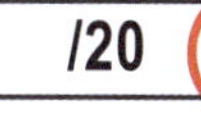 /20  0-8  10-14  16-20

# Grammar & Punctuation

AC9E3LA02, AC9E3LA06

## Sentences – Simple and compound

Remember! Every sentence has a subject and a verb. A simple sentence has one subject and one verb.

*Examples:*

Cane toads **are** not native animals.

subject verb

Cane toads **are** bad for the environment.

subject verb

A compound sentence is made up of two simple sentences joined by a joining word.

Joining words (also called conjunctions) include and, but, so, because, then and while.

*Examples:* Cane toads **are** not native animals, and they **are** bad for the environment.

We **need to get rid of** cane toads because they **are** bad for the environment.

**Join each pair of sentences. Choose from and, but, so or because. Write the new sentence underneath.**

1. **Cane toads are not native animals. They shouldn't even be here.**

2. **Animals shouldn't eat cane toads. They will die.**

3. **You're not bad for the environment. Cane toads are.**

4. **Cane toads eat the native animals' food. There is not enough food for them.**

5. **There were thousands of cane toads in my front yard. I couldn't count them.**

## Emotive words

In a persuasive discussion, the speaker uses emotive words to convince the listener to agree with them. They may exaggerate the situation or change a fact into opinion.

*Examples:* Fact – There were some cane toads in the front yard last night.

Exaggerated opinion – There were thousands of cane toads in my front yard.

**Read the sentences below. Write F for fact. Write O for opinion.**

6. _____ Cane toads are not native Australian animals.
7. _____ They shouldn't even be here.
8. _____ Cane toads harm the environment.
9. _____ They are poisonous, and if animals eat them, they will die.
10. _____ Cane toads destroy everything.
11. _____ They eat small Australian animals.
12. _____ They eat every bit of their food too.
13. _____ My dad says the only good cane toad is a dead one.
14. _____ It is true that we must protect the environment.
15. _____ I'm not sure if killing other living things is the right thing to do.

## Punctuation

Remember! A statement begins with a capital letter and ends with a full stop.

A question begins with a capital letter and ends with a question mark.

**Punctuate these sentences.**

16. how many cane toads did you see last night
17. why do you think cane toads are a pest
18. there are no native toads in Australia

*Score 2 points for each correct answer!* SCORE /36  0-16  18-30  32-36

TERM 2



TARGETING ENGLISH HOMEWORK YEAR 3 © PASCAL PRESS ISBN 978 1 925726 60 2

# Phonic & Word Knowledge

AC9E3LY06, AC9E3LY09, AC9E3LY11, AC9E3LY12

## The letter 'y'

The letter y can do the work of a consonant.
*Examples:* you, yard, yellow
It can do the work of a vowel.
*Examples:* my, fly, try; happy, baby, ugly
It can join with other vowels to form a vowel digraph and spell different vowel sounds.
*Examples:* they, day, boy, key, buy

**Say each word from the word bank. Listen to the different end sounds of the words.**

| Word bank | | | | | |
|---|---|---|---|---|---|
| they | my | why | ugly | say | any | way |
| humanely | really | boy | pony | valley | key |
| monkey | busy | enjoy | day | buy | try |
| study | annoy | fly | funny | tiny | |

**Choose words from the word bank to complete these sentences.**

1. There was a ______________ big cane toad at the door last night.
2. There aren't ______________ toads that are native to Australia.
3. It was ______________ watching my cat hide from a toad.
4. A toad hopped at Mum when she was putting the ______________ in the door.
5. We forgot to ______________ something for dinner at the shops.

## Tricky homophones

Homophones are words that sound the same but have different spellings and meanings. Look at these tricky homophones.
*Examples:* they're, their, there where, wear
hear, here your, you're

**Write the correct homophones from the brackets to complete these sentences.**

6. They left ______________ torch inside. (their, there)
7. They couldn't see ______________ they were going. (where, wear)
8. They could ______________ the toads hopping on the lawn. (hear, here)
9. Remember to bring ______________ bucket with you next time. (your, you're)
10. ______________ going to the movies after dinner. (They're, Their)
11. They will have to ______________ warm clothes as it's cool outside. (where, wear)
12. ______________ going to be late if you don't hurry. (Your, You're)

## Similar spelling, different sounds

Each of these words have the vowel trigraph ere (3 letters are used to spell one sound).
But in each word, the letters ere spell a different sound.
*Examples:* There rhymes with **air** and h**air**.
Here rhymes with **ear** and h**ear**.
Were rhymes with h**er** and f**ur**.

**Use blue to colour words that have the same vowel sound as there. Use green to colour words that have the same vowel sound as here. Use red to colour words that have the same vowel sound as were.**

chair deer sphere
bear nurse fern
ear bird pair
pearl spear gear

TERM 2

Score 2 points for each correct answer! SCORE /48 

AC9E3LY03, AC9E3LY04, AC9E3LY05, AC9S3U01

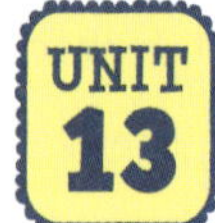

## Informative text – Diagrams



### Life Cycles of Insects

All living things grow and change. Compare the life cycles of these three insects.

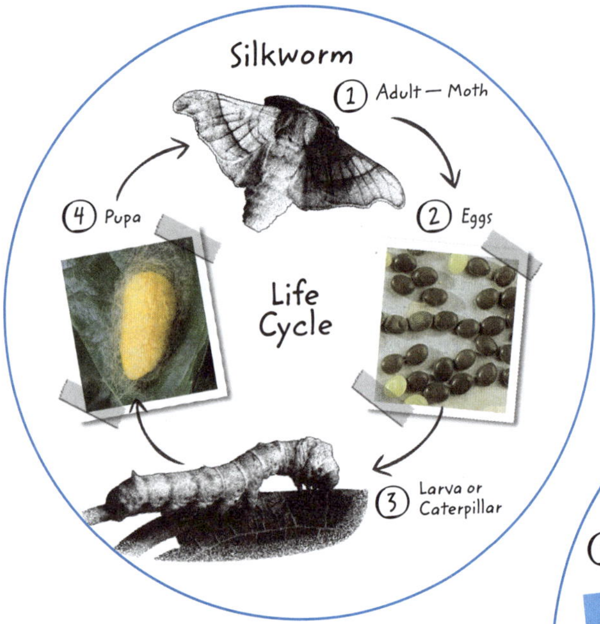
Silkworm
1 Adult – Moth
2 Eggs
3 Larva or Caterpillar
4 Pupa
Life Cycle

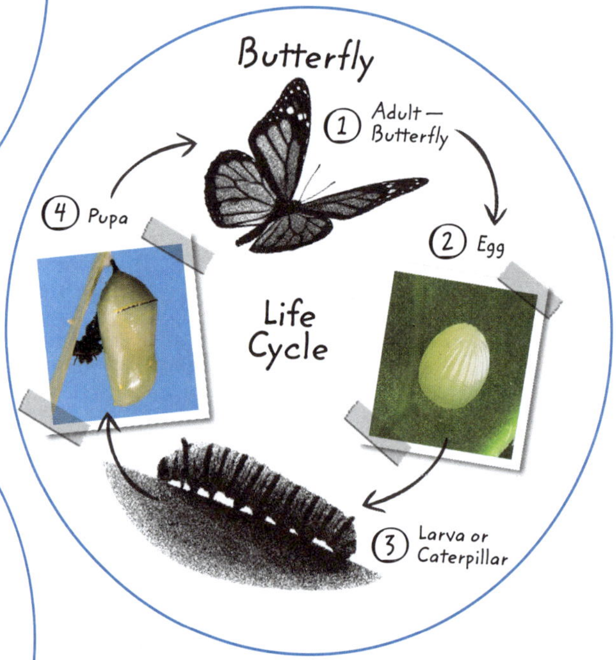
Butterfly
1 Adult – Butterfly
2 Egg
3 Larva or Caterpillar
4 Pupa
Life Cycle

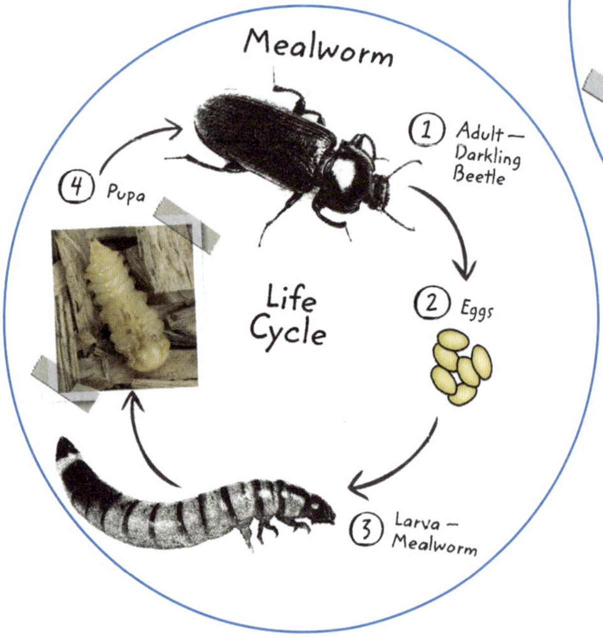
Mealworm
1 Adult – Darkling Beetle
2 Eggs
3 Larva – Mealworm
4 Pupa
Life Cycle

Source: *Stella the Silkworm*, *Cassie the Caterpillar* and *Max the Mealworm*, Pascal Press.


TARGETING ENGLISH HOMEWORK YEAR 3 © PASCAL PRESS ISBN 978 1 925726 60 2

# Reading & Comprehension

Shade the bubble next to the correct answer.

1. All three insects have the same four life stages: adult, egg, larva, pupa.
   - ◯ True
   - ◯ False

2. Which of these three insects lays the most eggs?
   - ◯ mealworm
   - ◯ butterfly
   - ◯ silkworm

3. Which insect does the mealworm turn into?
   - ◯ silk moth
   - ◯ butterfly
   - ◯ darkling beetle

4. What is another name for the larva of a butterfly?
   - ◯ mealworm
   - ◯ pupa
   - ◯ caterpillar

5. What is another name for the larva of a silk moth?
   - ◯ mealworm
   - ◯ pupa
   - ◯ caterpillar

6. What is the fourth life stage of all three insects called?
   - ◯ larva
   - ◯ pupa
   - ◯ egg

7. We know two of these insects by the name of their young. We know one by the name of its adult stage. Which insect do we know by its adult stage?
   - ◯ mealworm
   - ◯ butterfly
   - ◯ silkworm

8. What stage does each of these insects go through after it is a larva?
   - ◯ adult
   - ◯ pupa
   - ◯ egg

9. How many wings does a silk moth have?
   - ◯ two
   - ◯ four
   - ◯ unsure

10. How many wings does a butterfly have?
    - ◯ two
    - ◯ four
    - ◯ unsure

## What I'm reading

Title: ______________________

It's: ☐ a paper book/magazine/comic
☐ an audiobook
☐ online

It's: ☐ imaginative ☐ informative

Rating ☆ ☆ ☆ ☆ ☆

*Score 2 points for each correct answer!*

SCORE /20

TERM 2

AC9E3LA06, AC9E3LA07, AC9E3LA10

## Compound sentences

Remember! A compound sentence is made up of two simple sentences joined by a joining word.

Joining words (also called conjunctions) include and, but, so, for, yet, or and nor.

*Examples:* Silk moths are insects, **and** butterflies are insects too.

The larva of a silk moth is called a caterpillar, **but** the larva of a darkling beetle is called a mealworm.

**Join each pair of sentences. Choose from and, but or so. Write the new sentence underneath.**

1. **Silk moths lay eggs. Butterflies lay eggs too.**

   ______________________________

   ______________________________

   ______________________________

2. **Silkworm caterpillars turn into silk moths. Mealworms turn into darkling beetles.**

   ______________________________

   ______________________________

   ______________________________

3. **A butterfly laid these eggs. Butterfly larvae will hatch out of them.**

   ______________________________

   ______________________________

   ______________________________

4. **A young butterfly is called a larva. Sometimes it is called a caterpillar too.**

   ______________________________

   ______________________________

   ______________________________

5. **A young butterfly is called a caterpillar. A young darkling beetle is called a mealworm.**

   ______________________________

   ______________________________

   ______________________________

## Relating verbs

Relating verbs are used to link the information in a sentence. They show what things are or what things have. There is no action taking place.

Relating verbs include verbs like am, is, are, were, was, have, has.

*Examples:* A darkling beetle **is** an insect. Butterflies **have** four wings.

The verbs in these sentences are action or doing verbs.

*Examples:* Butterflies **lay** eggs. Mealworms **turn** into darkling beetles.

**Use relating verbs to complete these sentences. Choose from the words in the box above.**

6. A mealworm __________ the larva of the darkling beetle.
7. An adult butterfly __________ four wings.
8. Caterpillars __________ the young of some insects.
9. The adult __________ the first stage of an insect's life.
10. Silk moths __________ wings, but they cannot fly.

**For each sentence, write A if the bold verb is an action verb or R if it's a relating verb.**

11. __________ Butterflies **sip** nectar from flowers.
12. __________ Silkworm caterpillars **spin** a cocoon of silk.
13. __________ The larva of a darkling beetle **is** a mealworm.
14. __________ Adult butterflies **have** four wings.

*Score 2 points for each correct answer!*

SCORE  /28  0-12  14-22 24-28



TARGETING ENGLISH HOMEWORK YEAR 3 © PASCAL PRESS ISBN 978 1 925726 60 2

AC9E3LY06, AC9E3LY09, AC9E3LY10, AC9E3LY11

## Plurals

To make a word plural (more than one) we usually just add –s.

*Examples:* moth, moth**s**
caterpillar, caterpillar**s**

For words that end in s, ss, sh or ch, you add –es to make them plural.

*Examples:* batch, batch**es**
dish, dish**es**

When words end with a y after a consonant, change the y into i and add –es.

*Examples:* butterfly, butterfl**ies**
baby, bab**ies**

Some words have irregular plurals.

*Examples:* child, **children**
larva, **larvae**
pupa, **pupae**

**Match these singular (one) words to their plural (more than one) words.**

| | |
|---|---|
| 1 beetle | caterpillars |
| 2 moth | butterflies |
| 3 egg | pupae |
| 4 pupa | cycles |
| 5 caterpillar | beetles |
| 6 larva | larvae |
| 7 worm | moths |
| 8 butterfly | worms |
| 9 stage | eggs |
| 10 cycle | stages |

## Topic words

**The words in the box are important to know when reading about insects, especially mealworms, silkworms and butterflies.**

| | | | |
|---|---|---|---|
| adult | caterpillar | egg | mealworm |
| silkworm | beetle | cycle | insect |
| moth | stage | butterfly | darkling |
| larva | pupa | wings | |

**Can you find all 15 words in the grid? They go left to right and top to bottom. Some words overlap. Use different colours to highlight each word. As you find the words in the grid, write them on the lines below.**

| | | | | | | | | | | | |
|---|---|---|---|---|---|---|---|---|---|---|---|
| P | U | P | A | M | Y | S | T | A | G | E | C |
| A | W | B | R | E | S | H | I | J | A | G | T |
| Q | P | X | D | A | R | K | L | I | N | G | U |
| B | E | E | T | L | E | F | W | I | N | G | S |
| G | F | M | E | W | I | N | S | E | C | T | I |
| X | Q | O | R | O | D | P | I | O | L | T | O |
| C | A | T | E | R | P | I | L | L | A | R | B |
| Y | R | H | U | M | Z | N | K | J | R | C | V |
| C | A | D | U | L | T | C | W | D | V | K | Y |
| L | S | G | L | L | K | E | O | H | A | D | E |
| E | F | B | U | T | T | E | R | F | L | Y | B |
| W | H | Z | V | M | N | A | M | M | F | G | A |

11 ______
12 ______
13 ______
14 ______
15 ______
16 ______
17 ______
18 ______
19 ______
20 ______
21 ______
22 ______
23 ______
24 ______
25 ______

*Score 2 points for each correct answer!* SCORE /50

TERM 2

## Informative text – Explanation



### Keeping Warm – A First Nation's Perspective

First Nations Australians had many ways of keeping warm. One way was by making clothing. They made cloaks from the skins of animals such as quolls, platypus, sugar gliders, possums, kangaroos and emus. These skins were warm, and they kept the people dry.

Some of these cloaks were long. They would cover a person from their neck down to their feet. The type of cloak or clothing that was made depended on two things: where the people lived and the animal skins that were available.

To make the cloak, first the animal was skinned. Then the skin was attached to a flat surface. It was held in place with either wooden pins or echidna quills. All of the flesh was scraped off and eaten before the skin was allowed to dry. Nothing went to waste.

The cloaks were then decorated to make them look more beautiful. They used mussel and oyster shells to cut patterns in the leather. They used stone tools to beat it and make it softer and more comfortable.

The cloaks were painted using ochre and black pigment. The artwork often included symbols of the person's identity and Country.

In some parts of Australia, it was traditional for First Nations people to be buried in their cloak with their special things.

Source: Adapted from *Targeting Science*, Year 3, page 91, Pascal Press.


TARGETING ENGLISH HOMEWORK YEAR 3 © PASCAL PRESS ISBN 978 1 925726 60 2

# Reading & Comprehension

**Shade the bubble next to the correct answer. Write the answer on the line where appropriate.**

1. **What is this text mainly about?**
   - ◯ echidnas
   - ◯ Australian animals
   - ◯ cloaks made by First Nations Australians

2. **Why did First Nations Australians make cloaks?**
   - ◯ to keep warm and dry
   - ◯ to care for animals
   - ◯ to look beautiful

3. **The type of cloak made depended on two things. What were they? (Choose 2 answers.)**
   - ◯ where the people lived
   - ◯ what animal skins were available
   - ◯ how cold the people were
   - ◯ how many echidnas lived there

4. **What did First Nations Australians make their clothing from?**
   - ◯ cotton
   - ◯ animal skins
   - ◯ plastic

5. **What were the echidna quills used for?**
   - ◯ painting
   - ◯ holding the skin in place
   - ◯ spears

6. **What did First Nations Australians do with the animal flesh?**
   - ◯ ate it
   - ◯ used it to make cloaks
   - ◯ threw it away

7. **Why were the cloaks decorated with art?**
   - ◯ to be more comfortable
   - ◯ to be more beautiful
   - ◯ to be warmer

8. **What did First Nations Australians use to cut patterns in the leather?**
   - ◯ echidna quills
   - ◯ shells
   - ◯ knives

9. **What did First Nations Australians use to paint their cloaks?**
   - ◯ ochre and black pigment
   - ◯ paint
   - ◯ stones

10. **Are the traditions of First Nations peoples the same all over Australia?**
    - ◯ Yes
    - ◯ No
    - ◯ Unsure

11. **What do you know?**

    What is leather made from? What do you know is made from leather?

    ______________________________________________

    ______________________________________________

    ______________________________________________

    ______________________________________________

    ______________________________________________

    ______________________________________________

    ______________________________________________

TERM 2

## What I'm reading

Title: ______________________________

It's: ☐ a paper book/magazine/comic
☐ an audiobook
☐ online

It's: ☐ imaginative ☐ informative

Rating ☆ ☆ ☆ ☆ ☆

*Score 2 points for each correct answer!* SCORE /22    

# Grammar & Punctuation



TERM 2

## Clauses

A clause is a group of words with a subject and a verb. The subject and the verb must agree. That means a singular subject must have a singular verb and a plural subject must have a plural verb.

Simple sentences consist of just one clause. There is one subject and one verb. A simple sentence makes sense on its own. It is a main clause.

*Example:* First Nations Australians **had** many ways of keeping warm.

subject verb

Compound sentences consist of two clauses. Each clause makes sense on its own. They are both main clauses. We separate the two simple sentences by using a comma before the conjunction (joining word).

*Example:*

The skins **were** warm, and they **kept** people dry.

clause 1 comma conjunction clause 2

Both clauses could be written as separate sentences.

*Example:* The skins **were** warm. They **kept** people dry.

**Read these sentences. Circle the verbs. Underline the subjects. Write S if it is a simple sentence. Write C if it is a compound sentence.**

1. _____ They made cloaks from the skins of animals.
2. _____ Some of the cloaks were long.
3. _____ They would cover a person from their neck down to their feet.
4. _____ The skin was held in place, and all the flesh was scraped off.
5. _____ They cut patterns in the leather, and they beat it with stone tools.

**Choose the correct verb from the brackets to complete each sentence. Remember! The subject and verb must agree.**

6. The man's cloak __________ very long. (was, were)
7. The cloaks __________ made of animal skin. (was, were)
8. Echidnas __________ long, sharp quills. (has, have)
9. An echidna ___________ long, sharp quills. (has, have)
10. The cloaks ___________ very warm. (is, are)
11. The people ___________ the cloaks with ochre and black pigment. (paint, paints)
12. Cloaks ___________ people from their head to their toes. (cover, covers)

## Commas

Commas (,) are used to separate the items in a list that is written in a sentence. We do not put a comma before and and the last item.

*Example:* They made cloaks from the skins of animals such as quolls, platypus, sugar gliders, possums, kangaroos and emus.

**Read these lists. Put in the missing commas.**

13. Cloaks are beautiful warm and comfortable.
14. Kangaroos wallabies possums wombats and koalas are all Australian animals.
15. To decorate their cloaks, First Nations Australians used quills stone tools ochre and black pigment.
16. First Nations Australians live in every state and territory in Australia, including New South Wales Victoria Queensland Tasmania South Australia Western Australia Northern Territory and the Australian Capital Territory.

*Score 2 points for each correct answer!* SCORE /32  0-14  16-26  28-32 

TARGETING ENGLISH HOMEWORK YEAR 3 © PASCAL PRESS ISBN 978 1 925726 60 2

AC9E3LY06, AC9E3LY09, AC9E3LY10, AC9E3LY11

## Word endings – 'tion'

**Each of these words ends with –tion that sounds like 'shun'. Read the words. Circle the tion.**

| tion | nation | tradition |
|---|---|---|
| decoration | education | invitation |
| direction | vacation | potion |
| addition | caution | operation |
| emotion | lotion | motion |

**Choose a word from the table to complete each sentence.**

1. I got an ______________ to my friend's party.
2. The witch put frog legs and fish eggs in the ______________.
3. My sister always gets ______________ sickness when we go in the car.
4. We got lost because we didn't know which ______________ to go in.
5. Everyone is looking forward to our ______________ at the beach.

## Syllables

**Count the number of syllables in each word, then write them in the correct box.**

| | | | |
|---|---|---|---|
| wooden | skin | animal | comfortable |
| mussel | oyster | things | kangaroos |
| cloak | warm | surface | beautiful |
| person | traditional | echidna | stone |
| platypus | identity | available | Australia |

| One syllable | Two syllables |
|---|---|
| 6 | 11 |
| 7 | 12 |
| 8 | 13 |
| 9 | 14 |
| 10 | 15 |

| Three syllables | More than three |
|---|---|
| 16 | 21 |
| 17 | 22 |
| 18 | 23 |
| 19 | 24 |
| 20 | 25 |

## Word wheel

**Build words using the 3-letter blend in the centre of the wheel with the word endings in the spokes. Write the words you build on the lines.**

26. ______________________________
27. ______________________________
28. ______________________________
29. ______________________________
30. ______________________________
31. ______________________________
32. ______________________________
33. ______________________________

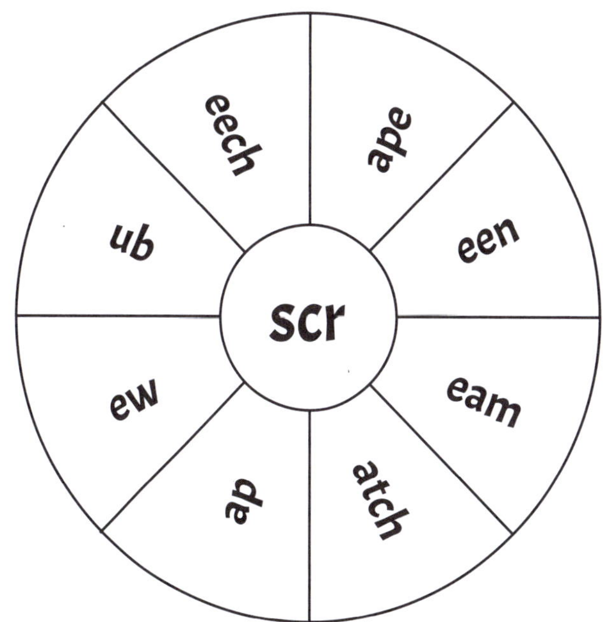


Score 2 points for each correct answer!

SCORE /66   

TERM 2

AC9E3LY03, AC9E3LY04, AC9E3LY05, AC9E3LE01

## Imaginative text – Science fiction



### In the Time Machine

This story is an excerpt from *A Step in Time*, Book 1 in the Time Quest series by Del Merrick. Read other chapters in the story in Units 7, 23 and 31.

Sid looks out of his time machine to see his friend, Bee, lying on the floor.

A black cat is rushing towards him. It jumps up onto the control panel, hitting buttons and levers.

The time machine begins to shake and hum.

Data flashes across the screen. The cat jumps out and heads for the open door.

Sid looks at the screen and knows the machine is already in countdown. He hits buttons and pushes levers, but he can't stop the shaking and humming.

"Bee!" he shouts. "BEE!"

Bee struggles to sit up. "Sid," she calls weakly. "Hit the red button!"

But Sid does not hear her.

He looks helplessly at the screen as the countdown continues.

... 5, 4, 3, 2, 1.

The door of the machine closes.

The shaking stops. The humming becomes louder, and the lights go out.

Sid's heart beats fast as he watches data flashing across the screen. He looks out the porthole and sees trees rush by,

... then clouds

... then empty blue sky.

Sid switches on Camera One and watches the screen. He can see the years rolling out before him like waves on a sea.

"Just like riding a surfboard," he chuckles as the machine passes through a circle of coloured lights.

Source: Excerpt from *A Step in Time*, Time Quest Series, Blake Education.

# Reading & Comprehension

TERM 2

**Use these clues to complete the crossword.**

**Across**

(3) Bee told Sid to hit the ______ button.
(5) Sid tries to stop the ______.
(6) A black ______ ran into the machine.
(9) Sid was in a ______ machine.
(10) Sid looked out through the ______.
(11) The machine started to shake and ______.
(12) Sid hit buttons and pushed ______.

**Down**

(1) Sid sees the countdown on the ______.
(2) Sid thought it was like riding a ______.
(4) ______ flashed across the screen.
(6) The machine went through a ______ of light.
(7) Sid built a time ______.
(8) The ______ in the machine went out.
(10) Sid had to ______ the levers.

| 1 | | 2 | | | | | | | 3 | | 4 |
|---|---|---|---|---|---|---|---|---|---|---|---|
| 5 | | | | | | | | | | | |
| | | | | | | | | | | | |
| | | | | | | 6 | | | | | |
| | | | | 7 | | | | | 8 | | |
| | | | | | | | | 9 | | | |
| | | | | | | | | | | | |
| 10 | | | | | | | | | 11 | | |
| | | | | | | | | | | | |
| | | | | | | | | | | | |
| | | | 12 | | | | | | | | |

## What I'm reading

Title: ______________________

It's: ☐ a paper book/magazine/comic
☐ an audiobook
☐ online

It's: ☐ imaginative ☐ informative

Rating ☆ ☆ ☆ ☆ ☆

*Score 2 points for each correct answer!* SCORE /28 0-12 14-22 24-28

# Grammar & Punctuation

AC9E3LA06, AC9E3LA07

## Direct speech

Remember! Writers tell us what people say to each other by using speech marks ("…"). The speech marks go at the beginning and end of what was said. The first spoken word always has a capital letter. A comma marks off the spoken words from the rest of the sentence. If the sentence has a question mark (?) or an exclamation mark (!), do not use a comma.

*Examples:* "Hit the red button!" Bee calls.

**Read these sentences. Underline the words that the character says. Circle the speech marks. Highlight the comma, question mark or exclamation mark.**

1. "Bee!" he shouts. "BEE!"
2. "Hit the red button!" Bee calls.
3. "Just like riding a surfboard," Sid chuckles.
4. "Where did that cat come from?" asks Bee.
5. "Watch out for the cat!" yells Bee.

## Saying verbs

Saying verbs show how people say things.

*Examples:* "Bee!" Sid **shouts.**

"Where did that cat come from?" **asks** Bee.

**Look at these saying verbs.**

| said | shouted | screamed | chuckled |
|---|---|---|---|
| cried | muttered | cried | asked |
| | mumbled | called | |

**Choose one of the saying verbs to complete each sentence.**

6. "Yikes! A monster!" ______________ Jamie.
7. "I don't want to go," ______________ Tan under his breath.
8. "This is such a funny story," ______________ Tema.
9. "I dropped my ice-cream," ______________ Sue.
10. "What time will you get there?" ______________ Bee.

## Compound clauses

Remember! A clause is a group of words with a subject and a verb.

Compound sentences consist of two clauses. Each clause makes sense on its own. We separate the two clauses by using a comma before the conjunction (joining word).

*Example:* The humming **becomes** louder, and the lights **go** out.

Both clauses could be written as separate sentences.

*Example:* The humming **becomes** louder. The lights **go** out.

Sometimes, when both clauses have the same subject, the subject is not repeated. It is understood.

*Example:* He **hits** buttons and **pushes** levers.

We understand that: He **hits** buttons and he **pushes** levers.

**Read these sentences. Circle the verbs. Underline the subjects. Where a subject is understood, draw a carat (^), and write the missing subject on the line.**

11. Sid looks at the screen and sees the countdown.

    ______________________________

12. The cat jumps out and heads for the open door.

    ______________________________

13. He looks out the porthole and sees trees rush by.

    ______________________________

14. Sid switches on Camera One and watches the screen.

    ______________________________

15. Bee is lying on the floor and sees the cat in the time machine.

    ______________________________

*Score 2 points for each correct answer!* SCORE  /30  0-12  14-24  26-30

TERM 2



TARGETING ENGLISH HOMEWORK YEAR 3 © PASCAL PRESS ISBN 978 1 925726 60 2

# Phonic & Word Knowledge

AC9E3LA08, AC9E3LY06, AC9E3LY09, AC9E3LY10, AC9E3LY11, AC9E3LY12

## Similar spelling, different vowel sound

The words rush and push end with the same letters, but they don't end with the same sound.

Rush has the short vowel sound 'u' as in but and jump.

Push has the short vowel sound 'oo' as in put and book.

**Read these words. Use red to circle the words with the 'u' sound as in rush. Use blue to circle the words with the 'oo' sound as in push.**

| | | | |
|---|---|---|---|
| 1 rush | 4 such | 7 clutch | 10 hutch |
| 2 push | 5 bush | 8 lush | 11 touch |
| 3 much | 6 butch | 9 mush | 12 cushion |

## The trigraph 'tch'

When three letters are used together to spell one sound, it is called a trigraph.

The trigraph 'tch' is used to spell the ch sound.

**Read these words. Draw lines to match them to the pictures.**

13  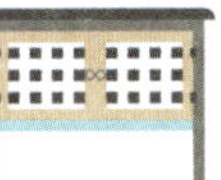 **witch**

14   **match**

15  **patch**

16  **hutch**

17  **watch**

18  **stitch**

**Add tch to these letters to make new words.**

19 ca_____ 20 ha_____ 21 ba_____

22 fe_____ 23 ske_____ 24 pi_____

25 di_____

## Verbs – Past tense

For most verbs, when we write the past tense, we simply add -ed to the base verb.

*Examples:*

look **looked** jump **jumped**

When the base verb ends with 'e', we leave off the 'e' and add -ed.

*Examples:*

like **liked** bake **baked**

When the base verb has one vowel followed by one consonant, we double the consonant before adding -ed and -ing.

*Examples:*

stop **stopped** hum **hummed**

Other verbs don't follow the usual pattern.

*Examples:*

begin **began** shake **shook**

**Choose from these past tense verbs to finish the sentences below.**

| | | | |
|---|---|---|---|
| hit | began | flashed | shouted |
| struggled | went | beat | saw |
| watched | shook | headed | hummed |

26 Today I shout at the sports carnival. Yesterday, I _______________ at the sports carnival.

27 The machines shake all over. Last week, the machines _______________ all over.

28 The cat heads out the door. The cat _______________ out the door last Monday.

29 I see my friends over there. I _______________ my friends over there yesterday.

30 We begin our new unit today. We _______________ our new unit last week.

*Score 2 points for each correct answer!* SCORE /60   

TERM 2

AC9E3LE02, AC9E3LE03, AC9E3LY03, AC9E3LY05

## TV show review: *Bluey*

TERM 2

### *Bluey*

You can watch *Bluey* on ABC iview.

Reviewed by Ben 9, Victoria.

Some people think Bluey is just for little kids. I disagree. I started watching Bluey when I was a little kid. I watched it with my big brother and my mum and dad. We still watch it together, and now I have a little sister who loves it too. So Bluey is for all ages.

Sometimes we think that Bluey's family is just like our family. It makes us laugh. We even have our favourite episodes. My little sister loves it when Bluey and Bingo dance and make their parents stop and dance too. She always wants to make us stop and dance.

Sometimes we play the games that Bluey's family plays. We even make up our own games too.

The music is fun. As soon as we hear the theme song, we grab our Bluey toys and get ready to watch. We laugh when Bingo sings because she sounds just like my little sister.

This is the only kids' show that my family loves to watch together. It helps us talk about things that are bothering us or things we like and don't like. I recommend it for all ages but especially for families to watch together.

If you love funny and clever TV shows as much as my family does, you'll love Bluey. It is very entertaining.

I give it 5 stars. 

TARGETING ENGLISH HOMEWORK YEAR 3 © PASCAL PRESS ISBN 978 1 925726 60 2

# Review

1 Have you watched any episodes of *Bluey*?

- ◯ Yes
- ◯ No
- ◯ Unsure

2 After reading this review, do you think you will watch some episodes of *Bluey*?

- ◯ Yes
- ◯ No
- ◯ Unsure

3 Which words or phrases in the review help you decide?

______________________________

______________________________

______________________________

4 List some TV shows that you like to watch. Circle your favourite.

______________________________

______________________________

______________________________

Now you can write a review of your favourite TV show so that others can decide whether to watch it or not.

1 About the TV show

Title: ______________________________

Where can you watch it?

______________________________

2 Circle the word that best describes the category of TV show.

comedy    science fiction    superhero
family    adventure    mystery
scary    detective    education
action    nature    history

If the type of TV show is not listed, write it here: ______________________________

3 How is the TV show presented? (Choose any that apply.)

- ◯ Animated
- ◯ Puppets
- ◯ Real people or animals
- ◯ People acting
- ◯ Other ______________________________

4 Which of these is true about the show?

- ◯ Each episode has a separate story or adventure.
- ◯ The episodes follow each other to tell one continuous story.
- ◯ Each episode has a series of mini stories or adventures.
- ◯ Other

______________________________

5 How long have you been watching the show?

______________________________

6 How often do you watch the show?

______________________________

7 Who do you watch the show with?

______________________________

8 Where do you watch the show?

______________________________

## The characters

9 What do you know about the main character, for example, their name, where they live, what they like doing, what they look like? Include anything you find interesting about the character.

______________________________

______________________________

______________________________

______________________________

______________________________

______________________________

______________________________

______________________________

______________________________

______________________________

TERM 2

# Review

AC9E3LE02, AC9E3LE03, AC9E3LY03, AC9E3LY05



(10) **What do you know about one of the supporting characters, for example, their name, where they live, what they like doing, what they look like? Include anything you find interesting about the character.**

(11) **Who is your favourite character?**

Why?

(12) **What sorts of things do the characters do in every episode?**

## The setting

(13) **When does the TV show take place?**

- ◯ in the past, a long time ago
- ◯ in the past, not long ago
- ◯ in the present
- ◯ in the future
- ◯ not sure

(14) **Where does the TV show take place? Is it a real location or a fictional place?**

(15) **List things that can be seen, heard or smelled in the location.**

Seen

Heard

Smelled



TARGETING ENGLISH HOMEWORK YEAR 3 © PASCAL PRESS ISBN 978 1 925726 60 2

## The story-lines (plot)

(16) Describe the types of things that happen in each episode or choose one episode and tell about it. Include what happens at the beginning, what problems occur and how the episode concludes or usually concludes.

(17) What do you like best about this TV show?

(18) Is this show like any other shows you have watched? If so, in what way?

(19) Who else might like to watch it? Who do you recommend it for?

(20) How many stars do you give it?

☆☆☆☆☆

Draw a picture of your favourite scene.

# Metamorphosis

Some animals make a very big change as they develop. This change is called metamorphosis.

**Butterfly: Complete Metamorphosis**

A butterfly develops in four stages: egg, larva, pupa and adult. The egg is laid on a plant.

A caterpillar, or larva, hatches from the egg. The caterpillar then becomes a pupa. The pupa sticks to a twig and forms a hard shell called a chrysalis. In the spring, an adult butterfly pushes out of the chrysalis.

**Dragonfly: Incomplete Metamorphosis**

A dragonfly develops in three stages: egg, nymph and adult. Dragonflies lay their eggs in water. When a nymph hatches from an egg, it does not have wings yet. The nymph grows and sheds its skin. This is called moulting. The nymph moults many times before it grows wings and leaves the water to fly off.

Source: *Targeting Science*, Year 3, page 22, Pascal Press.

**Shade the bubble next to the correct answer. Write the answer on the line where appropriate.**

1. **What does metamorphosis mean?**
   - ◯ a big change
   - ◯ a butterfly
   - ◯ a dragonfly

2. **Which animal goes through a complete metamorphosis as it grows?**
   - ◯ a butterfly
   - ◯ a dragonfly
   - ◯ a nymph

3. **Which animal goes through an incomplete metamorphosis as it grows?**
   - ◯ a butterfly
   - ◯ a dragonfly
   - ◯ a caterpillar

4. **How many stages of growth does a butterfly have?**
   - ◯ two
   - ◯ three
   - ◯ four

5. **How many stages of growth does a dragonfly have?**
   - ◯ two
   - ◯ three
   - ◯ four

6. **What is not a stage of the butterfly's growth?**
   - ◯ egg
   - ◯ larva
   - ◯ nymph
   - ◯ adult

7. **What is not a stage of the dragonfly's growth?**
   - ◯ egg
   - ◯ larva
   - ◯ nymph
   - ◯ adult

8. **Where does a butterfly lays its eggs?**
   - ◯ in a nest
   - ◯ on a plant
   - ◯ in the water

9. **Where does a dragonfly lays its eggs?**
   - ◯ in a nest
   - ◯ on a plant
   - ◯ in the water

10. **Where would you expect to see each of these animals?**

    butterflies: ____________________

    dragonflies: ____________________

*Score 2 points for each correct answer!* SCORE /20 0-8 10-14 16-20



TARGETING ENGLISH HOMEWORK YEAR 3 © PASCAL PRESS ISBN 978 1 925726 60 2

TERM 2 REVIEW

# Grammar & Punctuation

**Read these sentences. Underline the subject. Circle the verb. Highlight the topic words.**

1. A big change in animals is called metamorphosis.
2. Another name for caterpillar is larva.
3. A young dragonfly is a nymph.
4. Dragonfly nymphs moult many times.
5. A butterfly's pupa is called a chrysalis.

**Underline the adverbial phrases in each of these sentences. Circle the prepositions.**

6. A butterfly develops in four stages.
7. The egg is laid on a plant.
8. A caterpillar hatches from the egg.
9. An adult butterfly pushes out of the chrysalis in the spring.
10. I saw a dragonfly at the lake after school.

**Read these sentences. Underline the words that are spoken. Circle the saying verb. Highlight who is speaking. Write S for statement. Q for question. E for exclamation.**

11. _____ "Look! A butterfly!" said Tan.
12. _____ "I think it has just emerged," said Emma.
13. _____ "Why?" asked Tan.
14. _____ "Because it's waiting for its wings to dry," said Emma.

**Read these sentences. Circle the pronouns. Underline the nouns they refer to.**

15. Butterflies have wings, so they can fly.
16. When dragonflies hatch out of eggs, they are called nymphs.
17. It might be a dragonfly, but it doesn't breathe fire.
18. Children like to watch butterflies if they see them flying.

**Choose the correct verb for each sentence.**

19. A butterfly ________________ in four stages. (develop, develops)
20. Dragonfly nymphs ________________ many times. (moult, moults)
21. A butterfly ________________ its eggs on a plant. (lay, lays)
22. Dragonfly nymphs ________________ out of eggs. (hatch, hatches)
23. Some animals ________________ as they grow. (change, changes)

**Circle the adjectives in these sentences. On the line, write what the adjective is describing, e.g. colour, size, shape, number, sound, feelings or quality.**

24. Some animals change as they develop. (____________)
25. The pupa forms a hard shell called a chrysalis. (____________)
26. Dragonflies have transparent wings. (____________)
27. Metamorphosis is a big change animals make. (____________)

**Underline the adjectival phrase that describes the nouns in bold.**

28. The butterflies were attracted by the **scent** of the flowers.
29. The butterfly's pupa is on the **twig** near the top of the plant.

**Read this sentence. Underline the phrase that uses personification. Explain why it is an example of personification.**

30. The butterfly felt lonely as it flew from flower to flower.
31. Explain: ________________________________

________________________________

**Join these pairs of simple sentences to form compound sentences using and, but or so. Write the new sentence underneath.**

32. Butterflies have four life stages. Dragonflies have three life stages.

________________________________

________________________________

33. The butterfly's pupa sticks to a twig. It makes a hard shell.

________________________________

________________________________

34. A dragonfly grows wings. It can fly.

________________________________

________________________________

TERM 2

## Grammar & Punctuation

**Read the sentences below. Write F for fact. Write O for opinion.**

35. _____ Butterflies are the most beautiful insects.
36. _____ Butterflies have four life stages.
37. _____ Dragonflies have transparent wings.
38. _____ Dragonflies shouldn't be called dragonflies because they don't breathe fire.

**Use relating verbs to complete these sentences.**

39. A butterfly's pupa __________ called a chrysalis.
40. A dragonfly __________ four transparent wings.
41. Butterflies __________ four life stages.
42. There __________ many butterflies in the garden yesterday.

**Use action verbs to complete these sentences.**

43. Caterpillars __________ out of eggs.
44. Dragonfly nymphs __________ many times as they grow.
45. Butterflies __________ nectar from flowers.
46. Dragonflies __________ near water.

**Read these lists. Put in the missing commas.**

47. Butterflies have four life stages: egg caterpillar pupa and adult.
48. Dragonflies have three life stages: egg nymph and adult.
49. There are many different insects, including butterflies dragonflies moths beetles flies and mosquitos.
50. When we went to the lake, we saw butterflies dragonflies beetles and lots of flies.

Score 2 points for each correct answer!

## Phonic & Word Knowledge

**Read these sentences. Circle the words with an apostrophe. Write C for contraction. Write P for possession.**

1. _____ A dragonfly nymph can't fly because it has no wings.
2. _____ A butterfly's wings are usually colourful.
3. _____ When we went to the lake, we didn't see any spiders.

**Read these words. Underline the consonant digraph or blend. Write two more words that begin with the same digraph or blend.**

4. shed ____________________ ____________________
5. spring ____________________ ____________________
6. plant ____________________ ____________________
7. grow ____________________ ____________________
8. change ____________________ ____________________

**Use different colours to draw lines linking pairs of rhyming words.**

| | |
|---|---|
| 9. fly | grows |
| 10. hose | door |
| 11. change | thing |
| 12. four | high |
| 13. wing | range |
| 14. word | worse |
| 15. chair | hear |
| 16. spear | bird |
| 17. fern | pear |
| 18. nurse | burn |

TERM 2



TARGETING ENGLISH HOMEWORK YEAR 3 © PASCAL PRESS ISBN 978 1 925726 60 2

# Phonic & Word Knowledge

Read these words. Write **S** if you hear the **s sound**. Write **Z** if you hear the **z sound**.

19. _____ **grows**
20. _____ **wings**
21. _____ **flies**
22. _____ **plants**

Count the number of **syllables** in each word, then write them in the correct box.

| | | | |
|---|---|---|---|
| nymph | butterfly | adult | grow |
| metamorphosis | dragonfly | pupa | larva |
| eggs | develop | chrysalis | development |
| moulting | caterpillar | change | |

| One syllable | Two syllables |
|---|---|
| 23. | 27. |
| 24. | 28. |
| 25. | 29. |
| 26. | 30. |

| Three syllables | More than three |
|---|---|
| 31. | 35. |
| 32. | 36. |
| 33. | 37. |
| 34. | |

Say each word from the word bank. Listen to the different sounds represented by the **letter y**. Choose words from the word bank to complete the sentences.

| | | | | |
|---|---|---|---|---|
| butterfly | chrysalis | many | fly | yet |
| nymph | you | dragonfly | very | young |

38. A caterpillar forms a pupa called a _____________.
39. If you go to the lake, _______________ might see dragonflies.
40. There are not _______________ butterflies in the garden this year.
41. A young dragonfly is called a _____________.
42. Animals have wings so they can _____________.

Write the correct **homophones** from the brackets to complete these sentences.

43. Butterflies can fly when _____________ wings are dry. (their, there)
44. I didn't know _____________ I might find some butterflies. (where, wear)
45. I listened hard, but I couldn't _____________ the butterflies flying. (hear, here)
46. If _____________ looking for dragonflies, you'll find them near water. (your, you're)

Write the **plural** for each of these words. Look out for irregular plurals.

47. butterfly _______________
48. wing _______________
49. child _______________
50. pupa _______________
51. change _______________
52. nymph _______________

Write **past tense verbs** to complete these sentences.

53. Yesterday, I __________ a butterfly emerge from its pupa. (watch)
54. When we were at the lake, I __________ ten dragonflies. (see)
55. The dragonfly nymph __________ many times before it had wings. (moult)
56. The butterfly __________ from flower to flower. (flit)
57. The caterpillar __________ into a pupa. (change)
58. The dragonflies __________ around the lake. (fly)

*Score 2 points for each correct answer!*

TERM 2

AC9E3LY03, AC9E3LY04, AC9E3LY05, AC9E3LE02

## Imaginative text – Fable

### The Hare and the Tortoise

One day a hare was bragging to all the animals.

"I can run faster than anyone," he said. "Who is brave enough to race me?"

"I'll race you," said a tortoise.

"But you're just a tortoise," said the hare. "You could never beat me."

"I'd like to try," said the tortoise.

"You're on," said the hare.

The animals told the hare and the tortoise where to race.

"On your marks. Get set. Go!" said the fox.

The hare took off, faster than the wind. The tortoise plodded along, slow and steady. As soon as the hare could no longer see the tortoise behind him, he lay down in the shade of a tree.

"That tortoise will never catch me," he said and went to sleep.

After a while, the tortoise caught up to the hare. He saw the hare sleeping, but he didn't stop. He just kept going. Soon he reached the finish line.

When the hare woke up, he couldn't see the tortoise anywhere.

"What a slowcoach," he said.

When he got to the finish line, he was surprised to see that the tortoise was already there. "You're not the fastest," said all the animals. "Tortoise is the winner."

TARGETING ENGLISH HOMEWORK YEAR 3 © PASCAL PRESS ISBN 978 1 925726 60 2

# Reading & Comprehension

**Shade the bubble next to the correct answer. Write the answer on the line where appropriate.**

1. **Who thought he was the fastest animal?**
   - ◯ the hare
   - ◯ the tortoise
   - ◯ the fox

2. **Who had a race?**
   - ◯ the hare, the tortoise and the fox
   - ◯ the hare and the fox
   - ◯ the hare and the tortoise

3. **Who chose where the race would be held?**
   - ◯ the hare
   - ◯ the fox
   - ◯ the tortoise
   - ◯ the other animals

4. **What did the hare do when he got out of sight?**
   - ◯ lay down and went to sleep
   - ◯ kept on going
   - ◯ laughed at the hare

5. **What did the tortoise do when he saw the hare sleeping?**
   - ◯ He had a sleep too.
   - ◯ He kept on going.
   - ◯ He woke the hare up.

6. **Who won the race?**
   - ◯ the hare
   - ◯ the tortoise
   - ◯ the fox

7. **Why did the hare lie down to have a sleep?**
   - ◯ He was tired after all the running.
   - ◯ He didn't think the tortoise would catch up to him.
   - ◯ He wanted to wait for the tortoise to catch up.

8. **Why did the tortoise win the race?**
   - ◯ He could run faster than the hare.
   - ◯ He kept on going and didn't stop.
   - ◯ The hare went to sleep, but the tortoise kept on going.

9. **How do you think the tortoise felt at the end of the race?**
   - ◯ proud
   - ◯ disappointed
   - ◯ embarrassed

10. **How do you think the hare felt at the end of the race?**
    - ◯ proud
    - ◯ disappointed
    - ◯ embarrassed

11. **Summary**

Write a summary of the story in three or four sentences. Write what happens in the beginning, the middle and the end.

________________________________________

________________________________________

________________________________________

________________________________________

________________________________________

________________________________________

________________________________________

________________________________________

## What I'm reading

Title: ________________________________

It's: ☐ a paper book/magazine/comic
☐ an audiobook
☐ online

It's: ☐ imaginative ☐ informative

Rating ☆ ☆ ☆ ☆ ☆

*Score 2 points for each correct answer!* SCORE /22    

TERM 3

TARGETING ENGLISH HOMEWORK YEAR 3 © PASCAL PRESS ISBN 978 1 925726 60 2

# Grammar & Punctuation

AC9E3LA02, AC9E3LE03

## Comparative adjectives

Adjectives can be used to show how people or things compare to each other.

When two things are compared, you add the suffix -er.

*Example:* The hare is **fast**, but the antelope is **faster**.

When more than two things are compared, you add the suffix -est.

*Example:* The cheetah is the **fastest** of all.

These comparative adjectives are tricky:

| | | |
|---|---|---|
| good | better | best |
| bad | worse | worst |
| many | more | most |
| little | less | least |

**Add the suffixes -er and -est to these adjectives.**

| | er | est |
|---|---|---|
| 1 fast | ______ | ______ |
| 2 slow | ______ | ______ |
| 3 quick | ______ | ______ |
| 4 smart | ______ | ______ |
| 5 strong | ______ | ______ |

**Write the correct comparative adjective to complete each sentence.**

6 An elephant is ______ than a mouse. (big)

7 A tortoise is ______ than a horse. (small)

8 Tan is the ______ person in our class. (old)

9 My sister is ______ than I am. (tall)

10 Mitch is the ______ soccer player at our school. (good)

## Modal verbs

Modal verbs are helper verbs. They give us more information about the verbs that follow.

*Examples:* can could will would may might should must

Modal verbs can be used to show:

- how likely something is to happen. (The tortoise **might** win the race.)
- someone's ability to do something. (I **can** run faster than anyone.)
- if something must be done. (The tortoise **must** keep going.)
- if permission is given to do something. (The fox **can** start the race.)
- if something is planned to be done. (The fox **will** start the race.)

**Write modal verbs to complete these sentences.**

11 The hare ______ win if he keeps on running.

12 The hare ______ stop bragging to all the animals.

13 None of the other animals ______ race against the hare.

14 If the hare and the fox have a race, the hare ______ win.

15 The cheetah ______ win a race against any land animal.

16 If it rains, the race ______ be called off.

17 If he doesn't go to sleep, the hare ______ win the race.

18 When I am finished my homework, I ______ choose what to do.

*Score 2 points for each correct answer!* SCORE /36

0-16 18-30 32-36

TERM 3



TARGETING ENGLISH HOMEWORK YEAR 3 © PASCAL PRESS ISBN 978 1 925726 60 2

# Phonic & Word Knowledge

AC9E3LY06, AC9E3LY09, AC9E3LY10, AC9E3LY11, AC9E3LY12

## Words that end with 'gh'

These words end with the letters 'gh'. The letters 'gh' spell the 'f' sound.

*Examples:*

enou**gh** Who is brave **enough** to race me?
lau**gh** The hare won't **laugh** if the tortoise wins.
cou**gh** I stayed home because I had a runny nose and a **cough**.
rou**gh** The car bumped along the **rough** road.
tou**gh** The steak had been cooked too long and was very **tough**.

These words end with the letters 'gh'. The letters 'gh' are silent. They help spell the vowel sound.

*Examples:*

hi**gh** The sun was **high** in the sky.
bou**gh** The **bough** of the tree was bending in the wind.
dou**gh** The baker puts yeast in the **dough** to make pizza bases.
thi**gh** The cricket ball hit me on the **thigh**.
thou**gh** I can run fast. I can't swim fast **though**.

**Choose words from the gh list that rhyme with these words. Add others you know.**

1. stuff ______________________
2. try ______________________
3. off ______________________
4. calf ______________________
5. cow ______________________
6. go ______________________

## Homophones

Homophones are words that sound the same but have different meanings.

Sometimes they are spelled the same way.
*Examples*: lie, lie

Sometimes they are spelled differently.
*Examples*: hear, here

**Choose the correct homophone to complete these sentences.**

7. The children were told to brush their __________ before school. (hair, hare)
8. The __________ and the tortoise had a race. (hair, hare)
9. The tortoise __________ up to the hare and beat it. (caught, court)
10. Groups of children were playing handball on the tennis __________. (caught, court)
11. The tortoise __________ the hare, but it didn't stop. (saw, sore)
12. My thigh is __________ where the cricket ball hit it. (saw, sore)
13. I think __________ the fastest in the race. (your, you're)
14. I think __________ shoes are newer than mine. (your, you're)
15. I always tell the truth. I never __________. (lie, lie)
16. I had to __________ on the bed in the sick room because I wasn't well. (lie, lie)

## Word ladders

**Use the clues to change the top word into the bottom word, one letter at a time.**

**a**

| | | |
|---|---|---|
| | | **bull** |
| 17 | something that rings | |
| 18 | worn on the waist | |
| 19 | you do this on a drum | |
| | | bear |

**b**

| | | |
|---|---|---|
| | | **book** |
| 20 | a chef | |
| 21 | a stopper in a bottle | |
| 22 | used with a knife | |
| | | fort |

TERM 3

*Score 2 points for each correct answer!* SCORE /44    

# Reading & Comprehension

AC9E3LY03, AC9E3LY04, AC9E3LY05, AC9E3LE02, AC9HS3K06, AC9HP4P08, AC9HP4P10

## Informative text – Rules

### Trampolines

Many backyards have a trampoline. These are great fun when used properly. Some simple safety rules will make sure everyone has loads of fun.

## RULES FOR THE TRAMPOLINE

- Only one person at a time should be on the trampoline.
- Make sure there is always a partner or a 'spotter'. The spotter's job is to warn the trampoline user if they are moving off the centre of the mat.
- Bare feet should be used when on the trampoline.
- A trampoline should not be used if it is wet.
- Do not let anyone go underneath the trampoline.
- Only jump in the centre of the mat.
- Face the end of the frame when jumping on the trampoline.
- Focus your eyes on the trampoline. This will help control where you bounce.

Source: Adapted from *Passport to Safety*, Hazel Edwards & Goldie Alexander, Blake Education.

TERM 3



TARGETING ENGLISH HOMEWORK YEAR 3 © PASCAL PRESS ISBN 978 1 925726 60 2

# Reading & Comprehension

Shade the bubble next to the correct answer. Write the answer on the line where appropriate.

1. Why is it important to have rules for the trampoline? (Choose any that apply.)
   - ◯ to boss everyone around
   - ◯ to make it fun for everyone
   - ◯ to keep everyone safe
   - ◯ to ruin everyone's fun

2. How many people should be on the trampoline at the same time?
   - ◯ one
   - ◯ two partners – one to jump and one to spot
   - ◯ three
   - ◯ as many as you like

3. What is the purpose of the **spotter**?
   - ◯ to tell people when their time is up
   - ◯ to tell people when they are not in the centre of the trampoline
   - ◯ to make sure people are following the rules
   - ◯ to tell people when it's their turn

4. What should you wear on your feet when you are on the trampoline?
   - ◯ football boots
   - ◯ runners
   - ◯ nothing
   - ◯ socks

5. Why do you think a trampoline should not be used if it's wet?
   - ◯ It will be cold.
   - ◯ It will be slippery.
   - ◯ It will be noisy.
   - ◯ It won't be springy.

6. Why should people **not** go under the trampoline?
   - ◯ They might be hit by the person on the trampoline.
   - ◯ It's not time to play hide and seek.
   - ◯ Nobody wants them to have too much fun.
   - ◯ There might be spiders under there.

7. What do you call the part of the trampoline where people jump?
   - ◯ the frame
   - ◯ the mat
   - ◯ the bounce

8. Where should you face when you are jumping on the trampoline?
   - ◯ the end of the frame
   - ◯ the centre of the mat
   - ◯ your friends

9. What can you do to help control where you bounce?
   - ◯ Watch your feet.
   - ◯ Focus on the trampoline.
   - ◯ Look at your friends.

10. What do you think?

    Do you agree with the rule about only one person on a trampoline at a time? Explain.

    ______________________________________________
    ______________________________________________
    ______________________________________________
    ______________________________________________
    ______________________________________________
    ______________________________________________

TERM 3

## What I'm reading

Title: ______________________________

It's: ☐ a paper book/magazine/comic
☐ an audiobook
☐ online

It's: ☐ imaginative ☐ informative

Rating ☆ ☆ ☆ ☆ ☆

Score 2 points for each correct answer! SCORE /20 0-8 10-14 16-20

# Grammar & Punctuation

AC9E3LA02, AC9E3LA07, AC9E3LA10

## Sentences

Rules are usually written in short, sharp, simple sentences that tell you what to do.

Sometimes the subject 'you' is omitted. It is said to be understood that the rules are for you to follow.

*Examples:*

(You should make sure) only one person at a time is on the trampoline.

(You should) **only jump in the centre of the mat.**

The subject is omitted, and the sentences are shortened to make the rule more imperative and the message more important.

**Read these rules. Rewrite them, beginning each one with 'You should'. You may need to change the order of the words in the sentence.**

1. A trampoline should not be used if it is wet.

______________________________

2. Bare feet should be used when on the trampoline.

______________________________

3. Face the end of the frame when jumping on the trampoline.

______________________________

**Read these sentences. Rewrite them as rules, without 'You should'. You may need to change the order of the words in the sentence.**

4. You should always put your hand up if you want to ask a question.

______________________________

5. You should cover your mouth when you yawn.

______________________________

6. You should cross the road on a pedestrian crossing.

______________________________

## Modal words

Remember, modal verbs are helper verbs. In rules, they are used to tell us that something should or must be done.

*Examples:*

Bare feet **should** be used.

**Make sure** there is a 'spotter'.

Other modal words are also used to stress the importance of following the rules.

*Examples:*

only    always    warn    help

**Read these sentences. Underline the words and phrases that show the rule is important.**

7. Only one person at a time should be on the trampoline.
8. Do not run around the edge of the pool.
9. You must always use the ladder to go up the slippery slide.
10. Warning: the doors are closing.

## Adverbial phrases

Remember! An adverbial phrase tells us how, when, where and why things happen.

In the rules for the trampoline, adverbial phrases tell us where things should happen.

*Example:*

Only one person at a time should be (where) **on the trampoline.**

**Underline the adverbial phrases that tell where in these sentences.**

11. Do not go underneath the trampoline.
12. Focus your eyes on the trampoline.
13. The trampoline user should not move off the centre of the mat.

*Score 2 points for each correct answer!*

SCORE /26    
0-10 12-20 22-26

TERM 3



TARGETING ENGLISH HOMEWORK YEAR 3 © PASCAL PRESS ISBN 978 1 925726 60 2

# Phonic & Word Knowledge

UNIT 18

AC9E3LY06, AC9E3LY09, AC9E3LY10, AC9E3LY11, AC9E3LY12

## Letters spell different sounds – The letter 'c'

Remember, the letter 'c' can be used to represent different sounds: the hard 'ck' sound, as in cat; the soft 'c' sound, as in cent; the digraph 'ch', as in chips.

**Read these words. Underline c or ch. Write C if you hear the hard 'ck' sound, S if you hear the soft 'c' sound and CH if you hear 'ch' as in chips.**

1. centre _____
2. face _____
3. focus _____
4. control _____
5. bounce _____
6. choose _____
7. cold _____
8. copy _____
9. rich _____

## 'R' controlled vowel sounds 'ar', 'er' and 'or'

There are different ways of spelling each of the 'r' controlled vowel sounds, 'ar' as in star, 'er' as in fern, and 'or' as in corn.

*Examples*:

| | | | | |
|---|---|---|---|---|
| star | heart | grass | laugh | half |
| fern | bird | nurse | worm | pearl |
| corn | ball | door | sauce | thought |

**Read these words. Look at the letters in bold. Sort the words into the correct boxes.**

10. partner
11. person
12. centre
13. warn
14. sure
15. scarf
16. paw
17. surf
18. girl
19. fast
20. glass
21. hawk

| 'ar' vowel sound | 'er' vowel sound | 'or' vowel sound |
|---|---|---|
| | | |

## Syllables

**Count the number of syllables in each word. Write the number beside it.**

22. many _____
23. backyard _____
24. trampoline _____
25. properly _____
26. always _____
27. underneath _____
28. sure _____
29. person _____
30. anyone _____

## The suffix –er

Suffixes are syllables attached to the ends of words. Some syllables change verbs into nouns.

*Examples*:

One who **jumps** is a **jumper**.

One who **spots** is a **spotter**.

One who **races** is a **racer**.

The rules for adding the suffix –er are the same as for adding –ed and –ing.

**Add -er to the word in bold to make the noun for one who does the action. Write the word. Remember the rules.**

31. One who **sings** is a ____________________.
32. One who **teaches** is a ____________________.
33. One who **jogs** is a ____________________.
34. One who **writes** is a ____________________.

*Score 2 points for each correct answer!*

SCORE /68 | 0-32 | 34-62 | 64-68

TERM 3

AC9E3LY03, AC9E3LY04, AC9E3LY05, AC9E3LA09

## Imaginative text – A Play

### Pirate Treasure

**Characters:**

Narrator  Parrot  Jed  Captain Pete  Pirate Jack  Pirate Sal  Server

**Setting:** Inside Crazy Chicken's fast-food restaurant

Narrator: On Talk Like a Pirate Day, Jed found three pirates rummaging in a bin outside Crazy Chicken's. They were looking for treasure.

Parrot: Pieces of eight, pieces of eight!

Narrator: Jed told them they wouldn't find treasure in the bin, and he took them into the restaurant.

Server: Welcome to Crazy Chicken's. What would you like?

Captain Pete: Do you be having – treasure here?

Server: At Crazy Chicken's we treasure our 'Pieces of Eight', our crunchy, crisp, golden nuggets. Do you want to place an order?

Captain Pete: Treasure!

Pirate Jack: Gold!

Pirate Sal: Nuggets!

Jed: Aye, that's what we be having! Four serves, me good sir. Bring us your treasure!

Captain Pete: [to Jed] They will bring us 'The Treasure'?

Jed: Aye, Captain. Take a seat while I exchange a small bounty for the treasure.

Narrator: Jed paid for the meals with his pocket money.

Server: Thank you. Enjoy your meals. (muttering) I hate Talk Like a Pirate Day.

Narrator: The parrot watched from the windowsill.

Parrot: Pieces of eight, pieces of eight!

Narrator: Soon, the pirates and Jed were tucking into the golden nuggets.

Pirate Jack: (burping) That be one fine treasure!

Pirate Sal: That be the best treasure we've had for days!

Captain Pete: This be fine treasure, me lad, and you be one fine pirate. How would you like to join us on the high seas?

Jed: Um, thank you, Captain, but one day of talking like a pirate is enough for me.

Source: Adapted from *A Pirate for a Day* by Sandie Eldridge, Blake Education.





TARGETING ENGLISH HOMEWORK YEAR 3 © PASCAL PRESS ISBN 978 1 925726 60 2

# Reading & Comprehension

Write your answers on the lines provided.

① Where does the story take place? (setting)

② List **three** things you would see in the setting.

a

b

c

③ Who are the characters in the story?

④ List **three** things you know about each of these characters.

Jed

a

b

c

Captain Pete

a

b

c

⑤ What is the role of the narrator?

⑥ What were the pirates looking for in the bin?

⑦ Jed told the pirates they would find treasure in the restaurant. What was the treasure?

⑧ What words convinced the pirates there was treasure in the restaurant?

⑨ Look at the illustration.

Which of the characters is A?

Which of the characters is B?

Which of the characters is C?

How do you know?

⑩ What do you think?

Why do you think Jed didn't want to be a pirate?

What I'm reading

Title:

It's: ☐ a paper book/magazine/comic
☐ an audiobook
☐ online

It's: ☐ imaginative ☐ informative

Rating ☆☆☆☆☆

Score 2 points for each correct answer!

SCORE /20

TERM 3

AC9E3LA02, AC9E3LA06, AC9E3LA10

## Direct speech and saying verbs

Remember! In direct speech, writers usually tell us what people say to each other by using speech marks and saying verbs.

*Example*:

"Welcome to Crazy Chicken's. What would you like?" said the server.

In a play, the characters names are written on the left, and the words they say are written beside them. No speech marks or saying verbs are used.

**Rewrite these sentences from the play as direct speech. Remember to use the correct punctation and saying verbs.**

1. Server: Do you want to place an order?

_______________

_______________

2. Jed: Aye, that's what we be having! Four serves, me good sir.

_______________

_______________

3. Pirate Sal: That be the best treasure we've had for days!

_______________

_______________

4. Captain Pete: This be fine treasure, me lad, and you be one fine pirate.

_______________

_______________

## Sentences

Remember, a statement begins with a capital letter and ends with a full stop (.).

A question begins with a capital letter and ends with a question mark (?).

An exclamation begins with a capital letter and ends with an exclamation mark (!).

**Read through the play again and find the following:**

**Write two statements.**

5. _______________

_______________

6. _______________

_______________

**Write two questions.**

7. _______________

_______________

8. _______________

_______________

**Write two exclamations.**

9. _______________

_______________

10. _______________

_______________

## Adjectives – Feeling words

Remember, adjectives can be used to describe feelings. Although feeling words haven't been used in the play, we understand how the characters feel by what they say.

*Examples of feeling words:*

happy sad scared angry
surprised disgusted curious
proud amused bored
comfortable excited

**List adjectives to describe how Jed and the pirates were feeling at different times in the story.**

11. Jed _______________

_______________

12. Pirates _______________

_______________

*Score 2 points for each correct answer!* SCORE /24 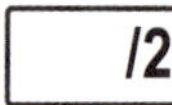 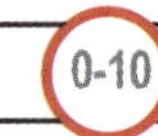 0-10  12-18  20-24

TERM 3



TARGETING ENGLISH HOMEWORK YEAR 3 © PASCAL PRESS ISBN 978 1 925726 60 2

# Phonic & Word Knowledge

AC9E3LY10, AC9E3LY12

## Opposites

| happy | bottom | sad | hard | bad |
|---|---|---|---|---|
| scared | that | surprised | bored | |
| quick | safe | inside | ashamed | none |
| proud | easy | top | good | end |
| this | all | outside | slow | start |

**There are 12 pairs of opposites in the box above. Write them on the lines.**

1. ______ ______
2. ______ ______
3. ______ ______
4. ______ ______
5. ______ ______
6. ______ ______
7. ______ ______
8. ______ ______
9. ______ ______
10. ______ ______
11. ______ ______
12. ______ ______

## Prefixes

A prefix is a letter or group of letters that is added to the beginning of a word.
The prefix un– means 'not' or 'the opposite of'.
*Examples:* plug **un**plug happy **un**happy

**Add the prefix un– to these words then write their meanings from the box.**

| not kind | not tidy | not fair | not safe |
|---|---|---|---|
| not surprised | not ashamed | not sure | |
| not healthy | not used | not able | |

13. ______sure ______
14. ______tidy ______
15. ______able ______
16. ______ashamed ______
17. ______safe ______
18. ______healthy ______
19. ______used ______
20. ______surprised ______
21. ______kind ______
22. ______fair ______

## Talk like a pirate

**In the play, there are pirate words and phrases that Jed and the pirates use. Write them here.**

*Example:* pieces of eight

23. ______
24. ______
25. ______
26. ______
27. ______
28. ______

## Word search

**Circle these high-frequency and pirate theme words in the grid:**

best, bounty, buy, chicken, drop, eight, gold, high, nuggets, pirates, serve, treasure

**Words go left to right or top to bottom.**

| G | C | H | I | C | K | E | N |
|---|---|---|---|---|---|---|---|
| O | E | I | G | H | T | P | U |
| L | I | G | R | B | A | S | G |
| D | D | H | T | E | B | E | G |
| T | R | E | A | S | U | R | E |
| B | O | U | N | T | Y | V | T |
| E | P | I | R | A | T | E | S |

29. When you have found all the words, the remaining letters, from left to right and top to bottom, will spell out a word. Write it here.

______

*Score 2 points for each correct answer!* SCORE /58   

TERM 3

AC9E3LY03, AC9E3LY04, AC9E3LY05, AC9HP4P10

## Persuasive text – Exposition

### Exercise is Good for You

Exercise is good for you. It helps to make you strong, fit and healthy. The best exercise makes you breathe faster and gets your heart pumping. You need to do at least 60 minutes of good exercise every day. Swimming, basketball, jogging, skating, biking or jumping rope are good ways to give your whole body a workout.

Exercise helps to make you flexible. When you are flexible, you can stretch your body and move in different ways.

Exercise helps to make you stronger. When you are strong, you can do push-ups, row a boat and run a race.

Exercise helps to keep you at a normal weight. Then you are more likely to eat well and do good exercise. Everyday tasks are easier and more fun too.

Exercise helps to make you feel good. When you exercise, special chemicals in your brain help you get rid of bad feelings. They help you feel calm.

Exercise helps you to sleep. After a good night's sleep, you wake up feeling rested and ready to start a new day.

Being fit and healthy is a better way to live.

TARGETING ENGLISH HOMEWORK YEAR 3 © PASCAL PRESS ISBN 978 1 925726 60 2

# Reading & Comprehension

**Shade the bubble next to the correct answer. Write the answer on the line where appropriate.**

1. **What is this article mainly about?**
   - ◯ playing sport
   - ◯ keeping calm
   - ◯ exercise

2. **Which of these things does exercise help with? (Choose any that apply.)**
   - ◯ strength
   - ◯ flexibility
   - ◯ feeling good
   - ◯ sleep

3. **What does the best exercise do? (Choose any that apply.)**
   - ◯ makes you feel sleepy
   - ◯ makes you breathe faster
   - ◯ makes you talk really fast
   - ◯ gets your heart pumping

4. **Which of these are good forms of exercise? (Choose any that apply.)**
   - ◯ reading
   - ◯ skating
   - ◯ playing video games
   - ◯ swimming
   - ◯ jumping rope
   - ◯ watching television

5. **Which word means you can stretch your body and move in different ways?**
   - ◯ strong
   - ◯ flexible
   - ◯ sleepy

6. **If you can do push-ups, row a boat or run a race, you are:**
   - ◯ strong.
   - ◯ flexible.
   - ◯ sleepy.

7. **When are you more likely to eat well and do good exercise? When you are:**
   - ◯ underweight.
   - ◯ normal weight.
   - ◯ overweight.

8. **How much exercise do you need to do every day?**
   - ◯ 1 hour
   - ◯ 2 hours
   - ◯ 3 hours

9. **What makes everyday tasks easier and fun to do?**
   - ◯ playing music
   - ◯ eating good food
   - ◯ exercise

10. **Which types of exercise do you enjoy most?**

_______________________________________

_______________________________________

TERM 3

## What I'm reading

Title: ______________________

It's: ☐ a paper book/magazine/comic
☐ an audiobook
☐ online

It's: ☐ imaginative ☐ informative

Rating ☆☆☆☆☆

Score 2 points for each correct answer! SCORE /20

# Grammar & Punctuation

AC9E3LA02, AC9E3LA06, AC9E3LY06, AC9E3LY10

## Compound sentences

Remember! Compound sentences consist of two clauses joined with a conjunction.

Conjunctions include and, but, so, yet.

*Example:* Exercise is good for you, **and** it helps you to live a better life.

Sometimes, if the clauses have the same subject, the subject is not repeated. It is understood.

*Example:* The best exercise makes you breathe faster and (it) gets your heart pumping.

**Use conjunctions to join these pairs of clauses into compound sentences.**

1. Exercise helps to make you flexible. You can stretch your body.

______________________________

______________________________

2. You can do push-ups. You can row a boat.

______________________________

______________________________

3. Exercise helps you to sleep. You wake up feeling rested.

______________________________

______________________________

4. The best exercise makes you breathe faster. It gets your heart pumping.

______________________________

______________________________

5. You will eat well. Everyday tasks will be easier.

______________________________

______________________________

## Emotive words

In a persuasive exposition, the writer uses emotive words to convince the reader to agree with them. They will be either positive or negative, depending on the writer's opinion.

*Examples:* good fantastic excellent
bad boring terrible

**Circle the emotive words in these sentences.**

6. Exercise is good for you.
7. Exercise helps to make you flexible.
8. Exercise helps to make you stronger.
9. Everyday tasks are easier and more fun to do.
10. When you exercise, special chemicals help you get rid of bad feelings.

## Comparative adjectives

Comparative adjectives can be used to compare abilities and feelings.

*Example:* You are **strong**. She is **stronger**.
I am the **strongest**.

When words end with 'y', you change the 'y' to 'i' before adding –er or –est.

*Example:* happy **happier** **happiest**

Remember, some comparative adjectives are tricky.

*Example:* good/better/best bad/worse/worst many/more/most little/less/least

And for some we don't add –er or –est. We use the words more and most.

*Example:* fun **more** fun **most** fun

**Complete the table of comparative adjectives.**

| Example: strong | stronger | strongest |
|---|---|---|
| fit | 11 | 12 |
| calm | 13 | 14 |
| ready | 15 | 16 |
| healthy | 17 | 18 |
| flexible | 19 | 20 |

*Score 2 points for each correct answer!* SCORE /40    

TERM 3



TARGETING ENGLISH HOMEWORK YEAR 3 © PASCAL PRESS ISBN 978 1 925726 60 2

## The letter 'x'

The letter 'x' is special because it doesn't often occur at the beginning of a word. It is usually in the middle or at the end of a word as in exercise or box. It makes a sound like 'ks'.

**Draw lines to match the words and pictures.**

1. fox
2. mixer
3. boxer
4. six
5. ox
6. text
7. sixty
8. T-Rex
9. lynx
10. taxi

**Choose from these words with the prefix ex– to complete the sentences.**

| exercise | example | exam | extra |
|---|---|---|---|
| exit | exciting | excellent | |
| excuse | exhale | excel | |

11. We will have an ______________ at the end of term to see what we have learned.
12. The boy made up an ______________ for why he was late.
13. Take a deep breath. Hold it. Now ______________.
14. Everyone should ______________ for 60 minutes every day.
15. I always ask for ______________ cheese on my pizza.

## Compound words

**Add ball or day to each of these words to make a compound word. Sometimes they will join at the front of the word and sometimes at the end.**

16. foot ______________
17. dream ______________
18. week ______________
19. gum ______________
20. every ______________
21. light ______________
22. basket ______________
23. meat ______________
24. eye ______________
25. birth ______________

## Verb tense – Adding –ed and –ing

For most verbs, we simply add –ed for past tense or –ing for present tense to the base verb.

*Example:* play   played   playing

When the base verb ends with 'e', we leave off the 'e' and add –ed or –ing.

*Example:* hope   hoped   hoping

When the base verb has one vowel followed by one consonant, we double the consonant.

*Example:* skip   skipped   skipping

Some verbs are irregular and the verb changes.

*Example:* give   gave

**Add endings to these base verbs to show past and present tense.**

| | Base verb (do) | Past tense (did) | Present tense (doing now) |
|---|---|---|---|
| 26 | exercise | | |
| 27 | pump | | |
| 28 | stretch | | |
| 29 | swim | | |
| 30 | make | | |

*Score 2 points for each correct answer!*

SCORE /60 0-28 30-54 56-60

TERM 3

  ISBN 978 1 925726 60 2

# Reading & Comprehension

AC9E3LY03, AC9E3LY04, AC9E3LY05, AC9S3U01

## Informative text – Report & Diagrams

### Survival Features of Snakes and Crocodiles

The Desert Death Adder and the Saltwater Crocodile are Australian reptiles.

The Desert Death Adder is one of the most venomous land snakes in the world. Its fangs are longer than those of most other venomous Australian snakes.

The Saltwater Crocodile is the largest of all living reptiles. An adult male can grow up to more than 5 m in length and weigh up to 1000 kg.

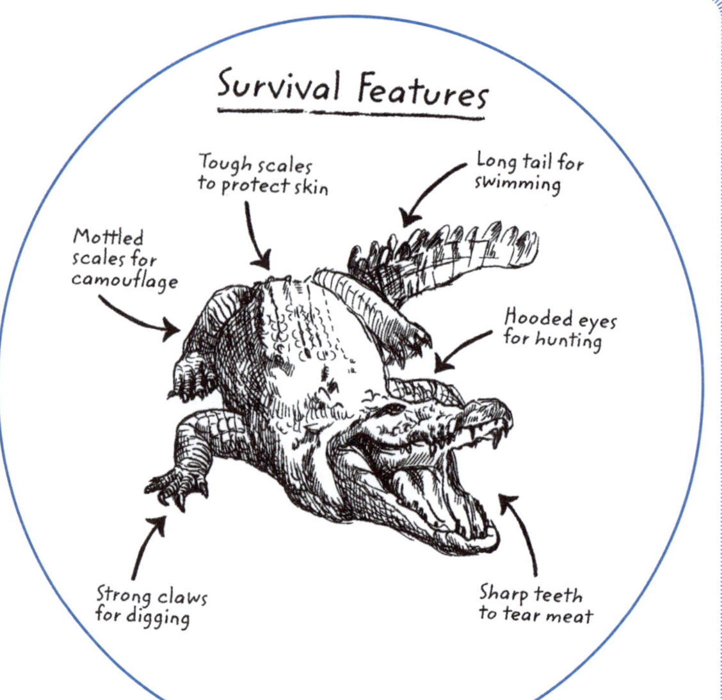


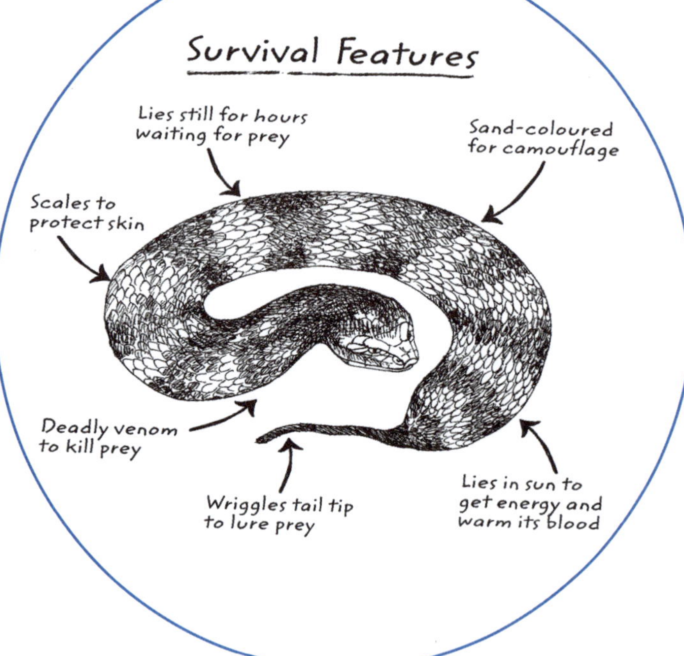


Source: Adapted from *Desmond the Death Adder* and *Crafty Crocodile*, Rebecca Johnson, Pascal Press.

TERM 3



TARGETING ENGLISH HOMEWORK YEAR 3 © PASCAL PRESS ISBN 978 1 925726 60 2

# Reading & Comprehension

Shade the bubble next to the correct answer.

1. **What type of animals is this article about?**
   - ◯ Australian mammals
   - ◯ Australian reptiles
   - ◯ Australian birds

2. **What do these two animals have in common? (Choose any that apply.)**
   - ◯ They are both Australian.
   - ◯ They are both reptiles.
   - ◯ They are both deadly.
   - ◯ They are both poisonous.
   - ◯ They both have scales.

3. **What is special about the Desert Death Adder?**
   - ◯ It is the longest snake in the world.
   - ◯ It is one of the most venomous land snakes in the world.
   - ◯ It is heavier than a crocodile.

4. **What is special about the Saltwater Crocodile?**
   - ◯ It is the largest reptile that ever lived.
   - ◯ It is the largest living reptile.
   - ◯ It has the longest fangs of any other reptile.

5. **What does a Desert Death Adder have for protection? (Choose any that apply.)**
   - ◯ scales
   - ◯ sand-coloured skin
   - ◯ venom
   - ◯ wriggly tail

6. **What does a Saltwater Crocodile have for protection? (Choose any that apply.)**
   - ◯ scales
   - ◯ strong claws
   - ◯ sharp teeth
   - ◯ wriggly tail

7. **What does the Desert Death Adder use its tail for?**
   - ◯ for digging
   - ◯ to lure prey
   - ◯ to swim

8. **What does the Saltwater Crocodile use its tail for?**
   - ◯ to dig
   - ◯ to lure prey
   - ◯ to swim

9. **Why does the Desert Death Adder lie in the sun?**
   - ◯ to rest
   - ◯ to warm up
   - ◯ to get a tan

10. **What does the Saltwater Crocodile use its hooded eyes for?**
    - ◯ to sleep
    - ◯ to see at night
    - ◯ to hunt

## What I'm reading

Title: ____________________

It's: ☐ a paper book/magazine/comic
☐ an audiobook
☐ online

It's: ☐ imaginative ☐ informative

Rating ☆ ☆ ☆ ☆ ☆

Score 2 points for each correct answer! SCORE /20

0-8 10-14 16-20

TERM 3

# Grammar & Punctuation

AC9E3LA06, AC9E3LA10, AC9E3LY10

## Adjectives with the suffix –ous

Adjectives that end with the suffix –ous usually mean 'full of' or having the quality.

*Examples:* venom**ous** = full of venom
danger**ous** = full of danger

But not all –ous adjectives build on a base word.

*Examples:* jeal**ous** anonym**ous**

**Read these –ous adjectives. Underline ous. Write their meaning.**

1. poisonous = ______________
2. mountainous = ______________
3. adventurous = ______________
4. humorous = ______________
5. famous = ______________
6. joyous = ______________
7. disastrous = ______________
8. hazardous = ______________

## Writing sentences

Labels on diagrams are often written in part sentences or sentence fragments. The subject may be missing and understood from the diagram.

*Example*: Wiggles tail tip to lure prey

The subject is understood: *The Desert Death Adder* wiggles its tail tip to lure prey.

**Write sentences using these sentence fragments.**

9. sharp teeth to tear meat

______________________________

10. sand-coloured for camouflage

______________________________

11. scales to protect skin

______________________________

12. strong claws for digging

______________________________

## Articles – a, an, the

The words a, an and the come before nouns. These words are called articles. They are often the first words in a noun group.

*Examples*:

**the** Desert Death Adder

**an** adult male

**a** Saltwater Crocodile

The word the refers to a particular person or thing. The is called the definite article.

A and an are used more generally. They do not relate to a particular person or thing. They are called indefinite articles.

A is used before a singular noun.
*Example*: **a** crocodile

An is used before a singular noun that begins with a vowel.
*Example*: **an** adder

**Choose a, an or the to complete these sentences.**

13. The Desert Death Adder will lie in _____ sun to warm up.
14. The Saltwater Crocodile has _____ long tail to help it swim.
15. The Saltwater Crocodile is _____ Australian reptile.
16. Scales help to protect _____ skin of Desert Death Adders.
17. The venom of _____ Desert Death Adder is deadly.
18. Mottled scales provide camouflage for _____ Saltwater Crocodiles.
19. The biggest reptile that is still living is _____ adult male Saltwater Crocodile.
20. Australian Death Adders live in _____ desert.

*Score 2 points for each correct answer!* SCORE  /40  0-18  20-34  36-40

TERM 3



TARGETING ENGLISH HOMEWORK YEAR 3 © PASCAL PRESS ISBN 978 1 925726 60 2

# Phonic & Word Knowledge

AC9E3LA10, AC9E3LY06, AC9E3LY12

## Topic words

**Draw lines to match these topic words to their meanings.**

| | |
|---|---|
| 1 reptile | a animals caught and killed by other animals for food |
| 2 adder | b a large sharp tooth |
| 3 venomous | c a venomous snake |
| 4 fangs | d a type of bait used for fishing or hunting |
| 5 prey | e a third eyelid covering the eye |
| 6 lure | f a cold-blooded animal that has scales and lays eggs |
| 7 camouflage | g continuing to live or exist |
| 8 mottled | h injects poison |
| 9 hooded | i marked with spots or smears of colour |
| 10 survival | j a means of hiding by blending in with surroundings |

## Three tricky words – desert, desert and dessert

Many people mix up the words desert, desert and dessert.

Two of the words look the same – desert and desert – but they sound different and have different meanings. Two of the words look different but they sound the same.

The first desert is a dry area of land, like where the Desert Death Adder lives. It is a noun, a naming word. It is pronounced as if it is spelt dez-ert. We stress the first syllable.

The second desert is a verb, a doing word. It means to leave or abandon something. There is a saying that rats desert a sinking ship. It is pronounced dee-zert. We stress the second syllable.

The third word, dessert, is something sweet, often eaten after a main course. You can remember it is the one with the double 's' for something sweet. It is a noun, but it is pronounced the same as the verb desert, meaning to leave.

**Choose the correct desert, desert or dessert to complete these sentences.**

11. Mum said I couldn't have ______________ until after dinner.
12. Many animals that live in the ______________ hide from the sun during the day.
13. I asked my friend to stay and not ______________ me in the playground.
14. I could not eat my ______________ because it was too sweet.
15. There is a lot of ______________ in the middle of Australia.
16. The old house was ______________ed and looked spooky at night.

**Each of these words is spelt incorrectly with an extra letter added. Rewrite the words correctly and write the extra letter on the lines below to find the answer to the riddle.**

17. repstile ______________
18. faangs ______________
19. andder ______________
20. preyd ______________
21. camouwflage ______________
22. luire ______________
23. mottcled ______________
24. hoodhed ______________
25. venomeous ______________
26. sursvival ______________

Why won't you ever go hungry in the desert?

Because of all the

__ __ __ __ __ __ __ __ __ __ there.

17 18 19 20 21 22 23 24 25 26

*Score 2 points for each correct answer!* SCORE /52

0-24

26-46

48-52

TERM 3

AC9E3LY03, AC9E3LY04, AC9E3LY05, AC9S3U02

## Informative text – Report

# Fossils

A fossil is the remains or marks of a plant or an animal that lived long ago. Living things decay when they die, but if their bones, shells or teeth are buried quickly by sediment, a fossil can form.

mould

Over millions of years, heavy layers of sediment pile up and harden into rock.

A mould is one kind of fossil. It is made when a plant or an animal rots away and leaves only its shape in the rock.

A cast is another kind of fossil.

cast

It is made when minerals fill a mould in the same shape as the plant or animal.

A trace fossil is made from things such as footprints or nests.

It tells scientists how the animals moved and lived.

**decay:** to break down or rot

**fossil:** remains or marks of a living thing that lived long ago

**mineral:** something found in nature that is not plant or animal

**sediment:** soil or sand that forms layers on land or under water

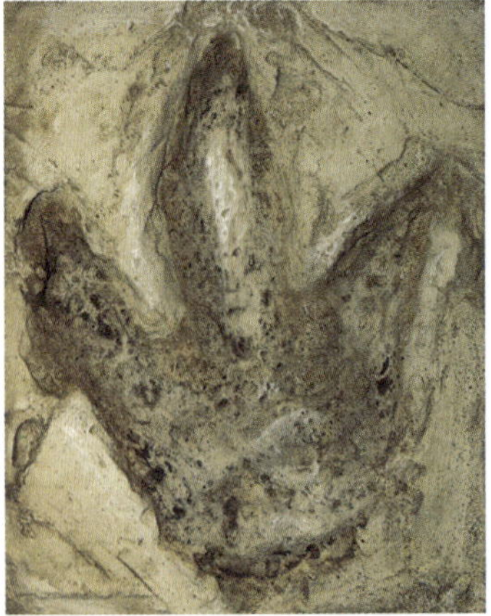

dinosaur's footprint

Source: *Targeting Science*, Year 3, page 41, Pascal Press.





TARGETING ENGLISH HOMEWORK YEAR 3 © PASCAL PRESS ISBN 978 1 925726 60 2

# Reading & Comprehension

**Shade the bubble next to the correct answer. Write the answer on the line where appropriate.**

1. **What is a fossil?**
   - ◯ a living thing
   - ◯ something that never lived
   - ◯ the remains of something that lived long ago
   - ◯ something decaying

2. **What happens to living things when they die?**
   - ◯ They decay.
   - ◯ They turn into fossils.
   - ◯ They are buried.

3. **What does decay mean?**
   - ◯ to get old
   - ◯ to break down or rot
   - ◯ to turn into a fossil

4. **Why are fossils important?**
   - ◯ They look cool.
   - ◯ They tell us about things that lived in the past.
   - ◯ Scientists like them.

5. **How long does it take for fossils to form?**
   - ◯ millions of years
   - ◯ ten years
   - ◯ a few weeks

6. **Which of these is not a type of fossil?**
   - ◯ mould
   - ◯ trace
   - ◯ draw
   - ◯ cast

7. **Draw lines to match the type of fossil to its description.**

| | |
|---|---|
| mould | marks left by things like footprints and nests |
| cast | the shape of a plant or animal in a rock |
| trace | minerals fill a mould in the shape of a plant or animal |

8. **What is a mineral?**
   - ◯ a plant
   - ◯ an animal
   - ◯ something found in nature that is not plant or animal

9. **What is sediment made up of?**
   - ◯ soil or sand
   - ◯ plants
   - ◯ animals

10. **Where could you go to see fossils?**

_______________________________________

_______________________________________

_______________________________________

TERM 3

## What I'm reading

Title: _______________________

It's: ☐ a paper book/magazine/comic
☐ an audiobook
☐ online

It's: ☐ imaginative ☐ informative

Rating ☆ ☆ ☆ ☆ ☆

Score 2 points for each correct answer!

SCORE /20    

# Grammar & Punctuation

AC9E3LA06, AC9E3LA07

## Subject–verb agreement

A subject and a verb must always agree. If the subject is singular, then the verb must be singular too. If the subject is plural (more than one), then the verb must be plural too.

*Examples:* **A** fossil (one) **is** the remains of a plant or animal that lived long ago.

Fossil**s** (more than one) **are** the remains of plants and animals.

It is often a helping verb that shows agreement with the subject.

| Singular helping verbs | |
|---|---|
| Present tense | am, is, do, does, has, have |
| Past tense | was, did, had |

| Plural helping verbs | |
|---|---|
| Present tense | are, have |
| Past tense | were, did, had |

**Choose the correct helping verb to complete these sentences.**

1. Animals and plants ______________ living things.
2. A mould ______________ one kind of fossil.
3. Traces ______________ fossils made from things like footprints.
4. A cast ______________ made when minerals fill a mould.

5 – 6 A fossil ______________ the remains of something that ______________ living long ago.

## Singular and plural verbs

Singular verbs that are not helping verbs usually have an -s added in the present tense. The plural verb in the present tense does not have an -s added.

*Examples:* **A** living thing (one) **decays** when it dies.

Living thing**s** (more than one) **decay** when they die.

We can see this in singular verbs like these: plays, writes, reads, rots, fills, tells, runs.

The plural forms of these verbs: play, write, read, rot, fill, tell, run.

**Write the correct form of the verb in brackets to complete these sentences.**

7. An animal ______________ away when it dies. (rot)
8. Plants ______________ away when they die. (rot)
9. Over time, a plant ______________ its shape in the rock. (leave)
10. Over time, animals decay and ______________ their shape in the rocks. (leave)
11. A fossil ______________ scientists how an animal moved and lived. (tell)
12. Fossils ______________ scientists how animals moved and lived. (tell)

## Commas

Remember, commas (,) are used to separate the items in a list that is written in a sentence. We do not put a comma before and or or and the last item.

*Example:* A fossil can form if their bones, shells or teeth are buried quickly by sediment.

**Read these lists. Put in the missing commas.**

13. Moulds casts and traces are all types of fossils.
14. A trace fossil is made from things such as footprints nests burrows tracks or trails.
15. Minerals like calcium potassium sodium and sulphur occur naturally in nature.
16. Scientists have found fossils of dinosaurs mastodons and sabre tooth tigers.
17. Fossils have been found in Australia in Winton Murgon Canowindra and other places.
18. Fossils can be found almost anywhere in rocks soil or clay.

*Score 2 points for each correct answer!* SCORE /36 0-16 18-30 32-36

TERM 3



TARGETING ENGLISH HOMEWORK YEAR 3 © PASCAL PRESS ISBN 978 1 925726 60 2

# Phonic & Word Knowledge

AC9E3LA10, AC9E3LY10, AC9E3LY11, AC9E3LY12

## Plurals

Remember, to make a word plural (more than one) we usually just add –s.

*Examples: fossil, fossils* *plant, plants*

Some words have irregular plurals.

*Examples: tooth, teeth* *leaf, leaves*

Write **plurals** for these words.

1. million ______
2. rock ______
3. mineral ______
4. footprint ______
5. leaf ______
6. nest ______
7. scientist ______
8. tooth ______
9. kind ______
10. mould ______

## Topic words

All the words in the box are words that are important to know when reading about fossils.

| fossil | plant | animal | millions | sediment | layers | mould | cast | scientist | |
|---|---|---|---|---|---|---|---|---|---|
| scientist | trace | mineral | rot | rock | decay | shape | mark | bury | bone | teeth |

Can you find all 20 words in the grid? They go left to right and top to bottom.

Some words overlap. Use different colours to highlight each word. Tick the words on the list as you find them.

11 – 30

| S | E | D | I | M | E | N | T | V | C | M | B |
|---|---|---|---|---|---|---|---|---|---|---|---|
| C | M | A | L | I | M | A | R | K | A | I | O |
| I | O | U | A | L | A | Y | E | R | S | N | N |
| E | U | B | P | L | A | N | T | L | T | E | E |
| N | L | A | N | I | M | A | L | D | S | R | T |
| T | D | E | R | O | C | K | B | E | H | A | E |
| I | F | R | O | N | S | S | U | C | A | L | E |
| S | F | O | S | S | I | L | R | A | P | I | T |
| T | L | T | R | A | C | E | Y | Y | E | S | H |

The letters that are not used, when read from left to right and top to bottom, will spell out a phrase.

31. Write the phrase here. ______

Score 2 points for each correct answer!

TERM 3

AC9E3LY03, AC9E3LY04, AC9E3LY05

## Imaginative text – Science fiction

### On the Way to Somewhere

This story is an excerpt from *A Step in Time*, Book 1 in the Time Quest series by Del Merrick. Read other chapters in the story in Units 7, 15 and 31.

Sid is in the time machine. He can see the years rolling out before him like waves on a sea.

"Just like riding a surfboard," he chuckles as the machine passes through a circle of coloured lights.

Suddenly, he sees a large chunk of rock heading his way. For a few seconds, he doesn't know what to do.

Then he remembers the rocket boosters. He hits the booster button. The machine is pushed upward with such speed that Sid is thrown to the floor.

He picks himself up and looks at the screen. It shows the rock is spinning away below him. Relieved, Sid switches off the boosters and sits back to enjoy the ride.

A voice crackles in his headset.

"Bee calling Sid. Bee calling Sid. Come in Sid."

Sid speaks into his headset. "BEE! I AM glad to hear your voice! This time travel is awesome!"

"What's happening, Sid?" Bee asks.

"I'm having a fantastic time, Bee. I'm on my way to somewhere, but I don't know where!" he says.

"Hit the ETA button," says Bee.

Sid hits the button and a date flashes on the screen.

"Looks like I'm heading for the Year 4088," he says cheerfully. "I'll have a look around and be back in no time."

Suddenly the wave communicator goes silent. Bee has lost contact with Sid.

All is quiet.

Source: Excerpt from *A Step in Time*, Time Quest series, Blake Education.

TERM 3



TARGETING ENGLISH HOMEWORK YEAR 3 © PASCAL PRESS ISBN 978 1 925726 60 2

# Reading & Comprehension

UNIT 23

Use these clues to complete the crossword.

**Across**

4. Sid remembered the rocket __________.
7. Sid said time travel was __________.
9. The machine went upward with __________.
11. Sid was __________ a time machine.
13. Sid hit the __________ boosters.
14. Bee lost ________ with Sid.
15. The __________ 4088 flashed on the screen.
16. Sid was in a time __________.

**Down**

1. Sid was pleased to hear Bee's __________.
2. Sid hears Bee's voice in his __________.
3. The wave __________ went silent.
4. The machine has a lot of ________ to push.
5. __________ is in control of the time machine.
6. It was very __________ when Sid lost contact with Bee.
8. __________ called Sid on the communicator.
10. The machine went through a __________ of light.
12. Sid could __________ hear Bee anymore.

| | | 1 | | | 2 | | | | | | 3 |
|---|---|---|---|---|---|---|---|---|---|---|---|
| 4 | | | | | | | 5 | | | | |
| | | | | | | | | | 6 | | |
| | | | | | | | | | | | |
| | | | | | | | | | | | |
| | | | 7 | | | | | | | | |
| | | 8 | | | | | | | | | |
| 9 | | | | | | 10 | | | | | |
| | | | | | | 11 | 12 | | | | |
| | | | | | | 13 | | | | | |
| | 14 | | | | | | | | | | |
| | | | | | | | | 15 | | | |
| 16 | | | | | | | | | | | |

TERM 3

## What I'm reading

Title: ______________________

It's: ☐ a paper book/magazine/comic
☐ an audiobook
☐ online

It's: ☐ imaginative ☐ informative

Rating ☆ ☆ ☆ ☆ ☆

*Score 2 points for each correct answer!* SCORE /34 0-14 16-28 30-34

# Grammar & Punctuation

AC9E3LA07, AC9E3LA08, AC9E3LE03

## Verbs

Remember! Verbs are words that tell us what is happening in a sentence. They tell us what the subject of the sentence is doing, thinking, saying and feeling.

*Examples*:

Sid **hits** the rocket booster button. (**doing**)

Sid **remembers** the rocket boosters. (**thinking**)

"What's happening, Sid?" Bee **asks**. (**saying**)

"Just like riding a surfboard," Sid **chuckles**. (**feeling** and **saying**)

There are also relating verbs.

Relating verbs help to link information in a sentence. They include verbs like am, is, are, were, was, have, has.

*Example*: Sid **is** in the time machine.

**Read these sentences. Underline the verb. Write D for doing, T for thinking, S for saying, F for feeling or R for a relating verb.**

1. _____ He switches off the boosters.
2. _____ Time travel is awesome.
3. _____ "A huge rock!" shouts Sid.
4. _____ "Which button?" wonders Sid.
5. _____ Sid enjoys time travel.
6. _____ Bee worries about Sid in the time machine.
7. _____ The wave communicator is quiet.
8. _____ Sid looks out the porthole.
9. _____ Sid remembers the rocket boosters.
10. _____ "The ETA button!" says Bee.

## Adjectives

Remember! Adjectives are words used to describe nouns. They work with a noun to tell us more about it. Adjectives are usually placed before a noun.

*Example*: Sid was having a **fantastic** time.

They can also follow a relating verb.

*Example:* Time travel is **awesome**.

**Read these sentences. Circle the adjectives. Underline the nouns they tell more about.**

11. I am glad to hear your voice.
12. Sid is relieved when the rock spins away.
13. Time travel is the best.
14. Sid has an enjoyable ride in the time machine.
15. Bee is glad to talk with Sid on the wave communicator.

## Adverbs

Adverbs tell us more about verbs. They add extra information about what people and things are doing. They tell us:

- how things are being done.
  *Example*: Bee speaks **loudly**.
- when things are happening.
  *Example*: **Suddenly** he sees a large chunk of rock.
- where things are happening.
  *Example*: Sid sits **back** in his seat.

**Read these sentences. Circle the adverbs. Underline the verbs they tell more about.**

16. The machine pushed upward.
17. The rock was spinning away.
18. Sid spoke cheerfully into the headset.
19. Sid left in the time machine yesterday.
20. Sid will be back soon.

*Score 2 points for each correct answer!*

SCORE /40   

TERM 3



TARGETING ENGLISH HOMEWORK YEAR 3 © PASCAL PRESS ISBN 978 1 925726 60 2

# Phonic & Word Knowledge

AC9E3LY06, AC9E3LY09, AC9E3LY11, AC9E3LY12

## Consonant sounds 'g' and 'j'

You know that the letter 'g' spells the sound you hear at the beginning of go and glad.

You know that the letter 'j' spells the sound you hear at the beginning of just and jump.

But sometimes the letter 'g' spells the 'j' sound. It is called the 'soft g' sound.

It makes the 'soft g' sound when it is followed by an 'e' as in gem, an 'i' as in giant or a 'y' as in gym.

It also makes the 'soft g' sound when it occurs in the middle or at the end of some words.

*Examples*: cage stage

The trigraph dge also spells the 'soft g' or 'j' sound as in judge or badge.

**Read these words. Listen to the sounds you hear. Sort them into the boxes.**

| gel | glue | gum | giant | enjoy | goat |
|---|---|---|---|---|---|
| green | fudge | bridge | edge | large | |
| mug | game | gate | just | gap | |

| 'hard g' sound as in **go** | |
|---|---|
| 1 | 5 |
| 2 | 6 |
| 3 | 7 |
| 4 | 8 |

| 'soft g' sound as in **gem** | |
|---|---|
| 9 | 13 |
| 10 | 14 |
| 11 | 15 |
| 12 | 16 |

## Silent letters 'g' and 'k'

**In these words, the letters g and k are silent. Draw lines to match the words and pictures.**

| | |
|---|---|
| 17 | gnome |
| 18 | gnat |
| 19 | sign |
| 20 | gnu |
| 21 | knight |
| 22 | knitting |
| 23 | knot |
| 24 | knife |

**Read these sentences. Underline the words that have a silent letter g or k.**

25 "I'm on my way to somewhere, but I don't know where!" said Sid.

26 Bree knew the wave communicator was broken when everything went quiet.

27 Bree had no knowledge of how to contact Sid again.

28 There was a sign on the control panel to tell Sid what to do.

29 The time machine was Sid's own design.

30 Sid hoped there would be no biting gnats on board.

## Homophones

**Choose the correct homophone to complete these sentences.**

31 Sid did not ______________ where he was going. (no, know)

32 The sailors went to ______________ in a yellow boat. (sea, see)

33 This gift is ______________ my mother. (for, fore, four)

34 I tied a ______________ in my shoelace. (not, knot)

35 Sid didn't know his ______________ to get home. (way, weigh)

*Score 2 points for each correct answer!*

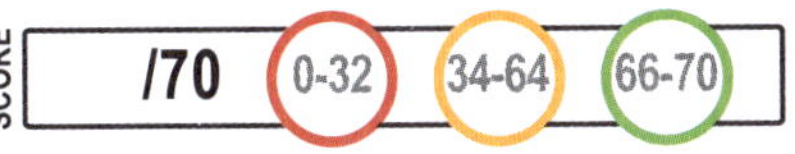


TERM 3

AC9E3LE02, AC9E3LE03, AC9E3LY03, AC9E3LY05

## Movie review: *The Magician's Elephant*

### *The Magician's Elephant*

You can watch *The Magician's Elephant* on Netflix.

Reviewed by Milly 9, Queensland.

I read the book *The Magician's* Elephant by Kate DiCamillo. I loved it, so I really wanted to see the movie. It is as good as I hoped it would be. It is an animated movie. I loved seeing all the characters come to life on the screen.

The movie is about a boy called Peter. He is an orphan. He lives with an old soldier called Vina. Vina tells Peter that his sister died when she was born, but Peter dreams she is alive. A fortune teller tells him that his sister is still alive. She says he has to follow an elephant to find his sister. First, he has to find the elephant.

On the way, he meets a lot of different people and has a lot of different adventures. A king tells him that he has to do three impossible tasks before he can have the elephant.

At first, I was surprised because the king wasn't in the book. But the king is funny and helpful, and I like him. I really like the ending too, but I'm not going to tell you how it ends. You'll have to watch the movie for yourself.

*The Magician's Elephant* is about finding your family, having hope and being brave. It is about doing impossible things. It's like a fairytale with a little bit of magic.

I think it is suitable for children who are over 7, especially if they have already read the book.

I give it 4 out of 5 stars because it is a little bit different from the book.

TERM 3

1. **Have you seen *The Magician's Elephant*?**
   - ◯ Yes
   - ◯ No
   - ◯ Unsure

2. **After reading this review, would you like to see *The Magician's Elephant*?**
   - ◯ Yes
   - ◯ No
   - ◯ Unsure

3. **Which words or phrases in the review help you decide?**

   ______________________________

   ______________________________

4. **List some movies that you have seen. Circle your favourite.**

   ______________________________

   ______________________________

   ______________________________

   ______________________________


TARGETING ENGLISH HOMEWORK YEAR 3 © PASCAL PRESS ISBN 978 1 925726 60 2

# Review

Now you can write a review of your favourite movie so that others can decide whether to watch it or not.

① About the movie

Title: ______________________

Where you can watch it:

______________________

② Circle the word that best describes the type of movie.

comedy   science fiction   superhero

family   adventure   mystery

scary   detective   action

fantasy   drama   musical

If the type of movie is not listed, write it here:

______________________

③ How is the movie presented? (Choose any that apply.)

◯ animated

◯ puppets

◯ real people or animals

◯ people acting

◯ other: ______________________

④ When did you see the movie?

______________________

⑤ Where did you watch it?

______________________

______________________

⑥ How many times have you seen it?

______________________

⑦ Who did you watch the movie with?

______________________

⑧ What made you choose to watch it the first time?

______________________

______________________

______________________

## The characters

⑨ What do you know about the main character, for example, their name, where they live, what they like doing, what they look like? Include anything you find interesting about the character.

______________________

______________________

______________________

______________________

______________________

______________________

______________________

______________________

TERM 3

⑩ **What do you know about one of the other characters, for example, their name, where they live, what they like doing, what they look like? Include anything you find interesting about the character.**

______________________________
______________________________
______________________________
______________________________
______________________________

⑪ **Who is your favourite character?**

______________________________

Why? ______________________________
______________________________
______________________________
______________________________
______________________________

## The setting

⑫ **When does the movie take place?**

- ◯ in the past, a long time ago
- ◯ in the past, not long ago
- ◯ in the present
- ◯ in the future
- ◯ not sure

⑬ **Where does the movie take place? Is it a real location or a fictional place?**

______________________________
______________________________
______________________________
______________________________
______________________________
______________________________

⑭ **List things that can be seen, heard or smelled in the location.**

Seen

______________________________
______________________________
______________________________
______________________________
______________________________
______________________________

Heard

______________________________
______________________________
______________________________
______________________________
______________________________
______________________________

Smelled

______________________________
______________________________
______________________________
______________________________
______________________________
______________________________

## The plot

⑮ **What happens in the beginning of the movie?**

______________________________
______________________________
______________________________
______________________________
______________________________
______________________________





TARGETING ENGLISH HOMEWORK YEAR 3 © PASCAL PRESS ISBN 978 1 925726 60 2

# Review

## Complication

⑯ What problem does the character have to overcome?

______________________________________________

______________________________________________

______________________________________________

______________________________________________

⑰ How does the movie end?

______________________________________________

______________________________________________

______________________________________________

______________________________________________

⑱ What is your favourite part of the movie?

______________________________________________

______________________________________________

______________________________________________

______________________________________________

Why? __________________________________________

______________________________________________

______________________________________________

______________________________________________

______________________________________________

⑲ Who else might like to watch this movie? Who do you recommend it for?

______________________________________________

______________________________________________

______________________________________________

______________________________________________

⑳ How many stars do you give it?

Draw your favourite part.

TERM 3

# Reading & Comprehension

## Safety Matters

It is important to have fun. It is also important to keep safe at the same time.

Safety matters. If you are sick or injured, you may need others to help you. You may be in bed or even in hospital for weeks. You may need help to move or do ordinary things like eat, get dressed or go to school.

You also need to know what to do if someone else gets hurt. There may be no-one else around who can help.

It is better to avoid accidents and injury to yourself and others. You can have adventures and play sport safely. You do this by avoiding danger zones, wearing the right gear for the activity and finding safer ways to play.

Source: Adapted from *Passport to Safety*, Hazel Edwards & Goldie Alexander, page 4, Blake Education.

**Shade the bubble next to the correct answer. Write the answer on the line where appropriate.**

1. **What must you do while having fun?**
   - ◯ dangerous stunts
   - ◯ keep safe
   - ◯ injure someone

2. **Can you stay safe and have fun at the same time?**
   - ◯ Yes
   - ◯ No
   - ◯ Unsure

3. **What may happen if you do not stay safe?**
   - ◯ You may have fun.
   - ◯ You may be injured.
   - ◯ You may make new friends.

4. **If you are injured, what might you need help with? (Choose any that apply.)**
   - ◯ walking
   - ◯ eating
   - ◯ getting dressed
   - ◯ going to school

5. **Which of these is usually the safest place to play?**
   - ◯ creek
   - ◯ road
   - ◯ playground

6. **What is meant by wearing the right gear?**
   - ◯ wearing appropriate clothing
   - ◯ changing gears on your bicycle
   - ◯ wearing only trending brand labels

7. **Which of these activities require special protective gear? (Choose any that apply.)**
   - ◯ riding a bicycle
   - ◯ swimming
   - ◯ reading a book
   - ◯ doing your homework
   - ◯ playing cricket

8. **Which of these people are not wearing the right gear? (Choose any that apply.)**

9. **What is an activity you do that requires special gear?**

   ______________________________

10. **List the special gear that is required for the activity.**

   ______________________________

   ______________________________

Score 2 points for each correct answer! SCORE /20 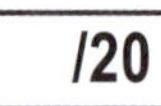 0-8  10-14  16-20

TERM 3



TARGETING ENGLISH HOMEWORK YEAR 3 © PASCAL PRESS ISBN 978 1 925726 60 2

# Grammar & Punctuation

**Write the correct comparative adjective to complete each sentence.**

1. You always need to wear the ____________ gear for the activity. (good)
2. Exercise can make you ____________. (strong)
3. Tan won every race because he was the ____________. (fast)
4. A playground is a ____________ place to play than the road. (safe)

**Write modal verbs to complete these sentences.**

5. You ____________ try to stay safe at all times.
6. If it rains, you ____________ exercise indoors.
7. You ____________ get stronger if you train every day.
8. If you don't like football, you ____________ like basketball.

**Rewrite this sentence as rules. Each rule will be short and begin with a verb.**

You can stay safe by avoiding danger zones, wearing the right gear for the activity and finding safer ways to play.

9. ____________________
10. ____________________
11. ____________________

**Circle the emotive words in these sentences.**

12. It is important to stay safe at all times.
13. It is better to avoid injury.
14. Safety matters.

**Underline the adverbial phrases that tell how, when, where or why in these sentences.**

15. It is important to keep safe at the same time.
16. You may need help to do everyday things.
17. You can stay safe by avoiding danger zones.
18. If you are badly injured, you may be in bed for weeks.

**Rewrite these sentences as direct speech. Remember to use the correct punctuation and saying verbs.**

19. Tan: Do you want to go down to the skatepark?

____________________

20. Tema: Sure! That sounds like fun.

____________________

21. Dad: Don't forget your safety gear!

____________________

**Unjumble these words to write a question, a statement and an exclamation. Remember to use the correct punctuation.**

22. are this Where we afternoon going

____________________

23. going the We skateboard to are park

____________________

24. fun is This

____________________

**Use conjunctions to join these pairs of clauses into compound sentences.**

25. It is important to have fun. It is important to stay safe at the same time.

____________________

26. You might get sick. You might be injured.

____________________

**Read these –ous adjectives. Underline 'ous'. Write their meaning.**

27. dangerous = ____________
28. advantageous = ____________
29. poisonous = ____________
30. perilous = ____________
31. hazardous = ____________
32. joyous = ____________

TERM 3

## Grammar & Punctuation

**Write the missing articles in this paragraph.**

33 – 37 When Tan and Tema went to ______ skateboard park, they saw ______ little child who was upset. They asked ______ child what was wrong. She said that ______ older girl had knocked her off her skateboard. She wasn't hurt, but it gave her ______ fright.

**Choose the correct helping verb to complete these sentences.**

38 Tan and Tema ______ playing at the skatepark.

39 Tema ______ practising some kick turns.

40 They ______ come to the park every day in the holidays.

**Read this list. Put in the missing commas.**

41 When you ride rollerskates, you need to wear rollerskates knee pads elbow pads wrist pads and a helmet.

**Read these sentences. Underline the verb. Write D for doing, T for thinking, S for saying, F for feeling or R for a relating verb. Circle the adverbs.**

42 ______ Tema rode his skateboard safely.

43 ______ "Awesome," Tan said loudly.

44 ______ "I am glad they are safe," Dad thought quietly.

**Read these sentences. Circle the adjectives. Underline the nouns they tell more about.**

45 Tema and Tan went to the local skatepark.

46 The skatepark was very busy.

47 Happy children were skating and having fun.

48 There wasn't one hurt child.

Score 2 points for each correct answer! SCORE /96  

## Phonic & Word Knowledge

**Choose one of the 'gh' words to complete each sentence.**

'gh' spells 'f' sound: enough laugh cough rough tough
'gh' is silent: high bough dough thigh though

1 One hour of exercise each day is __________.

2 Tema bragged he could jump as __________ as the tree.

3 Tan stayed home on Wednesday because he had a bad __________.

4 I like it when I make my own __________ for the pizza.

**Choose the correct homophone to complete these sentences.**

5 The children were allowed to skate on the tennis __________. (caught, court)

6 I __________ some children having fun at the skatepark. (saw, sore)

7 There is nowhere to ride skateboards __________. (hear, here)

**Read these words. Underline the letter 'c' or the letters 'ch'. Write C if you hear the hard 'ck' sound, S if you hear the soft 'c' sound and CH if you hear 'ch' as in chips.**

8 activity _____
9 centre _____
10 school _____
11 chomp _____
12 choose _____
13 city _____

**Read these words. Look at the letters in bold. Sort the words into the correct boxes.**

14 h**ear**t
15 l**au**gh
16 p**ear**l
17 s**ur**f
18 w**ar**m
19 b**ir**d
20 w**a**ter
21 h**al**f

| 'ar' vowel sound | 'er' vowel sound | 'or' vowel sound |
|---|---|---|
| | | |

**Count the number of syllables in each word. Write the number beside it.**

22 important _____
23 zones _____
24 safety _____
25 hospital _____
26 injury _____
27 activity _____



TARGETING ENGLISH HOMEWORK YEAR 3 © PASCAL PRESS ISBN 978 1 925726 60 2

# Phonic & Word Knowledge

Add **–er** to the word in bold to make the noun for one who does the action. Write the word. Remember the rules.

(28) One who **skates** is a ____________________.

(29) One who **jumps** is a ____________________.

(30) One who **runs** is a ____________________.

Draw lines to match **pairs of opposites.**

| | |
|---|---|
| (31) important | special |
| (32) ordinary | unadventurous |
| (33) right | unimportant |
| (34) adventurous | wrong |
| (35) safe | unhurt |
| (36) dangerous | worse |
| (37) better | risk-free |
| (38) hurt | unsafe |

Add the **prefix un–, in–** or **dis–** to these words to make their opposites.

(39) _____happy

(40) _____safe

(41) _____comfort

(42) _____complete

(43) _____ correct

(44) _____approve

Write words with the **letter 'x'** to complete these sentences.

(45) My little brother is __________ years old.

(46) We always have an __________ to see what we've learned.

(47) We put all the ingredients into the __________ bowl.

(48) Because the game was tied, it went into __________ time.

Write a word on the end of each of these words to make a **compound word.**

(49) butter__________

(50) foot__________

(51) day__________

Add the **correct form** of the word in brackets to complete these sentences.

(52) I am ____________ now. I ____________ every day this week. (exercise)

(53) I ____________ this morning. I will be ____________ again later. (swim)

Read these words. Listen to the **vowel sounds.** Write the word in the bag whose picture has the same vowel sound. Remember, vowel sounds can be spelled in different ways.

| | | | | |
|---|---|---|---|---|
| and | sick | need | same | what |
| some | time | bed | help | have |
| dressed | things | got | one | may |
| be | eat | safe | if | right |
| move | know | fun | zones | by |
| who | no | sock | can | school |

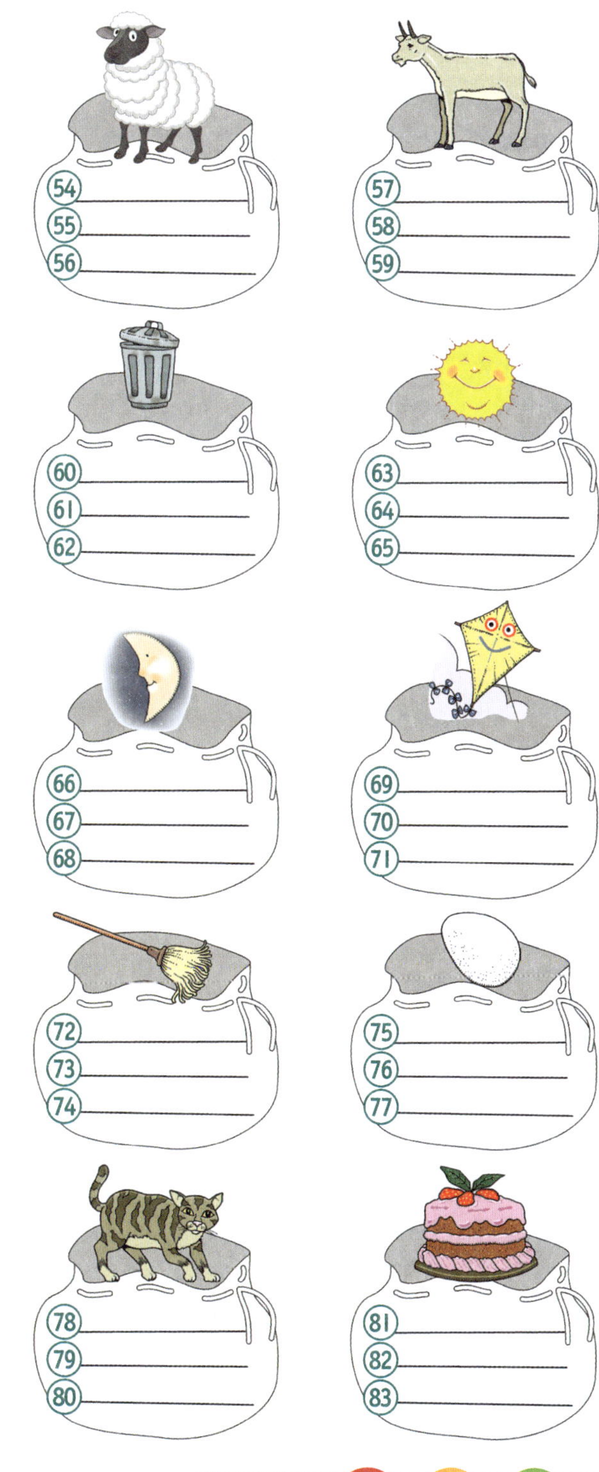

(54) ____________
(55) ____________
(56) ____________

(57) ____________
(58) ____________
(59) ____________

(60) ____________
(61) ____________
(62) ____________

(63) ____________
(64) ____________
(65) ____________

(66) ____________
(67) ____________
(68) ____________

(69) ____________
(70) ____________
(71) ____________

(72) ____________
(73) ____________
(74) ____________

(75) ____________
(76) ____________
(77) ____________

(78) ____________
(79) ____________
(80) ____________

(81) ____________
(82) ____________
(83) ____________

*Score 2 points for each correct answer!*

SCORE /166 0-80 82-160 162-166

TERM 3

AC9E3LA09, AC9E3LE01, AC9E3LE02, AC9E3LY03, AC9E3LY04, AC9E3LY05

## Imaginative text – Narrative

### The Holidays are Here!

Tessa loved spending school holidays on the farm with her great-grandparents. They were fun and made her laugh. Mum and Dad said they were 'real characters'.

"They're a bit unusual," Mum said as she packed Tessa's backpack for another visit.

Dad grinned. "You can say that again."

"You're a very lucky girl," Tessa's mum said.

"Not everyone your age has great-grandparents to visit."

The trip from the city to the country seemed to take forever. Even with puzzle books and colouring in to do, Tessa got so bored she fell asleep and had to be woken up when they finally arrived.

"Maybe she needs a kiss from a Prince Charming," she heard Great Grandpop Alfred say.

"You'd better go and get one of the frogs from the creek then," Great Grandma Em told him.

Tessa giggled. It was great to be back. Now she had two whole weeks of fun to look forward to. They had planned so many exciting things to do during their phone calls about her stay.

Source: Extract from *Getting Rid of Wrinkles*, Tina Raffa-Mulligan, Blake Education.





TARGETING ENGLISH HOMEWORK YEAR 3 © PASCAL PRESS ISBN 978 1 925726 60 2

# Reading & Comprehension

Shade the bubble next to the correct answer. Write the answer on the line where appropriate.

1 Who is the main character in this story?
- ◯ Tessa
- ◯ Great Grandpop Alfred
- ◯ Great Grandma Em

2 Where is Tessa spending the school holidays?
- ◯ at the beach
- ◯ on a farm
- ◯ in the city

3 Why does Tessa like spending time with her great-grandparents?
- ◯ They are old.
- ◯ They treat her like a princess.
- ◯ They have fun together.

4 What does Mum mean when she says they are **real characters**?
- ◯ They are cartoon characters come to life.
- ◯ They are pretend great-grandparents.
- ◯ They do funny and fun things.

5 What does the illustration show?
- ◯ Tessa is car sick from the long trip.
- ◯ Great Grandpop Alfred and Great Grandma Em are worried about Tessa.
- ◯ Tessa has heard her great-grandparents and thinks they are funny.

6 What did Tessa do on the way to the farm?
- ◯ puzzles and colouring
- ◯ games on a phone
- ◯ listened to music

7 What did Dad mean by, **"You can say that again"**?
- ◯ He didn't hear it.
- ◯ He agrees.
- ◯ He likes to repeat things.

8 Why did Tessa think it took forever to get to the farm?
- ◯ She was bored.
- ◯ She couldn't wait to get there.
- ◯ Her clock was broken.

9 What story did Tessa's great-grandparents joke about?
- ◯ Cinderella
- ◯ Sleeping Beauty
- ◯ Red Riding Hood

10 What do you know?

Do you know someone who is described as a **real character**? Who?

______________________________
______________________________
______________________________
______________________________

Why are they described as a **real character**?

______________________________
______________________________
______________________________
______________________________

TERM 4

## What I'm reading

Title: ______________________________

It's: ☐ a paper book/magazine/comic
☐ an audiobook
☐ online

It's: ☐ imaginative ☐ informative

Rating ☆ ☆ ☆ ☆ ☆

Score 2 points for each correct answer! SCORE /20

# Grammar & Punctuation

AC9E3LA02, AC9E3LA07, AC9E3LE03

## Emotive words

Writers use different words, including adjectives, verbs and nouns to build an image of a character in our minds. These words help us learn more about Tessa's great-grandparents.

*Examples*: characters (noun)
unusual (adjective)
giggled (verb)

**Read these sentences. Circle the words that help us learn more about Tessa's great-grandparents and how she feels about them. Write N if the word is a noun, A for an adjective and V for a verb.**

1. _____ Tessa loved spending school holidays on the farm with her great-grandparents.
2. _____ They were fun.
3. _____ Tessa was a very lucky girl.
4. _____ It was great to be back.
5. _____ They had planned so many exciting things to do.
6. _____ Dad grinned when he thought about Tessa's great-grandparents.

## Adverbs

Remember! Adverbs tell us more about verbs. They tell us how things are being done, when things are happening or where things are happening.

**Underline the verbs and circle the adverbs in these sentences. Circle how, when or where.**

7. They finally arrived at the farm. (how, when, where)
8. The trip from the farm took forever. (how, when, where)
9. Tessa spoke excitedly about her holiday. (how, when, where)
10. Great Grandpop Alfred joked frequently. (how, when, where)
11. Tessa giggled quietly at Great Grandpop Alfred's jokes. (how, when, where)
12. Tessa loved going away for the holidays. (how, when, where)

## Adverbial phrases

Remember! Adverbial phrases also tell us more about verbs. They tell us how things are being done, when things are happening, where things are happening or why things are happening. A phrase is a group of words that usually begins with a preposition.

Here are some prepositions.

*Examples:*

| at | in | until | from | between |
|---|---|---|---|---|
| on | to | under | with | near |
| for | above | | | |

**Add a preposition from the box to complete these sentences.**

13. Tessa loved spending school holidays _______________ the farm.
14. Mum packed Tessa's backpack _______________ the holidays.

15. They drove away _______________ the city.
16. Tessa fell asleep _______________ the car.
17. Great Grandpop Alfred made Tessa laugh _______________ his silly jokes.
18. It is a long time _______________ the holidays.
19. Tessa walked _______________ her great-grandparents.
20. Not everyone your age has great-grandparents _______________ visit.

*Score 2 points for each correct answer!* SCORE /40 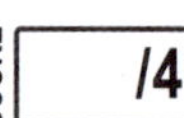 0-18  20-34   36-40

TERM 4



TARGETING ENGLISH HOMEWORK YEAR 3 © PASCAL PRESS ISBN 978 1 925726 60 2

AC9E3LY09, AC9E3LY10

## Words that end in 'y'

**Say each word in the word bank. Listen to the different end sounds of the words.**

| say | many | holiday | city | funny |
|---|---|---|---|---|
| lucky | lonely | stay | finally | |
| country | every | they | | |

**Choose words from the word bank to complete these sentences.**

1. Tessa went to her great-grandparents' farm for a ______________.
2. After a long drive, they ______________ arrived.
3. Tessa visited her great-grandparents ______________ holiday.
4. Tessa laughed at all Great Grandpop Alfred's ______________ jokes.
5. Tessa was very ______________ to have great-grandparents.

## Plurals of words that end in 'y'

When a word ends with a y after a vowel (ay, ey, oy or uy), just add -s to make the plural (more than one).

*Examples*:

day days stay stays

When a word ends in a y after a consonant, change the y into an i and add -es to make the plural.

*Examples*:

city cities country countries

**Rewrite these words as plurals.**

6. holiday ______________
7. party ______________
8. toy ______________
9. monkey ______________
10. ferry ______________
11. key ______________
12. family ______________
13. fairy ______________
14. baby ______________
15. jelly ______________

## Adverbs of manner

Adverbs that tell us how things are being done are called adverbs of manner. Many adverbs of manner are built from adjectives by adding the suffix -ly.

*Examples*:

quick**ly** loud**ly**

When the adjective ends in y, you usually change the y to i before adding -ly.

*Examples*:

luck**ily** angr**ily**

**Rewrite these adjectives by adding the suffix -ly to make adverbs.**

16. funny ______________
17. sleepy ______________
18. kind ______________
19. slow ______________
20. joking ______________
21. soft ______________
22. greedy ______________
23. late ______________
24. boring ______________
25. excited ______________

## Compound words

**Draw lines to match words that combine to form compound words.**

| | |
|---|---|
| 26. back | one |
| 27. grand | time |
| 28. every | yard |
| 29. summer | pack |
| 30. farm | parents |

Score 2 points for each correct answer! SCORE /60 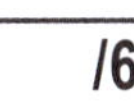   

TERM 4

## Informative text – Procedure

# Make Your Own Fossil

**What you need:**

- petroleum jelly
- plaster of Paris
- water
- bowl and spoon
- cardboard
- leaves and shells

**What you do:**

1. Coat a leaf and a shell with petroleum jelly. Set them aside.
2. Follow the directions to mix the plaster and the water. Have an adult help you.
3. Spread some plaster on the cardboard. Use enough plaster so that you can press the leaf and the shell into it.
4. Press the coated leaf and shell gently into the plaster. Try not to move them once they are in the plaster.
5. Let the plaster dry overnight. When it is dry, carefully remove the leaf and the shell.

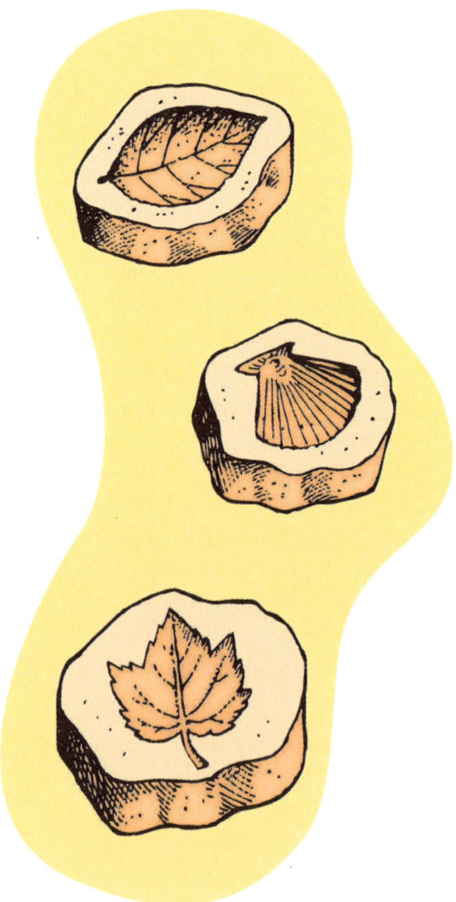

Source: *Targeting Science*, Year 3, page 47, Pascal Press.




TARGETING ENGLISH HOMEWORK YEAR 3 © PASCAL PRESS ISBN 978 1 925726 60 2

# Reading & Comprehension

**Shade the bubble next to the correct answer. Write the answer on the line where appropriate.**

1. **Which of these do you need to make a fossil?**
   - ◯ raspberry jelly
   - ◯ petroleum jelly
   - ◯ jelly beans

2. **Which of these do you not need to make a fossil?**
   - ◯ cardboard
   - ◯ water
   - ◯ sugar

3. **What does the word coat mean in step 1?**
   - ◯ a jacket
   - ◯ cover
   - ◯ cut

4. **What does the procedure suggest you use to make fossils?**
   - ◯ bones
   - ◯ pages of a book
   - ◯ shells

5. **What do you mix with water?**
   - ◯ petroleum jelly
   - ◯ plaster of Paris
   - ◯ cardboard

6. **How do you know how much water to use?**
   - ◯ guess
   - ◯ read the direction on the plaster of Paris packet

7. **What is another word for directions?**
   - ◯ instructions
   - ◯ north, south, east, west
   - ◯ rules

8. **How thick should you spread the plaster?**
   - ◯ less than 1 cm
   - ◯ about 1 cm
   - ◯ more than 1 cm

9. **How long do you leave the plaster to set?**
   - ◯ 1 hour
   - ◯ 6 hours
   - ◯ overnight

10. **What do you think?**

    Why do you need to coat the leaves and shells with petroleum jelly?

    ______________________________________________

    ______________________________________________

    ______________________________________________

    ______________________________________________

    ______________________________________________

    ______________________________________________

    ______________________________________________

TERM 4

## What I'm reading

Title: ______________________________

It's: ☐ a paper book/magazine/comic
☐ an audiobook
☐ online

It's: ☐ imaginative ☐ informative

Rating ☆ ☆ ☆ ☆ ☆

Score 2 points for each correct answer! SCORE /20

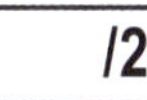

0-8

AC9E3LA07

## Commands

The instructions, or method, in a procedure tell you what to do. They are a series of commands that begin with verbs. The subject you is not stated. It is understood.

*Examples:*

**Coat** a leaf and a shell with petroleum jelly. **Set** them aside.

(You) **coat** a leaf and a shell with petroleum jelly. (You) **set** them aside.

**Reread the instructions for making your own fossil. Circle the doing words that begin each command. Write them on these lines.**

① ______________________

______________________

______________________

______________________

**Think of what you might do once you have made a fossil. Add words to these doing verbs to write instructions for others to follow. Then write one of your own. Remember to use full stops at the end of each command.**

② Take______________________

______________________

③ Show______________________

______________________

④ Display______________________

______________________

⑤ ______________________

______________________

______________________

TERM 4

## Lists

Items to be used in a procedure are usually listed under each other using bullet points.

Instructions to be followed are usually listed under each other using numbers.

If the items are listed in a sentence, commas (,) are used to separate them. We do not put a comma before and or or and the last item.

*Example:* If their bones, shells or teeth are buried quickly by sediment, a fossil can form.

**Write the items in these sentences as lists with bullet points.**

⑥ To make your own fossil, you need leaves, shells, feathers, bones, bark or flower petals.

| For fossils, you need: |
|---|
| |
| |
| |
| |
| |
| |

⑦ If you don't have plaster of Paris, you can use flour and water, clay, plasticine or modelling clay.

| No plaster of Paris, then use: |
|---|
| |
| |
| |
| |
| |
| |

⑧ Scientists study the remains of animals that lived long ago, including their bones, teeth, footprints, feathers, fur and trails.

| Scientists study remains of: |
|---|
| |
| |
| |
| |
| |
| |

**Add the missing commas in this paragraph.**

⑨ A scientist who studies fossils is called a paleontologist. There are many types of fossils, including seashells footprints wood leaf impressions nests and even burrows.

*Score 2 points for each correct answer!* SCORE /18    

TARGETING ENGLISH HOMEWORK YEAR 3 © PASCAL PRESS ISBN 978 1 925726 60 2

# Phonic & Word Knowledge

AC9E3LY06, AC9E3LY09, AC9E3LY10

## Plurals

Remember! To make a word plural (more than one), we usually just add -s.

When words end in s, ss, sh or ch, you add -es to make them plural.

When words end with a y after a consonant, you change the y into i and add -es.

And some words have irregular plurals.

*Examples:*

child, children    fish, fish

To make the plural of many words that end in f or fe, you change the f or fe to v, and then add -es.

*Examples:*

leaf, leaves    wife, wives

**Write these words as plurals.**

1. loaf ______
2. half ______
3. child ______
4. fly ______
5. hoof ______
6. shell ______
7. branch ______
8. knife ______
9. calf ______
10. sheep ______

## Homonyms

Homonyms are words that sound alike and are spelt alike but have different meanings.

*Examples:*

You wear a **coat** over other clothes. (noun)

You **coat** the leaf with petroleum jelly. (verb)

**Choose the correct meaning for the words in bold in each of these sentences. Write A or B.**

**A** a part of a tree    **B** allows

11. ____ The boy always **leaves** the plaster to dry overnight.
12. ____ The boy raked the dry **leaves** into a pile.

**A** place    **B** become firm

13. ____ Put the jelly in the fridge to **set**.
14. ____ When you are finished, **set** your fossil on the shelf for display.

**A** an insect    **B** move through the air

15. ____ Nobody wants to find a dead **fly** in their lunch.
16. ____ It would be fun to **fly** in the air like a bird.

## Syllables

**Count the number of syllables in each word, then write them in the correct box.**

| | | | |
|---|---|---|---|
| leaf | shells | direction | paleontologist |
| plaster | cardboard | television | follow |
| petroleum | spread | gently | carefully |
| procedure | scientific | bowl | overnight |

| One syllable | Two syllables |
|---|---|
| 17 | 21 |
| 18 | 22 |
| 19 | 23 |
| 20 | 24 |

| Three syllables | More than three |
|---|---|
| 25 | 29 |
| 26 | 30 |
| 27 | 31 |
| 28 | 32 |

*Score 2 points for each correct answer!* SCORE /64 0-30 32-58 60-64

TERM 4

# Reading & Comprehension



## Imaginative text – Haiku poems

### The Seasons

Early morning sun
Birds chirrup by the window
Wake up sleepy head.

Purple hills shimmer
Dark clouds gobble up blue skies
Storms pummel grey streets.

Golden leaves tremble
Falling lifeless to the ground
Green leaves hold on tight.

Bare branches shiver
Dead leaves crackle underfoot
Icy winds blow cold.



**Write your answers on the lines provided.**

1. What **season** does each haiku poem describe?

   Verse 1 ____________________
   Verse 2 ____________________
   Verse 3 ____________________
   Verse 4 ____________________

2. Which words in the **spring** haiku poem tell you it is about spring? List 2 or 3. Explain how you know.

3. Which words in the **summer** haiku poem tell you it is about summer? List 2 or 3. Explain how you know.

4. Which words in the **autumn** haiku poem tell you it is about autumn? List 2 or 3. Explain how you know.

5. Which words in the **winter** haiku poem tell you it is about winter? List 2 or 3. Explain how you know.

6. What does **chirrup** mean?

7. Why are the hills **purple**?

8. Why are some leaves golden and some leaves green?

9. Why do the leaves **crackle** underfoot?

10. What do you know?

Are the seasons you experience the same as the seasons described in the poems? Explain why.

Spring:

Summer:

Autumn:

Winter:

### What I'm reading

Title:

It's: ☐ a paper book/magazine/comic
☐ an audiobook
☐ online

It's: ☐ imaginative ☐ informative

Rating ☆☆☆☆☆

Score 2 points for each correct answer! SCORE /20 0-8 10-14 16-20

# Grammar & Punctuation

AC9E3LE03, AC9E3LE04

## Personification

Writers use personification to make something that is not human seem to behave in a way that is human.

*Example:* Green leaves hold on tight.

The leaves (noun) have been personified. Hold (verb) is a human behaviour.

**Look back at the haiku poems. List an example of personification in each of these verses. Circle the noun. Underline the verb.**

1. Verse 2 ______________________________
______________________________

2. Verse 4 ______________________________
______________________________

**Read these sentences. Circle the noun that has been personified. Underline the verb.**

3. Kites dance in the breeze.
4. The blinking 'open' sign refused to let us pass.
5. The book jumped off the shelf and into my heart.
6. The phone insisted that I answer it straightaway.
7. The tiny boats played hide and seek in the waves.
8. The moon looked down kindly on the lonely travellers.

**Write sentences to personify each of these nouns.**

9. stars ______________________________
______________________________
______________________________

10. vine ______________________________
______________________________
______________________________

11. water ______________________________
______________________________
______________________________

12. game ______________________________
______________________________
______________________________

TERM 4

## Adjectives

Remember! Adjectives are words used to describe nouns. In haiku and other poetry they can help to create the atmosphere or mood. The mood created by the adjectives is different for each season's haiku.

*Examples*:

**dark** clouds  **golden** leaves  **icy** winds

**Read these sentences. Circle the adjectives. Underline the nouns they tell more about.**

13. Birds chirruped and told the sleepy head to wake up.
14. The purple hills shimmered in the distance.
15. The green leaves held on tight to the trees.
16. Icy winds blew cold through the valley.
17. The full moon lit the way.
18. The angry wind tossed everything about.
19. The sun shower tiptoed across the playground.
20. Hats and sunscreen promised protection against the harsh sunlight.

*Score 2 points for each correct answer!*

SCORE /40  0-18  20-34  36-40



TARGETING ENGLISH HOMEWORK YEAR 3 © PASCAL PRESS ISBN 978 1 925726 60 2

# Phonic & Word Knowledge

AC9E3LY06, AC9E3LY09

## Onomatopoeia

Onomatopoeia is a word that imitates or sounds like the noise it describes.

*Examples*: moo oink baa neigh snap sizzle pop crackle pummel chirrup crash bang screech grunt roar buzz boom splash beep clatter thud creak giggle beep

**Say each word in the word bank. Choose words from the word bank to complete these sentences.**

1. I heard the ______________ when the cold water met the hot barbecue plate.
2. There was an enormous ______________ when the car stopped suddenly.
3. I knew a cow was around the corner when I heard a loud ______________.
4. When my balloon landed on the cactus, it went ______________.

5. I heard the ______________ because my phone was set to vibrate.
6. I knew the bird had dived into the water when I heard the ______________.
7. The stairs went ______________, ______________, ______________ with every step.
8. There was a great ______________ when the cutlery drawer was tipped upside down.
9. The truck went ______________, ______________, ______________ as it reversed.
10. My grandpa tries not to ______________ when he gets up, but he always does.

## Alliteration

Alliteration is the repetition of the same sound in words that are close together. It is usually at the beginning of words, but it can occur within words.

*Examples*: **B**are **b**ranches **b**end and **b**ow in the **b**iting wind.

**Read these sentences. Circle the sound that is repeated.**

11. The greedy green goblin gets angry if someone gobbles his gourmet food.
12. Many mighty magicians make mean monsters meek.
13. The sea serpent slides silently through the still waters.
14. Ten tiny turtles try to catch the turning tide before it's too late.
15. Dreadful dragons dreamed up dastardly deeds to destroy and dominate.

## Syllables

A haiku is a poem written on three lines. It has 5 syllables on the first line, 7 syllables on the second line and 5 syllables on the last line. That makes 17 syllables in all.

**Choose one of the sentences in exercises 11–15. Count the number of syllables. Rewrite it as a haiku poem with a total of 17 syllables, 5 on the first line, 7 on the second and 5 on the third.**

16. ______________________________

______________________________

______________________________

______________________________

______________________________

*Score 2 points for each correct answer!* SCORE /32

TERM 4

AC9E3LY03, AC9E3LY04, AC9E3LY05, AC9E3LE02

## Persuasive text – Advertisement

# Zip It Lightning Hoverboard!

Impress your friends!
Take our new hoverboard for a spin!
You'll never settle for a skateboard again.

### Australia's most popular hoverboard

"My 9-year-old loves her new Zip It hoverboard. She could ride it as soon as she got it, and she'd never ridden one before. I love all its safety features. I don't have to worry about her when she goes for a ride!"

*Jane D.*

**SAVE!**
**Be one of the first 100 to order online and receive a $50 discount.**

Fun to ride!

**Best Hoverboard for kids**

**Safety approved. Lifetime guarantee.**
**Safest battery on the market.**

Easy to learn!





TARGETING ENGLISH HOMEWORK YEAR 3 © PASCAL PRESS ISBN 978 1 925726 60 2

Shade the bubble next to the correct answer. Write the answer on the line where appropriate.

1. What is being advertised?
   - ◯ a hoverboard
   - ◯ a skateboard
   - ◯ a hovercraft

2. Which of these things allows you to play music on the hoverboard?
   - ◯ LED lights
   - ◯ rechargeable battery
   - ◯ Bluetooth speaker

3. What is the brand name of the hoverboard?
   - ◯ New Hoverboard
   - ◯ Zip It Hoverboard
   - ◯ Best Hoverboard

4. What do you have to do to get a discount?
   - ◯ order now
   - ◯ order online
   - ◯ buy two

5. How much is the discount?
   - ◯ half price
   - ◯ 50% off
   - ◯ $50

6. According to the advertisement, what are the benefits of the advertised hoverboard? (Choose any that apply.)
   - ◯ safety approved
   - ◯ safest battery on the market
   - ◯ lifetime guarantee
   - ◯ better than a skateboard
   - ◯ cheap

7. What does **eco-friendly** mean?
   - ◯ It's safety approved.
   - ◯ You will have lots of friends if you have one.
   - ◯ It's easy to learn.
   - ◯ It's not harmful to the environment.
   - ◯ It will make you feel good about yourself.

8. Which of these features allows the advertiser to use the term **eco-friendly** about the hoverboard? (Choose any that apply.)
   - ◯ most popular hoverboard
   - ◯ LED lights
   - ◯ rechargeable battery
   - ◯ bluetooth speakers

9. Which of these things did a reviewer **not** say about the Lightning Hoverboard?
   - ◯ It's inexpensive.
   - ◯ It's easy to ride.
   - ◯ It has good safety features.
   - ◯ Her child loves it.

10. What do you think?

    Would you want a hoverboard after reading this advertisement? Explain.

    ______________________________
    ______________________________
    ______________________________
    ______________________________
    ______________________________
    ______________________________

## What I'm reading

Title: ______________________________

It's: ☐ a paper book/magazine/comic
☐ an audiobook
☐ online

It's: ☐ imaginative ☐ informative

Rating ☆ ☆ ☆ ☆ ☆

Score 2 points for each correct answer! SCORE /20 0-8 10-14 16-20

TERM 4

# Grammar & Punctuation

AC9E3LA02, AC9E3LA06, AC9E3LA10

## Emotive words

Advertisers use emotive words and strong adjectives to convince people to purchase their goods or services.

*Examples:* new easy best most popular

**Circle the emotive words in these sentences.**

1. You will impress your friends when you ride your new Zip It Lightning Hoverboard.
2. The Lightning Hoverboard is the latest and greatest in the Zip It range.
3. My 9-year-old loves her new Zip It hoverboard.
4. Hoverboards are more fun than skateboards.
5. The Zip It Lightning Hoverboard is the best on the market.

## Sentences and sentence fragments

Remember! A sentence is a group of words that makes sense on its own. It has a subject and a verb. Sometimes the subject is understood.

*Example*: (You) impress your friends!

A sentence fragment is part of a sentence. Sentence fragments are often used in advertisements. While they don't make sense on their own, they make sense in the context of the advertisement.

*Examples*: Safety approved. Eco-friendly!

**Read these groups of words. Write S for sentence. Write F for sentence fragment.**

6. _____ I love all its safety features.
7. _____ Lifetime guarantee.
8. _____ LED lights!
9. _____ Take our new hoverboard for a spin!
10. _____ Play music from your phone as you zip around!
11. _____ Easy to learn!
12. _____ Fun to ride!

**Choose three sentence fragments from the above exercises. Add words to change them into complete sentences.**

13. ______________________________

14. ______________________________

15. ______________________________

## Exclamation marks

Exclamation marks (!) are often used in advertisements to add impact to the features or statements. They are most often used in sentence fragments but can also be used at the end of sentences.

**Finish these sentences and sentence fragments with full stops or exclamation marks.**

16. New safety features
17. The best hoverboard in the world
18. You will enjoy riding your hoverboard around the neighbourhood
19. The first 100 customers to order online will receive a $50 discount
20. You won't believe how much fun riding a hoverboard can be

*Score 2 points for each correct answer!*

SCORE /40 0-18 20-34 36-40

TERM 4



TARGETING ENGLISH HOMEWORK YEAR 3 © PASCAL PRESS ISBN 978 1 925726 60 2

AC9E3LY10

## Prefixes

A prefix is a letter or group of letters that is added to the beginning of a word. When it is added to the beginning of a word, the meaning of the word changes.

The prefixes in– and un– mean 'not' or 'the opposite of'.

*Examples*: expensive, inexpensive
common, uncommon

We usually know whether to use in– or un– by having heard the words used.

*Examples*: kind, unkind (not inkind)
visible, invisible (not unvisible)

**Write the correct prefix in– or un– to change the meaning of the word in bold in these sentences.**

1. Hoverboards can be _____**safe** if you don't know what you are doing.
2. Liam could not go on his hoverboard because he was _____**well**.
3. Heather could not go on her hoverboard because her work was _____**complete**.
4. You must _____**tie** your shoelaces before you take them off.
5. Tan was very _____**flexible** when it came to warm-up exercises.

## Prefix re–

The prefix re– means to 'do again'.

*Examples*: charge, **re**charge    write, **re**write

**Add the prefix re– to these words.**

| | |
|---|---|
| 6. _____do | 11. _____run |
| 7. _____use | 12. _____join |
| 8. _____turn | 13. _____heat |
| 9. _____tell | 14. _____read |
| 10. _____make | 15. _____build |

## Compound words

Remember! A compound word is two words joined together to make one word.

*Example:* hover + **board** = hover**board**

**Add board to each of these words to make a new compound word.**

16. skate ____________________
17. black ____________________
18. base ____________________
19. sail ____________________
20. head ____________________
21. surf ____________________
22. over ____________________
23. white ____________________
24. card ____________________
25. out ____________________

**Which board word are these?**

26.  ____________

27.  ____________

28.  ____________

29.  ____________

30.  ____________

Score 2 points for each correct answer! SCORE /60 0-28 30-54 56-60

TERM 4

## Informative text – Report

# Types of Rocks

**There are three main types of rocks.**

| Sedimentary Rocks | Igneous Rocks | Metamorphic Rocks |
| --- | --- | --- |
| Sedimentary rocks are formed over many years. They are formed out of sediments or tiny pieces of rock and soil. Streams and rivers carry a lot of sediment to larger bodies of water, where it settles at the bottom. The water and earth above the sediments squeeze them and cement them together. Millions of years later, they form into solid rock. It is called sedimentary rock because it is made from sediments. | Igneous rocks are formed by volcanoes. When hot molten rock is inside a volcano, it is called magma or lava. When it cools and hardens, it forms igneous rocks. Igneous rocks can form on the Earth's surface or somewhere within the Earth's crust. | Metamorphic rocks are formed deep under the surface of the Earth. They are formed by huge amounts of heat and pressure. The heat from the Earth's core and the huge weight of the rocks and soil cause rocks to melt and change. These changed rocks were once other types of rocks such as sedimentary or igneous rocks. They are now called metamorphic rocks because they have been changed. |
| **Examples of sedimentary rocks:** | **Examples of igneous rocks:** | **Examples of metamorphic rocks:** |
|  |  |  |
|  |  |  |
|  |  |  |
|  |  |  |
| |  | |
| • Limestone<br>• Coal<br>• Sandstone<br>• Shale | • Basalt<br>• Granite<br>• Quartz<br>• Pumice<br>• Tuff | • Gneiss<br>• Marble<br>• Slate<br>• Schist |

Source: *Targeting Science*, Year 3, page 33, Pascal Press.





TARGETING ENGLISH HOMEWORK YEAR 3 © PASCAL PRESS ISBN 978 1 925726 60 2

# Reading & Comprehension

**Shade the bubble next to the correct answer. Write the answer on the line where appropriate.**

1. **How many main types of rocks are there?**
   - ◯ one
   - ◯ three
   - ◯ thirteen
   - ◯ hundreds

2. **Which of these is not a type of rock?**
   - ◯ sedimentary
   - ◯ rocky road
   - ◯ igneous
   - ◯ metamorphic

3. **What type of rock is basalt?**
   - ◯ sedimentary
   - ◯ igneous
   - ◯ metamorphic

4. **Which of these is an igneous rock?**
   - ◯ marble
   - ◯ sandstone
   - ◯ tuff

5. **Which of these is not a metamorphic rock?**
   - ◯ marble
   - ◯ basalt
   - ◯ schist

6. **What type of rocks are formed from lava from volcanoes?**
   - ◯ sedimentary
   - ◯ igneous
   - ◯ metamorphic

7. **What type of rocks are formed from sediments?**
   - ◯ sedimentary
   - ◯ igneous
   - ◯ metamorphic

8. **What type of rocks are formed by heat and pressure?**
   - ◯ sedimentary
   - ◯ igneous
   - ◯ metamorphic

9. **Choose the best meaning for metamorphic.**
   - ◯ melting
   - ◯ changing
   - ◯ staying the same

10. **What do you know?**

    Different types of rock are used in our homes and other buildings. List the types of rocks you know about and where you have seen them.

    ______________________________
    ______________________________
    ______________________________
    ______________________________
    ______________________________
    ______________________________
    ______________________________
    ______________________________
    ______________________________
    ______________________________

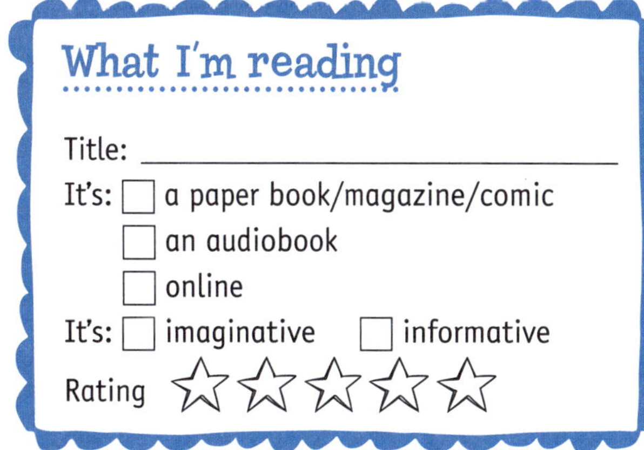


TERM 4

Score 2 points for each correct answer! SCORE /20

# Grammar & Punctuation

AC9E3LA06, AC9E3LA07, AC9E3LA10

## Subject–verb agreement

Remember! A subject and a verb must always agree. A singular subject must have a singular verb. A plural (more than one) subject must have a plural verb.

When a group of things is recognised as one, it has a singular verb.

*Example:* A lot of sediment (one lot) **is** carried by rivers and streams.

Verbs may be one word.

*Example*: forms

Verbs may be verbs groups with a main verb and a helper or auxiliary verb.

*Example*: **is** formed

**Write a verb or verb group to complete these sentences.**

1. Metamorphic rocks _______________ by huge amounts of heat and pressure.
2. Sedimentary rocks _______________ millions of years to form.
3. Igneous rocks _______________ on the surface or under the ground.
4. Limestone _______________ a type of sedimentary rock.
5. Basalt and granite _______________ types of igneous rock.
6. Water and earth _______________ the sediments together.

## Noun groups

A noun group is a group of words built around a noun. Noun groups give more information about the main noun.

Noun groups may include articles, such as a, an, the.

They may include adjectives, such as **sedimentary** rock.

They may include adjectival phrases.

*Example:* The water and earth **above the sediments** squeeze them and cement them together.

**Circle the nouns and underline the noun groups in these sentences.**

7. Hot molten rock forms inside volcanoes.
8. A metamorphic rock is made by heat from the Earth's core.
9. It takes millions of years for sedimentary rocks to form.
10. Hot molten rock inside a volcano is called magma or lava.
11. A metamorphic rock forms under the surface of the Earth.
12. Sandstone is a type of sedimentary rock.

## Lists and commas

Items in a group are often listed under each other. They may be listed with or without bullet points or numbers.

If the items are listed in a sentence, commas (,) are used to separate them. We do not put a comma before and or or and the last item.

*Example:* Igneous rocks include basalt, granite, quartz, pumice **and** tuff.

**Write sentences to list sedimentary and metamorphic rocks.**

13. _______________________________________________

_______________________________________________

_______________________________________________

_______________________________________________

_______________________________________________

14. _______________________________________________

_______________________________________________

_______________________________________________

_______________________________________________

_______________________________________________

*Score 2 points for each correct answer!* SCORE  /28  0-12  14-22  24-28

TERM 4



TARGETING ENGLISH HOMEWORK YEAR 3 © PASCAL PRESS ISBN 978 1 925726 60 2

AC9E3LA08, AC9E3LY09, AC9E3LY10

## Adding endings to words that end in 'y'

Remember! When a noun ends with a y after a vowel (ay, ey, oy or uy), just add -s to make the plural (more than one).

*Examples*:

day days stay stays

When a word ends in a y after a consonant, change the y into an i and add -es to make the plural.

*Examples*:

body bodies country countries

The rules are similar for adding endings to vowels, except we don't change the y to i before adding -ing.

*Examples*:

stay stays stayed staying

carry carries carried carrying

Some vowels have irregular past tense verbs.

*Examples*:

buy buys bought buying

**Rewrite these words as plurals.**

1. body ______
2. baby ______
3. donkey ______
4. sky ______
5. library ______
6. story ______
7. key ______
8. journey ______
9. factory ______
10. day ______

**Add endings to these base verbs to show present tense and past tense. The first is done for you. Watch out for irregular verbs.**

| | Base verb (do) | Past tense (did) | Present tense (doing now) |
|---|---|---|---|
| | carry | carried | carrying |
| 11 | play | | |
| 12 | hurry | | |
| 13 | try | | |
| 14 | fly | | |
| 15 | buy | | |
| 16 | empty | | |
| 17 | enjoy | | |
| 18 | cry | | |
| 19 | copy | | |
| 20 | reply | | |

## Syllables

**Count the number of syllables in each word, then write them in the correct box.**

sedimentary metamorphic igneous
sediments rocks streams
surface Earth pressure
volcano magma geologist

| One syllable | Two syllables |
|---|---|
| 21 | 24 |
| 22 | 25 |
| 23 | 26 |

| Three syllables | More than three |
|---|---|
| 27 | 30 |
| 28 | 31 |
| 29 | 32 |

Score 2 points for each correct answer! SCORE /64    

TERM 4

AC9E3LY03, AC9E3LY04, AC9E3LY05, AC9S3U02, AC9HS3K01

## Informative text – Report

### Uses of Rocks – A First Nations' Perspective

First Nations peoples have used rocks and stones for making weapons and grinding tools for thousands of years. Rocks are hard and durable. These properties make them perfect for making axes, spearheads and other weapons and utensils. The edges of the rocks can be sharpened and ground to make thin blades or sharp points.

Rocks such as ochre are ground to a fine powder and mixed with water to make paint.

Grinding stones were used to grind and crush different materials. Bulbs, berries, seeds, insects and flowers were placed between a large lower stone and a smaller upper stone.

Flaked stone tools were made by hitting a piece of stone, called a core, with a 'hammerstone', which was often a pebble. This would cause the rock to 'flake' leaving a sharp-edged rock that could then be fastened to timber using resin or other plant and animal materials.

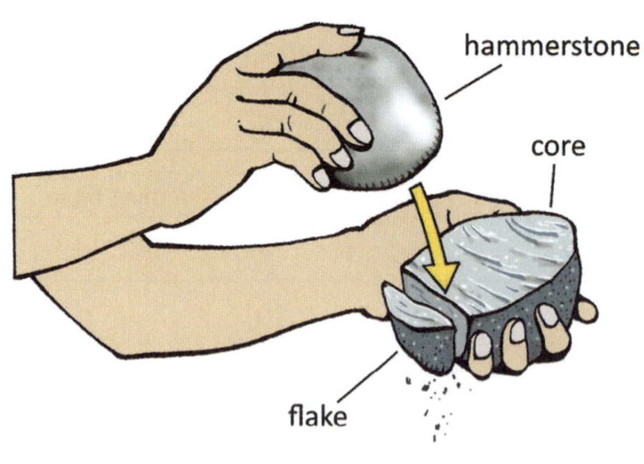


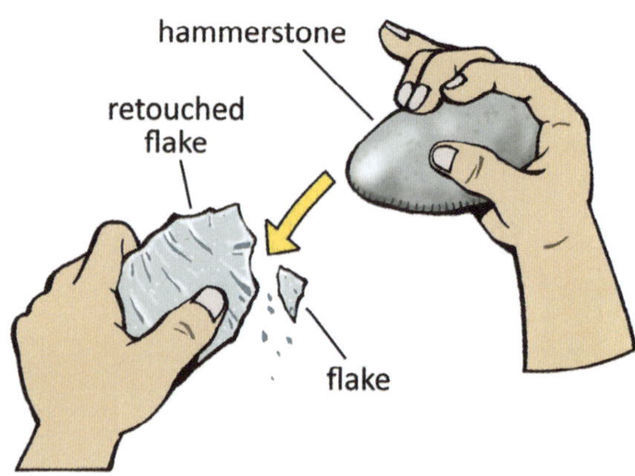


Source: Adapted from *Targeting Science*, Year 3, page 40, Pascal Press.




TARGETING ENGLISH HOMEWORK YEAR 3 © PASCAL PRESS ISBN 978 1 925726 60 2

# Reading & Comprehension

Shade the bubble next to the correct answer. Write the answer on the line where appropriate.

1. How long have First Nations peoples been using rocks and stones?
   - ◯ a few years
   - ◯ hundreds of years
   - ◯ thousands of years

2. Which of these do First Nations peoples use rocks and stones for? (Choose any that apply.)
   - ◯ weapons
   - ◯ tools
   - ◯ paint

3. Which properties make rocks and stones perfect for making weapons?
   - ◯ hard and durable
   - ◯ sharp and flat
   - ◯ easy to grind

4. Which rocks do First Nations peoples use to make paint?
   - ◯ hammerstones
   - ◯ ochre
   - ◯ grinding stones

5. Which stones are used to crush different materials?
   - ◯ hammerstones
   - ◯ ochre
   - ◯ grinding stones

6. How many stones were used to grind different materials?
   - ◯ one
   - ◯ two
   - ◯ three

7. What was a hammerstone used with?
   - ◯ a core
   - ◯ a pebble
   - ◯ a grinding stone

8. What was a hammerstone used to make?
   - ◯ ochre
   - ◯ grinding stones
   - ◯ flaked stone tools

9. What was a **flake**, a sharpened stone, fastened to?
   - ◯ animals
   - ◯ timber
   - ◯ plants

10. What do you think?

    Why is water added to ochre to make paint?

    ______________________________________________
    ______________________________________________
    ______________________________________________
    ______________________________________________
    ______________________________________________
    ______________________________________________
    ______________________________________________
    ______________________________________________
    ______________________________________________
    ______________________________________________
    ______________________________________________

TERM 4

## What I'm reading

Title: ______________________________

It's: ☐ a paper book/magazine/comic
☐ an audiobook
☐ online

It's: ☐ imaginative ☐ informative

Rating ☆☆☆☆☆

Score 2 points for each correct answer! SCORE /20

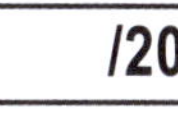

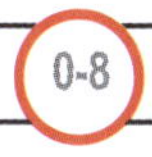

# Grammar & Punctuation

AC9E3LA08, AC9E3LA10

## Adverbial phrases

Remember! Adverbial phrases also tell us more about verbs. They tell us how things are being done, when things are happening, where things are happening or why things are happening. A phrase is a group of words that usually begins with a preposition.

Here are some prepositions:

above at before between by
during for in into near
off on over since to
under until with

**Underline the adverbial phrases in these sentences. Circle the prepositions. Write how, when, where or why the adverbial phrase tells.**

1. Rocks and stones have been used for making weapons and tools. (__________)
2. The edges of rocks are sharpened to make thin blades or sharp points. (__________)
3. First Nations peoples have used rocks and stones for thousands of years. (__________)
4. Ochre is mixed with water. (__________)
5. Flowers were placed between two stones. (__________)
6. Flaked stone tools were made by hitting stones together. (__________)
7. The sharp-edged rock could be fastened to timber. (__________)
8. First Nations peoples lived in Australia before Europeans arrived in 1788. (__________)

## Lists and commas

Remember! When items are listed in a sentence, commas (,) are used to separate them. We do not put a comma before and or or and the last item.

When items are listed under each other, they may be listed with or without bullet points or numbers.

**Write the items in these sentences as lists using bullet points.**

9. Rocks and stones are used for making axes, spearheads, other weapons, utensils and paint.

   Uses of rocks and stones

   ______________________________
   ______________________________
   ______________________________
   ______________________________
   ______________________________

10. Bulbs, berries, seeds, insects and flowers were ground using grinding stones.

   ______________________________

   Items for grinding

   ______________________________
   ______________________________
   ______________________________
   ______________________________
   ______________________________

**Read these sentences with lists. Add commas where they are needed.**

11. The First Nations peoples of Australia eat a wide variety of plant food, including fruit nuts seeds vegetables roots and grasses.
12. The First Nations peoples of Australia eat a wide variety of meat, including kangaroos possums emus goannas turtles fish and shellfish.
13. The First Nations peoples use every part of the wattle tree in different ways, including the leaves bark seeds roots flowers sap and wood.

*Score 2 points for each correct answer!* SCORE /26 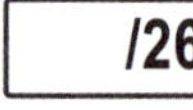 0-10  12-20  22-26 

TERM 4



TARGETING ENGLISH HOMEWORK YEAR 3 © PASCAL PRESS ISBN 978 1 925726 60 2

# Phonic & Word Knowledge

AC9E3LY09, AC9E3LY11

## Silent 't'

In the word fasten, which means to hold tight or close, the letter t is silent.

It is also silent in these words:

castle Christmas butcher listen
often nestle ballet soften
moisten hasten

**Choose one of the words with a silent 't' to complete each sentence.**

1. First Nations peoples use resin to _______________ sharp rocks to timber.
2. First Nations peoples add water to _______________ the ochre.
3. It is important to _______________ carefully to what others are saying.
4. We must _______________ our seatbelts when we travel by car or plane.
5. If you put butter in the sun, it will _______________.

## Hard g and soft g

Remember! Hard g is the sound you hear at the beginning of **g**rind and **g**round.

Soft g is when it makes the same sound as the letter **j** in **j**ump.

*Examples*: lar**ge** ed**ge**

**Read these words. They all have the soft g sound.**

badge edge hedge ridge
bridge fridge lodge large
smudge fudge nudge judge
cage stage budgie gentle
legend urgent

**Write the word to match each picture.**

6. _______________
7. _______________
8. _______________
9. _______________
10. _______________
11. _______________

## The letter 'c' and the digraph 'ch'

Remember! The letter c can be used to represent different sounds: the hard 'ck' sound, as in **c**ore; the 'soft c' sound, as in pie**c**e; the digraph 'ch', as in **ch**ips.

The diagraph ch can also represent different sounds: the hard 'ck' sound, as in o**ch**re and s**ch**ool; the 'sh' sound, as in bro**ch**ure and **ch**arade; and the 'ch' sound, as in **ch**ips.

**Read these words. Underline the letter c or the letters ch. Listen to the sound. Sort the words into the boxes.**

ochre piece school change chef
lunch chemist city chute
machine chess cent

| 'ck' sound | 'soft c' sound |
|---|---|
| 12 | 15 |
| 13 | 16 |
| 14 | 17 |
| **'ch' sound** | **'ch' sound** |
| 18 | 21 |
| 19 | 22 |
| 20 | 23 |

Score 2 points for each correct answer! SCORE /46 0-20 22-40 42-46

TERM 4

AC9E3LY03, AC9E3LY04, AC9E3LY05

## Imaginative text – Science fiction

# Destination 4088

This story is an excerpt from *Pluto's First Mission*, Book 6 in the Time Quest series by Del Merrick. Read other chapters in the story in Units 7, 15 and 23.

Sid is lost somewhere in his time machine. Benson and Bee have built another time machine to go and look for him. Only Benson is going. Bee wishes she could go too, but someone has to stay behind for communication.

Benson sits at the control panel. He presses several levers, then the START button. The machine begins to shake and hum.

"All systems go," says Benson into his headset. "I just have to enter a time zone."

"Try 4088," says Bee, remembering it was one of the last things Sid said before he disappeared.

Benson punches in 4088 and presses ENTER.

The lights go out. He looks out the porthole and sees trees rush by,

... then clouds,

... then empty, blue sky.

"Pluto has landed!" says Benson into his headset. He checks the time scanner – 4088. "I'll take a look around, Bee, and get back to you."

Benson steps down into a strange world of long, glass-topped buildings and people in silver suits on solar wave riders. He sees a building that looks like a silver bubble. It has skylights and one door that opens like a drawbridge. Two men stand guard, like soldiers.

He scans the bubble with his x-ray glasses. There, in an empty room below the skylight, is Sid.

Source: Excerpt from *Pluto's First Mission*, Time Quest series, Blake Education.

TERM 4



TARGETING ENGLISH HOMEWORK YEAR 3 © PASCAL PRESS ISBN 978 1 925726 60 2

# Reading & Comprehension

**Use these clues to complete the crossword.**

**Across**

1. Sid was lost _________.
3. One door opened like a _________.
6. Bee _________ what Sid said.
8. Benson looked at the scanner to _________ where he landed.
9. Benson sat at the control _________.
11. Benson travelled forwards in _________.
13. The lights went _________ in the time machine.
14. "All _________ go," said Benson.
15. Benson looked out through a _________.

**Down**

1. Benson was going to look for _________.
2. "Pluto has landed," said _________.
4. _________ wished she could go with Benson.
5. A silver building has _________.
7. Benson was travelling in a new time _________.
8. The START button is on the _________ panel.
10. Benson spoke into his _________.
12. Benson landed in a different time _________.

| 1 | | | | | | | | | | | |
|---|---|---|---|---|---|---|---|---|---|---|---|
| | | | | | | | | | 2 | | |
| 3 | | | | 4 | | | | | | | |
| | | | | | | | | | | | 5 |
| | 6 | | 7 | | | | | | | | |
| | | | | | | | | | | | |
| 8 | | | | | | | 9 | | | | |
| | | | | | 10 | | | | | | |
| | | 11 | | | | | | | 12 | | |
| | | | | | | | | | | | |
| | | | | | | | | | | | |
| 13 | | | | | 14 | | | | | | |
| | | | | | | | | | | | |
| | | 15 | | | | | | | | | |

TERM 4

## What I'm reading

Title: ______________________

It's: ☐ a paper book/magazine/comic
☐ an audiobook
☐ online

It's: ☐ imaginative ☐ informative

Rating ☆ ☆ ☆ ☆ ☆

Score 2 points for each correct answer! SCORE /34

0-14 16-28 30-34

# Grammar & Punctuation

AC9E3LA06, AC9E3LA07, AC9E3LY06

## Verbs

Remember! Verbs are words that tell us what is happening in a sentence. They tell us what the subject of the sentence is doing, thinking, saying and feeling.

There are also relating verbs that help to link information in a sentence.

**Read these sentences. Circle the verbs. Write D for a doing verb, T for a thinking verb, S for a saying verb, F for a feeling verb or R for a relating verb.**

1. _____ Sid is lost somewhere in his time machine.
2. _____ Benson and Bee built another time machine.
3. _____ Bee wishes she could go too.
4. _____ Benson sits at the control panel.
5. _____ "All systems go," says Benson.
6. _____ Bee remembered what Sid told her.
7. _____ Two men stand guard, like soldiers.
8. _____ "Have you found Sid?" asks Bee.
9. _____ Benson thought the world looked strange.
10. _____ The building has skylights and one door.

## Compound sentences

Remember! Compound sentences consist of two clauses joined with a conjunction.

Conjunctions include and, but, so, yet.

Sometimes the subject of the second clause is not repeated if it is the same as in the first clause. It is 'understood'.

**Read these compound sentences. Underline the verbs in each clause. Rewrite each clause as a simple sentence. Remember to use capital letters and full stops.**

11. Sid is lost in his time machine, and Bee and Benson don't know where.
12. ______________________________
13. ______________________________
14. Bee wishes she could go, but someone has to stay behind.
15. ______________________________
16. ______________________________
17. Benson presses the START button so the machine will start.
18. ______________________________
19. ______________________________
20. Benson looked everywhere, yet he couldn't see Bee.
21. ______________________________
22. ______________________________

**Join these pairs of simple sentences to form compound sentences.**

23. The people wore silver suits. They rode on solar wave riders.

______________________________

24. The building looked like a silver bubble. It had skylights on the top.

______________________________

Score 2 points for each correct answer! SCORE /48   

TERM 4



TARGETING ENGLISH HOMEWORK YEAR 3 © PASCAL PRESS ISBN 978 1 925726 60 2

# Phonic & Word Knowledge

AC9E3LY06, AC9E3LY10

## Prefixes

Remember! A prefix is a letter or group of letters that is added to the beginning of a word. When it is added to the beginning of a word, the meaning of the word changes.

Like the prefixes in– and un–, the prefix dis– also means 'not' or 'the opposite of'.

*Example*: appear, **dis**appear

Sid told Bee a number before he disappeared.

**Add the prefix dis– to the words in bold to make a word that means the opposite of.**

1. Benson did not know if he could **trust** the strangers. Until he was certain, he would ______________ them.
2. Benson usually chose to **like** rather than ______________ new people he met.
3. Bee and Benson need to **obey**, not ______________ their orders.
4. To ensure that germs don't **infect** the time machine, Benson will ______________ it.
5. Bee and Benson always **agreed** on what to do. They never ______________.
6. Benson was always **honest** and told the truth. He was never ______________.

**Choose the correct prefix un–, in– or dis– to make the opposite of these words.**

7. happy ______________
8. active ______________
9. comfortable ______________
10. arm ______________
11. respectful ______________
12. correct ______________

## Compound words

Remember! A compound word is two words joined together to make one word.

*Example:* butter + **fly** = butter**fly**

Sometimes compound words are joined by hyphens.

*Example:* wishy-washy    far-fetched

**There are eight compound words in the story. Can you find them all? Write them on these lines.**

13. ______________
14. ______________
15. ______________
16. ______________
17. ______________
18. ______________
19. ______________
20. ______________

**Rewrite these words by adding light to make new compound words.**

21. sky ______________
22. candle ______________
23. moon ______________
24. sun ______________
25. tail ______________
26. head ______________
27. search ______________
28. flash ______________
29. high ______________
30. flood ______________

**Read this paragraph. Ten (10) words have been spelled incorrectly. Circle them. Write them correctly on the lines below.**

Side is lost sumwhere in time. Bee and Benson maid a knew time mashine to look for him. Benson went in the machine, but Bee staid beehind. Benson landed in a strange werld wear everythink looked different.

31 – 40

______________ ______________
______________ ______________
______________ ______________
______________ ______________
______________ ______________

*Score 2 points for each correct answer!*

SCORE /80 0-38 40-74 76-80

TERM 4

AC9E3LE02, AC9E3LE03, AC9E3LY03, AC9E3LY05

## Video game review: *Super Mario Odyssey*

### Super Mario Odyssey

*Super Mario Odyssey* is a platform game for Nintendo Switch.

Reviewed by Rowan 9, Tasmania.

*Super Mario Odyssey* is an excellent game. I can't stop playing it. I only stop if Mum tells me I have to go outside or do something else.

Super Mario has to rescue Princess Peach. Bowser has kidnapped her. Again. And he says they're going to get married. She definitely doesn't want to marry Bowser.

Bowser sends the Broodals – they're really weird – to stop Mario. But Mario uses his hat, called Cappy, to capture them. Get it – *cap*ture? When his hat lands on anything, he can control it.

Mario travels around, going to lots of different kingdoms. His airship is called Odyssey. He gets power by collecting Power Moons in the kingdoms. He can get coins too for buying things.

It can be a bit annoying at times. But mostly, it's really fun.

The graphics are really good, and I like the music and sound effects too. They're great, just like in the other Super Mario games.

I think any kids over 6 could play this game. Young kids might have trouble with the controls. My little brother did at first, but he finally got the hang of it.

I give it 5 out of 5 stars because it really is another awesome Super Mario game. They definitely are my favourites.

1. **Have you played *Super Mario Odyssey*?**
   - ◯ Yes
   - ◯ No
   - ◯ Unsure
2. **After reading this review, would you like to play *Super Mario Odyssey*?**
   - ◯ Yes
   - ◯ No
   - ◯ Unsure
3. **Which words or phrases in the review help you decide?**

   ______________________________
   ______________________________
   ______________________________
4. **List some video games that you have played. Circle your favourite.**

   ______________________________
   ______________________________
   ______________________________





TARGETING ENGLISH HOMEWORK YEAR 3 © PASCAL PRESS ISBN 978 1 925726 60 2

# Review

**Now you can write a review of your favourite video game so that others can decide whether to play it or not.**

① **About the video game**

Title: ____________________

What do you need to play it?

____________________

② **Circle the word that best describes the type of video game.**

platform action battle sports racing
adventure puzzle role-playing
simulator action-adventure fighting
education

If the type of game is not listed, write it here:

____________________

③ **When did you first play the game?**

____________________

____________________

④ **Where did you play it?**

____________________

____________________

⑤ **How many times have you played it?**

____________________

⑥ **How often do you play it?**

____________________

⑦ **Why did you choose to play it the first time?**

____________________

____________________

⑧ **What is the main thing you like about the game?**

____________________

____________________

⑨ **Do any of your friends or family play this game?**

◯ Yes
◯ No
◯ Unsure

Explain why they choose to play or not play this game if you know.

____________________

____________________

____________________

____________________

____________________

## What is the game about?

⑩ **What is the game mainly about? What do you have to do in the game? What is the goal? What do you have to do to be successful?**

____________________

____________________

____________________

____________________

____________________

____________________

____________________

____________________

____________________

____________________

____________________

____________________

____________________

____________________

____________________

# Review

## Abilities

⑪ **Are there any special abilities you have in the game or actions you can take, for example, jump, fly, capture things with your cap? Explain.**

## Characters

⑫ **Are there any characters in the game? What do you know about them, for example, their name, where they live, what they like doing, what they look like? Include anything you find interesting about the characters.**

⑬ **Who is your favourite character?**

Why?

## The setting

⑭ **When does the game take place?**

- ◯ in the past, a long time ago
- ◯ in the past, not long ago
- ◯ in the present
- ◯ in the future
- ◯ not sure

Where does the game take place? Is it a real location or a fictional place?

⑮ **List things that can be seen, heard or smelled in the location.**

Seen

Heard

Smelled





TARGETING ENGLISH HOMEWORK YEAR 3 © PASCAL PRESS ISBN 978 1 925726 60 2

## Review

⑯ **What do you think of the graphics?**

⑰ **What do you think of the music?**

⑱ **What is your favourite part of the game?**

Why?

⑲ **Who else might like to play this game? Who do you recommend it for?**

⑳ **How many stars do you give it?**

☆☆☆☆☆

Draw your favourite part.

TERM 4

# Reading & Comprehension

## A Super-Special Chocolate Cake

Tessa was staying with her great-grandparents on the farm. The first thing Tessa did was help Great Grandma Em bake a super-special chocolate cake for dessert.

Tessa had to hide under the table while everything went into the huge mixing bowl.

"Don't peek," Great Grandma Em said. "It's a secret recipe. Not even you can see what goes into the mixture."

"You wouldn't want to know anyway," Great Grandpop chuckled. "She learned it from a witch and it's full of magic things. Em thinks it will make her skin as smooth as a baby's bottom."

Great Gran snorted. "Nibble dust!" She put the last of the mixture in the cake tin. Then she popped it into the oven to bake. She gave Tessa the bowl and spoon to lick. "I don't give two hoots about wrinkles."

Source: Extract from *Getting Rid of Wrinkles*, Teena Raffa-Mulligan, Blake Education.

**Shade the bubble next to the correct answer. Write the answer on the line where appropriate.**

1. **Why was Tessa at the farm?**
   - ◯ She lives there.
   - ◯ She was visiting her great-grandparents.
   - ◯ She wanted to feed the animals.

2. **What was the first thing Tessa did at the farm?**
   - ◯ helped make a cake
   - ◯ fed the animals
   - ◯ nibbled on a bowl of dust

3. **What sort of cake did Tessa and her great-grandmother make?**
   - ◯ a magic cake
   - ◯ a chocolate cake
   - ◯ a mud cake

4. **Why did Tessa and her great-grandmother make the cake?**
   - ◯ for her birthday
   - ◯ for desert
   - ◯ for dessert

5. **How did Tessa help her great-grandmother make the cake?**
   - ◯ She put all the ingredients in the bowl.
   - ◯ She mixed all the ingredients.
   - ◯ She hid under the table.

6. **Why do you think Tessa had to hide under the table?**
   - ◯ She was scared.
   - ◯ Great Gran didn't want her to see what was going into the cake.
   - ◯ She was misbehaving.

7. **What did Great Grandpop say went into the cake?**
   - ◯ nibble dust
   - ◯ witches' brews
   - ◯ magic stuff

8. **What did Great Grandpop say Great Grandma Em hoped the cake would do?**
   - ◯ make her wrinkly
   - ◯ remove her wrinkles
   - ◯ make her a baby

9. **What do you think nibble dust means?**

   ______________________________

   ______________________________

10. **What do you think I don't give two hoots about wrinkles means?**

    ______________________________

    ______________________________

*Score 2 points for each correct answer!* SCORE /20 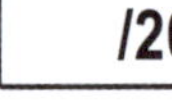   
0-8 10-14 16-20

TERM 4


TARGETING ENGLISH HOMEWORK YEAR 3 © PASCAL PRESS ISBN 978 1 925726 60 2

# Grammar & Punctuation

**Circle the emotive words in these sentences. Write N if the word is a noun, A for an adjective and V for a verb.**

1. ____ Tessa helped Great Grandma Em bake a super-special chocolate cake for dessert.
2. ____ She learned it from a witch and it's full of magic things.
3. ____ Great Gran snorted.

**Underline the verbs and circle the adverbs in these sentences. Circle how, when or where.**

4. They made a chocolate cake first. (how, when, where)
5. Tessa stayed quietly under the table. (how, when, where)
6. Great Gran sat down on the chair. (how, when, where)

**Add an adverbial phrase to each of these sentences. Circle the prepositions.**

7. Tessa was staying ________________________.
8. Tessa hid ________________________.
9. Great Gran cooked the cake ________________________.

**Think of 3 things Tessa might do at the farm. Write them as commands. Circle the verbs (doing words) that begin each command.**

10. ________________________
11. ________________________
12. ________________________

**Write a sentence with a list of at least 5 things you can see in the illustration of Great Gran's kitchen. Rember to use commas.**

13. ________________________
________________________

**Write sentences to personify each of these nouns.**

14. cow
________________________
________________________

15. chicken
________________________
________________________

**Read these sentences. Circle the adjectives. Underline the nouns they tell more about.**

16. Tessa and Great Grandma Em baked a super-special chocolate cake for dessert.
17. Great Grandma Em put the secret ingredients into the huge mixing bowl.
18. The first thing Tessa did was bake a cake.

**Read these groups of words. Write S for sentence. Write F for sentence fragment.**

19. ______ Don't peek!
20. ______ It's a secret recipe.
21. ______ Nibble dust!
22. ______ full of magic things

**Write a verb or verb group to complete these sentences.**

23. Tessa ______________ staying at the farm with her great-grandparents.
24. Great Grandpop always ______________ jokes.
25. When they ______________ the cake, Tessa ______________ under the table.

**Circle the nouns and underline the noun groups in these sentences.**

26. They baked a super-special chocolate cake for dessert.
27. Everything went into the huge mixing bowl.
28. Great Gran put the cake into the hot oven to bake.

TERM 4

## Grammar & Punctuation

**Read these sentences. Circle the verbs. Write D for a doing verb, T for a thinking verb, S for a saying verb, F for a feeling verb or R for a relating verb.**

29. _____ "No peeking," said Great Gran Em.
30. _____ Tessa wondered why she was under the table.
31. _____ Great Grandpop relaxed in his rocking chair.
32. _____ Tessa hid under the table.
33. _____ Tessa is on the farm with her great-grandparents.

**Rewrite this compound sentence as two simple sentences.**

They mixed the ingredients together, and Great Gran put the cake in the oven.

34. ______________________________
35. ______________________________

**Rewrite these sentences as direct speech. Remember to use the correct punctuation and saying verbs.**

36. Great Gran: You sit under the table while I put in the secret ingredients.

______________________________

37. Great Grandpop: Em thinks the cake will hide all her wrinkles.

______________________________

38. Tessa: This is the best cake ever. I wish I knew what went in it.

______________________________

Score 2 points for each correct answer!

SCORE /76 0-36 38-70 72-76

## Phonic & Word Knowledge

**Rewrite these words as plurals.**

1. bowl ______________________________
2. witch ______________________________
3. baby ______________________________
4. recipe ______________________________
5. half ______________________________
6. fish ______________________________

**Rewrite these adjectives by adding the suffix –ly to make adverbs.**

7. hungry ______________________________
8. kind ______________________________
9. smooth ______________________________
10. careless ______________________________
11. secret ______________________________
12. quiet ______________________________

**Read these compound words. Write the two words that form them.**

13. daylight __________ + __________
14. super-special __________ + __________
15. summertime __________ + __________
16. grandchildren __________ + __________

**These words are homonyms. They have two different meanings. One meaning is a noun, the other is a verb. Choose a homonym. Write two sentences to show the different meanings. Write N for noun and V for verb.**

| bear | lie | bat |
|---|---|---|
| clip | book | try |

17. ______________________________

18. ______________________________

TERM 4



TARGETING ENGLISH HOMEWORK YEAR 3 © PASCAL PRESS ISBN 978 1 925726 60 2

# Phonic & Word Knowledge

TERM 4 REVIEW

Count the number of **syllables** in each word, then write them in the correct box.

huge grandparents special chocolate dessert cake grandmother everything ingredients mixture bowl misbehaving

| One syllable | Two syllables |
|---|---|
| 19 | 22 |
| 20 | 23 |
| 21 | 24 |

| Three syllables | More than three |
|---|---|
| 25 | 28 |
| 26 | 29 |
| 27 | 30 |

Write a word with **onomatopoeia** to complete these sentences.

31 The floorboards ____________ as I tiptoed up the stairs.

32 There was a mighty ____________ as the lightning flashed.

33 I heard a ____________ as the rock hit the water.

Read these sentences. Circle the **sound** that is **repeated**.

34 Great Gran grabbed the goat that was gobbling the vegetables in her garden.

35 Tessa taught the tiny turtle to turn in its tank.

Explain the **meanings** of these words with prefixes.

36 uncomfortable ____________________

____________________

37 incorrect ____________________

____________________

38 disqualified ____________________

____________________

Add endings to these base verbs to show **present tense** and **past tense**. The first is done for you. Watch out for irregular verbs.

| | Base verb | Past tense | Present tense |
|---|---|---|---|
| | carry | carried | carrying |
| 39 | bake | | |
| 40 | hide | | |
| 41 | see | | |
| 42 | pop | | |

Read these words. Underline the **letter 'c'** or the **letters 'ch'**. Listen to the sound. Sort the words into the boxes. (Two words will be in two boxes.)

special recipe magic chuckled piece chocolate secret chef lunch city chute machine cent witch

| 'ck' sound | 'soft c' sound |
|---|---|
| 43 | 47 |
| 44 | 48 |
| 45 | 49 |
| 46 | 50 |

| 'ch' sound | 'sh' sound |
|---|---|
| 51 | 55 |
| 52 | 56 |
| 53 | 57 |
| 54 | 58 |

Score 2 points for each correct answer! SCORE /116

TERM 4

# MY READING LIST

**Name:** ______________________

______________________

| | Title | Author | Rating | Date |
|---|---|---|---|---|
| 1 | | | ☆☆☆☆☆ | |
| 2 | | | ☆☆☆☆☆ | |
| 3 | | | ☆☆☆☆☆ | |
| 4 | | | ☆☆☆☆☆ | |
| 5 | | | ☆☆☆☆☆ | |
| 6 | | | ☆☆☆☆☆ | |
| 7 | | | ☆☆☆☆☆ | |
| 8 | | | ☆☆☆☆☆ | |
| 9 | | | ☆☆☆☆☆ | |
| 10 | | | ☆☆☆☆☆ | |
| 11 | | | ☆☆☆☆☆ | |
| 12 | | | ☆☆☆☆☆ | |
| 13 | | | ☆☆☆☆☆ | |
| 14 | | | ☆☆☆☆☆ | |
| 15 | | | ☆☆☆☆☆ | |
| 16 | | | ☆☆☆☆☆ | |
| 17 | | | ☆☆☆☆☆ | |
| 18 | | | ☆☆☆☆☆ | |
| 19 | | | ☆☆☆☆☆ | |
| 20 | | | ☆☆☆☆☆ | |
| 21 | | | ☆☆☆☆☆ | |
| 22 | | | ☆☆☆☆☆ | |
| 23 | | | ☆☆☆☆☆ | |
| 24 | | | ☆☆☆☆☆ | |
| 25 | | | ☆☆☆☆☆ | |
| 26 | | | ☆☆☆☆☆ | |
| 27 | | | ☆☆☆☆☆ | |
| 28 | | | ☆☆☆☆☆ | |
| 29 | | | ☆☆☆☆☆ | |
| 30 | | | ☆☆☆☆☆ | |
| 31 | | | ☆☆☆☆☆ | |
| 32 | | | ☆☆☆☆☆ | |



TARGETING ENGLISH HOMEWORK YEAR 3 © PASCAL PRESS ISBN 978 1 925726 60 2

# Answers

## Term 1

## Unit 1

### Page 3 Reading & Comprehension

1 afternoon tea time
2 Chocolate crackles were Grandpa's favourites. All the ingredients were in the cupboard. They knew what to do. They wanted to make Grandpa happy.
3 to help them set
4 happy
5 two
6 He started to laugh.
7 baking powder
8 icing sugar
9 They didn't want to froth at the mouth.
10 Answers will vary.

### Page 4 Grammar & Punctuation

1 circled
2 not circled
3 not circled
4 circled
5-6 Answers will vary.
7 circled
8 circled
9 underlined
10 underlined
11–12 Answers will vary.
13–14 Answers will vary.
15 "What did you put in the chocolate crackles?"
16 Why did the elephant cross the road?
17 The mouse ran between the elephant's legs.
18 It was time to get a new fence.
19 A milk truck has a horn and gives milk.
20 They are afraid of the worldwide web.
21 He had no body to go with.

### Page 5 Phonic & Word Knowledge

1 day, made
2 tea, cheeks
3 white, like
4 both, role
5 you, use
6–10 Answers will vary.
11–22 Green: while, whale, what, white, which, wheel, when, whether
Yellow: whole, who, whose, whom
23 tables
24 books
25 pencils
26 times
27 ingredients
28 eyes
29 ingredients
30 eye
31 pencils
32 times

## Unit 2

### Page 7 Reading & Comprehension

1 an item of food
2 a tool to use
3 a way to do things
4 4
5 Answers will vary.
6 180 °C
7 wash them
8 so children don't hurt themselves with sharp knives; so children don't burn themselves
9 1¼ hours
10 15 minutes
11 Ingredients: bacon, onion, milk, chives, potato, butter
Utensils: pan, board, fork, tablespoon, bowl, tray, knife, masher
Crossed out: cork, better, table, light, pencil, silk

### Page 8 Grammar & Punctuation

1 Do you like baked potatoes?
2 Do you like onions and bacon on potatoes?
3 We had baked potatoes for lunch on Sunday.
4 Sometimes we add corn instead of bacon to our baked potatoes.
5 circled
6 not circled
7 not circled
8 circled
9 Turn, Wash, Prick, Put, Cook, Chop, Fry, Drain, Take, Slice, Scoop, Put, Add, Mash, Stir, Pile, Put, Place
10–13 Answers will vary.
14 What will we have for lunch today? I know. Let's make baked potatoes! They are my favourite. Do you like baked potatoes too? Which would you prefer?

### Page 9 Phonic & Word Knowledge

1 bake, place
2 be, heat
3 knife, slice
4 bowl, coal
5 you, use
6 knife
7 help
8 add
9 place
10 hot
11 I am turning on the oven. I turned on the oven.
12 I am mixing in the onion. I mixed in the onion.
13 I am mashing the potato. I mashed the potato.
14 I am adding the milk. I added the milk.
15 I am scooping out the potato. I scooped out the potato.
16 Sentence: I like to eat baked potatoes.

| U | N | T | I | L | I | W | L |
|---|---|---|---|---|---|---|---|
| I | K | H | A | R | E | I | E |
| T | H | E | M | P | U | T | T |
| F | O | Y | E | H | A | H | T |
| O | N | C | E | A | B | A | K |
| R | E | D | P | L | O | T | A |
| T | O | E | S | F | R | O | M |

## Unit 3

### Page 11 Reading & Comprehension

1 at his Gran's house
2 in the back room
3 alone
4 the hall
5 His Gran tucked him in too tight.
6 an old toy
7 a teddy
8 old; long, floppy ears; striped body
9 to fall asleep
10 Answers will vary.

### Page 12 Grammar & Punctuation

1 slept
2 shone
3 wriggled
4 saw
5 got
6 was sleeping
7 was coming
8 had tucked
9 had made
10 didn't look
11 was wriggling; past
12 will keep; future
13 is sleeping; present
14 S
15 C

### Page 13 Phonic & Word Knowledge

1 shop, chop
2 shin, chin, thin
3 chat, that
4 wish, with, wing
5 such, sung
6 gash, gang
7 B
8 B
9 B
10 D
11 D
12 D
13 B
14 B
15 hallway
16 motorway
17 airway
18 causeway
19 clearway
20 stairway

## Unit 4

### Page 15 Reading & Comprehension

1 *Time Out!*
2 Eddie Woo and Jess Black
3 Pan Macmillan, 2022
4 9781760982997
5 Eddie Woo
6 He loves maths, adventure and solving mysteries. His best friends Rusty and DT do too. They work together as a team of super-sleuths.
7 Rusty and DT
8 Answers will vary, e.g. adventure, mystery, fun.
9 Yes. The reviewer says it's a great book and gave it 5 stars.
10 Answers will vary.

ANSWERS

# Answers

## Page 16 Grammar & Punctuation

1 PN
2 CN
3 PN
4 PN
5 PN
6 CN
7 CN
8 PN
9 CN
10 CN
11 Eddie Woo is a maths teacher. He lives in Sydney, Australia. He likes to help people learn maths. He posts a lot of maths lessons on YouTube. He writes a lot of books about mathematics too.

In the book, *Time Out*, Eddie Woo is the main character. His best friends are Rusty and DT. The character in the book is not the real Eddie Woo. But just like the real Eddie Woo, he likes maths and likes to solve problems too.

12–15 Answers will vary.
16 fun, love, exciting, win, great, 5 stars
17 Positive (green): funny, exciting, fantastic, unbelievable, great, best, wonderful
Negative (red): strange, boring, dreadful, scary, horrible, worst

## Page 17 Phonic & Word Knowledge

1 screw
2 stew
3 moon
4 glue
5 fruit
6 school
7 boot
8 flute
9 suit
10 sleuth
11 to
12 clue
13 suitable
14 two
15 soon
16 worm
17 bird
18 surf
19 nurse
20 pearl
21 shirt
22 church
23 skirt
24 fern
25 Earth
26 ice, S
27 character, C, C
28 place, S
29 chicken, CH,C
30 school, C
31 discover, C
32 city, S
33 clue, C
34 search, CH

## Unit 5

## Page 19 Reading & Comprehension

1 in a takeaway store
2 No/Maybe
3 Answers will vary, e.g. It says delivery or pick-up./Some takeaway stores have a few tables outside.
4 fast food
5 six
6 burger with the lot
7 Answers will vary, e.g. It has more on it.
8 by phone, online, in-store
9 Answers will vary, e.g. by car, by bicycle, by foot.
10 Answers will vary, e.g. It takes time for the food to be delivered after it's cooked.

## Page 20 Grammar & Punctuation

1 Wash
Polish
Vacuum
Wash the windows
2 feed the cat
walk the dog
water the plants
relax
3 swimmers
towel
bathing cap
sunscreen
4 Mobile phones
Headphones
Speakers
Computers
5 At school, we do maths, reading, writing, HASS, PE and art.
6 I play soccer after school on Monday, Wednesday and Friday.
7 My friends Kristin, Casey, Jamie, Trang and Tema came over to my house last night.
8 At the shop, I bought some bread, milk, apples, bananas and ice-cream.
9 To make a cake, you need flour, butter, sugar, eggs, milk and salt.
10 This is the best book I've ever read. It's funny, sad, scary and spooky.
11 after noon
12 barbecue
13 mayonnaise
14 vanilla
15 chocolate
16 strawberry

## Page 21 Phonic & Word Knowledge

1 batter, happen, traffic
2 glitter, swimmers, ribbon, middle. wriggle
3 scallop, bottle, soccer, shopping
4 pepper, letter
5 butter, bubble, sudden, funny
6 happen
7 bottle
8 bubble
9 traffic
10 funny
11 1
12 2
13 2
14 1
15 2
16 1
17 scallops C
18 cod C
19 sticks C
20 cutlets C
21 chicken CH, C
22 crumbed C
23 chop CH
24 chocolate CH, C
25 crab C

## Unit 6

## Page 23 Reading & Comprehension

1 No
2 1935
3 Hawaii
4 to eat the sugarcane beetles
5 No
6 The cane toads didn't like the sugarcane beetles.
7 Queensland
8 Queensland, New South Wales, Northern Territory, Western Australia
9 They are ugly.
10 kindly

## Page 24 Grammar & Punctuation

1 Cane toads like dark and damp **places**.
2 Make your home a toad-free **zone**.
3 **Farmers** in North Queensland grow sugar cane.
4 Australia is a wide, brown **land**.
5 It is important to keep your pets away from the poisonous cane **toads**.
6 Beetles were eating the sugar cane.
7 Cane toads eat small animals.
8 They like dark and damp places.
9 Farmers in North Queensland grow sugar cane.
10 Beware! Dogs and cats may chase cane toads.
11–18 Australia is home to more than 200 native frogs. Most Australian frogs are not found anywhere else in the world. Australia has no native toads. The only toad in Australia is the cane toad. It is a pest. It eats Australian frogs. It eats their food too. Most Australian frogs are not poisonous, but the cane toad is poisonous. It has poison glands on its back and neck.

ANSWERS



TARGETING ENGLISH HOMEWORK YEAR 3 © PASCAL PRESS ISBN 978 1 925726 60 2

# Answers

## Page 25 Phonic & Word Knowledge

1 hide
2 beetles
3 zone
4 cute
5 came
6 wanted, wanting
7 arrived, arriving
8 hopped, hopping
9 jumped, jumping
10 lived, living
11 catch, caught
12 make, made
13 bring, brought
14 eat, ate
15 hide, hid
16 lay, laid

## Unit 7

## Page 27 Reading & Comprehension

| | | | | | | ¹T | | | | | | | |
|---|---|---|---|---|---|---|---|---|---|---|---|---|---|
| | | | | | | I | | | | | | | |
| | ²C | O | ³M | M | U | N | I | C | ⁴A | T | O | R | |
| | H | | A | | | | | | N | | | | |
| | E | | C | | | | ⁵E | G | G | | ⁶P | | |
| | C | | H | | | | | | R | | O | | |
| | K | | I | | ⁷B | A | C | K | Y | A | R | D | |
| | | | N | | | | | | | | T | | |
| | ⁸S | H | E | D | | | | ⁹N | I | G | H | T | |
| | T | | | | | | | | | | O | | |
| | ¹⁰O | U | T | S | I | D | E | | ¹¹B | | L | | |
| | R | | | | | | | ¹²L | E | V | E | R | S |
| ¹³S | M | E | K | K | L | E | S | | E | | | | |

## Page 28 Grammar & Punctuation

1 "I think we've done it," says Sid.
2 "This is one mean machine!" says Bee.
3 "Wave communicator. Check!" calls Bee.
4 "Does the tracking system work?" asks Bee.
5 "Check the control panel first," says Bee.
6 "Our machine is ready to go," said Sid.
7 "Where will you go?" asked Bee.
8 "Tracking system. Check!" called Bee.
9 "Should we make sure the door locks?" asked Bee.
10 "I've already checked the door," said Sid.
11 dark, empty
12 glass
13 tin
14 wall
15 backyard
16 control

## Page 29 Phonic & Word Knowledge

1 B
2 B
3 B
4 D
5 D
6 D
7 B
8 D
9 B
10 B
11 B
12 B
13 D
14 B
15 2
16 1
17 2
18 5
19 2
20 2
21 3
22 3
23 1
24 2
25 emp + ty
26 al + most
27 sys + tem
28 con + trol
29 rub + bing
30 step + ping
31 an + gry
32 light + ning
33 thun + der
34 rum + bles

## Unit 8

## Pages 30–33 Book Review

Answers will vary.

## Term 1 Review

## Page 34 Reading & Comprehension

1 at his Gran's house
2 mothballs, lavender
3 yes
4 sweet
5 scared
6 Jeepers Creepers
7 scratching
8 behind the curtains
9 Answers will vary.
10 Answers will vary.

## Page 35 Grammar & Punctuation

1 circled
2 not circled
3 not circled
4 circled
5–6 Answers will vary.
7 circled
8 circled
9 underlined
10 underlined
11–12 Answers will vary.
13 Turn off the light, Toby!
14 Hold Batbat tight, Toby.
15 Be brave, Toby!
16 Stay still and listen, Toby.
17 is noticing, present
18 felt, past
19 was telling, past
20 is coming, present
21 will feel, future
22 Toby PN
23 Olivia PN
24 house CN
25 Jeepers Creepers PN
26 Gran PN
27 Batbat PN
28–31 Answers will vary.
32 Toby looked under the bed, behind the curtains, on the chair and behind the door.
33 Toby liked sweet things like strawberries, watermelon, oranges and lavender.
34 Olivia told Toby stories about goblins, dragons, Jeepers Creepers and other monsters.
35 frightened
36 worried
37 courageous
38 peaceful
39 happy
40 the smell of lavender and mothballs
41 the back room
42 Toby's toy teddy from long ago
43 Olivia told monster stories.
44 Toby liked the sweet smell of lavender and mothballs.
45 Toby held Batbat tight.
46 back
47 sweet
48 scratching
49 "I wish I didn't have to sleep here on my own," said Toby.
50 "Don't be such a baby!" said Olivia.
51 "What do you think is making the noise?" asked Gran.

## Pages 36–37 Phonic & Word Knowledge

| | | | | | |
|---|---|---|---|---|---|
| 1 | Batbat | stay | back | place | scratch |
| 2 | sleep | sweet | sheets | smell | felt |
| 3 | like | him | stiff | with | fright |
| 4 | told | hope | on | moth | whole |
| 5 | up | you | use | puff | but |

6 fright
7 with
8 whole
9 sleep
10 but
11 sheets
12 beds
13 mothballs
14 curtains
15 moths
16 noises
17 wheel
18 chop
19 shed
20 thumb
21 B
22 D
23 B
24 D
25 D
26 D
27 D
28 B
29 mothballs
30 grandmother
31 stairway
32 butterfly
33 moon
34 fern
35 glue
36 nurse
37 bird
38 pearl
39 fruit
40 worm
41 piece S
42 curtains C
43 cheese CH
44 ice S
45 match CH
46 clue C
47 staying, stayed
48 sleeping, slept
49 hoping, hoped
50 noticing, noticed
51 feeling, felt
52 shining, shone
53 2
54 1
55 3
56 3
57 2
58 3
59 1
60 2

ANSWERS

# Answers

## Term 2

## Unit 9

### Page 39 Reading & Comprehension

1 Emma
2 Emma's sneezes
3 sisters
4 Emma
5 the first day of the holidays
6 Alice's hair flew up into a cone on the top of her head.
7 She moved slowly like a tortoise.
8 Her hair made a cone shape on the top of her head.
9 shocked
10 Answers will vary, e.g. Someone could get hurt./Bad things happen.
11 Answers will vary.

### Page 40 Grammar & Punctuation

1 like
2 on
3 in
4 in
5 at
6 under
7 off
8 on
9 E "Argh!" screamed Alice.
10 Q "What's the matter?" asked Mum.
11 E "Look what Emma did to my hair!" replied Alice.
12 Q "How did she do that?" enquired Mum.
13 S "I sneezed," admitted Emma. "That's all."
14 S "A sneeze can't do that," said Mum.
15 S "My sneeze did," stated Emma.

### Page 44 Phonic & Word Knowledge

1 doesn't, C
2 won't, C
3 Emma's, P
4 Alice's sister's, P
5 shouldn't, C
6 can't, C
7 else's, P
8 elephant's, P
9 he is
10 does not
11 could not
12 cannot
13 you have
14 I would
15 Everything
16 Nothing
17 anything
18 something
19 scatter – Answers will vary, e.g. scoop, scone.
20 sneeze – Answers will vary, e.g. snoop, snap.
21 blanket – Answers will vary, e.g. black, blue.
22 sprang – Answers will vary, e.g. sprint, sprinkle.
23 floor – Answers will vary, e.g. flavour, flower.
24 slowly – Answers will vary, e.g. slap, slam.

## Unit 10

### Page 43 Reading & Comprehension

1 matter
2 three
3 has weight and takes up space
4 molecules
5 solid
6 liquid
7 gas
8 solid
9 liquid
10 gas

### Page 44 Grammar & Punctuation

1 Molecules are the tiny parts that make up all matter.
2 Your shoes are made up of matter.
3 A gas is invisible.
4 Millions of molecules are in a tiny pinhead.
5 Everything is made of matter.
6 Your hair is a solid.
7 The helium in a balloon is a gas.
8 Honey is my favourite liquid.
9 When you leave solids alone, they stay in the same shape.
10 You cannot see air, but you can see what it does.
11 Chocolates will melt if they are left in the sun.
12 A solid will not change unless you do something to it.
13 Liquids may flow fast, or they may flow slowly.
14 People cannot see air, but they can see what it does.
15 stays
16 is
17 are
18 are

### Page 45 Phonic & Word Knowledge

1 tum + my
2 sun + screen
3 can + not
4 on + ly
5 quick + ly
6 bal + loon
7 e + ven
8 slow + ly
9 ga + ses
10 ho + ney
11 li + quids
12 bro + ken
13 syl + la + bles
14 a + ny + thing
15 e + ver + y + thing
16 con + tain + er
17 e + ver + y + where
18 in + for + ma + tion
19 beetle
20 candle
21 window
22 pirate
23 pencil
24 captain
25 cabbage
26 spider
27 carpet

## Unit 11

### Page 47 Reading & Comprehension

1 the Owl and the Pussy-Cat
2 to sea
3 a beautiful pea-green boat
4 some honey, and plenty of money
5 Answers will vary, e.g. They liked each other.
6 get married
7 a ring
8 the land where the bong-tree grows
9 a pig
10 a turkey
11 Answers will vary.

### Page 48 Grammar & Punctuation

1 some, number
2 elegant, quality
3 small, size
4 sweet, sound (or quality)
5 one, number
6 runcible
7 Answers will vary.
8 of the moon
9 on the hill
10 of bong-trees
11–13 Examples: The Owl sang to a small guitar./Pussy said, "Let us be married." /A Piggy-wig stood with a ring at the end of his nose./ The pig said he'd sell his ring./The turkey married them./They dined on mince and slices of quince./They danced by the light of the moon.

### Page 49 Phonic & Word Knowledge

1 honey
2 away
3 grows
4 sing
5 mince
6 spoon
7 star
8 land
9 stood
10 above
11 S
12 L
13 S
14 L
15 S
16 L
17 sing
18 bong-trees
19 wings
20 fangs
21 long
22 sang
23 bong-trees
24 sang
25 long
26 wings
27 Z
28 Z
29 S
30 Z

## Unit 12

### Page 51 Reading & Comprehension

1 cane toads
2 collected cane toads
3 thousands
4 They are ugly.
5 It's mean.
6 have always lived in Australia, weren't brought here
7 No
8 No
9 kindly
10 Answers will vary.

ANSWERS



TARGETING ENGLISH HOMEWORK YEAR 3 © PASCAL PRESS ISBN 978 1 925726 60 2

# Answers

## Page 52 Grammar & Punctuation

1. Cane toads are not native animals, so they shouldn't even be here.
2. Animals shouldn't eat cane toads because they will die.
3. You're not bad for the environment, but cane toads are.
4. Cane toads eat the native animals' food, so there is not enough food for them.
5. There were thousands of cane toads in my front yard, and I couldn't count them.
6. F
7. O
8. F
9. F
10. O
11. F
12. O
13. O
14. F
15. O
16. How many cane toads did you see last night?
17. Why do you think cane toads are a pest?
18. There are no native toads in Australia.

## Page 53 Phonic & Word Knowledge

1. really
2. any
3. funny
4. key
5. buy
6. their
7. where
8. hear
9. your
10. They're
11. wear
12. You're

13–24 there: chair, bear, pair
here: ear, deer, sphere, spear, gear
were: fern, nurse, bird, pearl

## Unit 13

## Page 55 Reading & Comprehension

1. True
2. silkworm
3. darkling beetle
4. caterpillar
5. caterpillar
6. pupa
7. butterfly
8. pupa
9. four
10. four

## Page 56 Grammar & Punctuation

1. Silk moths lay eggs, and butterflies lay eggs too.
2. Silkworm caterpillars turn into silk moths, but mealworms turn into darkling beetles.
3. A butterfly laid these eggs, so butterfly larvae will hatch out of them.
4. A young butterfly is called a larva, and sometimes it is called a caterpillar too.
5. A young butterfly is called a caterpillar, but a young darkling beetle is called a mealworm.
6. is
7. has
8. are
9. is
10. have
11. A
12. A
13. R
14. R

## Page 57 Phonic & Word Knowledge

1. beetles
2. moths
3. eggs
4. pupae
5. caterpillars
6. larvae
7. worms
8. butterflies
9. stages
10. cycles

11–25

| P | U | P | A | M | Y | S | T | A | G | E | C |
|---|---|---|---|---|---|---|---|---|---|---|---|
| A | W | B | R | E | S | H | I | J | A | G | T |
| Q | P | X | D | A | R | K | L | I | N | G | U |
| B | E | E | T | L | E | F | W | I | N | G | S |
| G | F | M | E | W | I | N | S | E | C | T | I |
| X | Q | O | R | O | D | P | I | O | L | T | O |
| C | A | T | E | R | P | I | L | L | A | R | B |
| Y | R | H | U | M | Z | N | K | J | R | C | V |
| C | A | D | U | L | T | C | W | D | V | K | Y |
| L | S | G | L | L | K | E | O | H | A | D | E |
| E | F | B | U | T | T | E | R | F | L | Y | B |
| W | H | Z | V | M | N | A | M | M | F | G | A |

## Unit 14

## Page 59 Reading & Comprehension

1. cloaks made by First Nations Australians
2. to keep warm and dry
3. where the people lived/what animal skins were available
4. animal skins
5. holding the skin in place
6. ate it
7. to be more beautiful
8. shells
9. ochre and black pigment
10. No
11. Answers will vary.

## Page 60 Grammar & Punctuation

1. S They made cloaks from the skins of animals.
2. S Some of the cloaks were long.
3. S They would cover a person from their neck down to their feet.
4. C The skin was held in place, and all the flesh was scraped off.
5. C They cut patterns in the leather, and they beat it with stone tools.
6. was
7. were
8. have
9. has
10. are
11. paint
12. cover
13. Cloaks are beautiful, warm and comfortable.
14. Kangaroos, wallabies, possums, wombats and koalas are all Australian animals.
15. To decorate their cloaks, First Nations Australians used quills, stone tools, ochre and black pigment.
16. First Nations Australians live in every state and territory in Australia including, New South Wales, Victoria, Queensland, Tasmania, South Australia, Western Australia, Northern Territory and the Australian Capital Territory.

## Page 61 Phonic & Word Knowledge

1. invitation
2. potion
3. motion
4. direction
5. vacation

| One syllable | Two syllables | Three syllables | More than three |
|---|---|---|---|
| 6 skin | 11 wooden | 16 animal | 21 comfortable |
| 7 things | 12 mussel | 17 kangaroos | 22 traditional |
| 8 cloak | 13 oyster | 18 beautiful | 23 identity |
| 9 warm | 14 surface | 19 echidna | 24 available |
| 10 stone | 15 person | 20 platypus | 25 Australia |

26–33 scrape, screen, scream, scratch, scrap, screw, scrub, screech

# Answers

## Unit 15

### Page 63 Reading & Comprehension

| | | | | | | | | | | | |
|---|---|---|---|---|---|---|---|---|---|---|---|
| 1 S | | 2 S | | | | | | | 3 R | E | 4 D |
| 5 C | O | U | N | T | D | O | W | N | | | A |
| R | | R | | | | | | | | | T |
| E | | F | | | | 6 C | A | T | | | A |
| E | | B | | 7 M | | I | | | 8 L | | |
| N | | O | | A | | R | | 9 T | I | M | E |
| | | A | | C | | C | | | G | | |
| 10 P | O | R | T | H | O | L | E | | 11 H | U | M |
| U | | D | | I | | E | | | T | | |
| S | | | | N | | | | | S | | |
| H | | | 12 L | E | V | E | R | S | | | |

### Page 64 Grammar & Punctuation

1 "Bee!" he shouts. "BEE!"
2 "Hit the red button!" Bee calls.
3 "Just like riding a surfboard," Sid chuckles.
4 "Where did that cat come from?" asks Bee.
5 "Watch out for the cat!" yells Bee.
6 shouted
7 muttered
8 chuckled
9 cried
10 asked
11 Sid looks at the screen and ^ sees the countdown. (Sid)
12 The cat jumps out and ^ heads for the open door. (the cat)
13 He looks out the porthole and ^ sees trees rush by. (he)
14 Sid switches on Camera One and ^ watches the screen. (Sid)
15 Bee is lying on the floor and ^ sees the cat in the time machine. (Bee)

### Page 65 Phonic & Word Knowledge

1 red
2 blue
3 red
4 red
5 blue
6 blue
7 red
8 red
9 red
10 red
11 red
12 blue
13 hutch
14 stitch
15 match
16 watch
17 witch
18 patch
19 catch
20 hatch
21 batch
22 fetch
23 sketch
24 pitch
25 ditch
26 shouted
27 shook
28 headed
29 saw
30 began

## Unit 16

### Pages 66–69 Review

Answers will vary.

## Term 2 Review

### Page 70 Reading & Comprehension

1 a big change
2 a butterfly
3 a dragonfly
4 four
5 three
6 nymph
7 larva
8 on a plant
9 in the water
10 Answers may vary, e.g. butterflies in the garden, dragonflies near water.

### Pages 71–72 Grammar & Punctuation

1 A big change in animals is called metamorphosis.
2 Another name for caterpillar is larva.
3 A young dragonfly is a nymph.
4 Dragonfly nymphs moult many times.
5 A butterfly's pupa is called a chrysalis.
6 A butterfly develops in four stages.
7 The egg is laid on a plant.
8 A caterpillar hatches from the egg.
9 An adult butterfly pushes out of the chrysalis in the spring.
10 I saw a dragonfly at the lake after school.
11 E "Look! A butterfly!" said Tan.
12 S "I think it has just emerged," said Emma.
13 Q "Why?" asked Tan.
14 S "Because it's waiting for its wings to dry," said Emma.
15 they, butterflies
16 they, dragonflies
17 it, dragonfly
18 they, children; them, butterflies
19 develops
20 moult
21 lays
22 hatch
23 change
24 some, number
25 hard, quality
26 transparent, colour
27 big, size
28 of the flowers
29 near the top of the plant
30 felt lonely
31 Butterflies don't have feelings.
32 Butterflies have four life stages, but dragonflies have three life stages.
33 The butterfly's pupa sticks to a twig, and it makes a hard shell.
34 A dragonfly grows wings, so it can fly.
35 O
36 F
37 F
38 O
39 is
40 has
41 have
42 were
43 hatch
44 moult
45 sip
46 live
47 Butterflies have four life stages: egg, caterpillar, pupa and adult.
48 Dragonflies have three life stages: egg, nymph and adult.
49 There are many different insects, including butterflies, dragonflies, moths, beetles, flies and mosquitos.
50 When we went to the lake, we saw butterflies, dragonflies, beetles and lots of flies.

### Pages 72–73 Phonic & Word Knowledge

1 can't, C
2 butterfly's, P
3 didn't, C
4 shed – Answers will vary, e.g. shade, shame, shadow, sheep.
5 spring – Answers will vary, e.g. sprout, spread, sprain, sprint.
6 plant – Answers will vary, e.g. play, plank, please, plight.
7 grow – Answers will vary, e.g. green, grasp, grace, grind.
8 change – Answers will vary, e.g. chocolate, cheese, chips, choice.
9 high
10 grows
11 range
12 door
13 thing
14 bird
15 pear
16 hear
17 burn
18 worse
19 Z
20 Z
21 Z
22 S

ANSWERS


TARGETING ENGLISH HOMEWORK YEAR 3 © PASCAL PRESS ISBN 978 1 925726 60 2

# Answers

## Page 73 Phonic & Word Knowledge (cont.)

| One syllable | Two syllables | Three syllables | More than three |
|---|---|---|---|
| 23 nymph | 27 adult | 31 butterfly | 35 metamorphosis |
| 24 grow | 28 pupa | 32 dragonfly | 36 development |
| 25 eggs | 29 larva | 33 develop | 37 caterpillar |
| 26 change | 30 moulting | 34 chrysalis | |

38 chrysalis
39 you
40 many
41 nymph
42 fly
43 their
44 where
45 hear
46 you're
47 butterflies
48 wings
49 children
50 pupae
51 changes
52 nymphs
53 watched
54 saw
55 moulted
56 flitted
57 changed
58 flew

## Term 3

## Unit 17

### Page 75 Reading & Comprehension

1 the hare
2 the hare and the tortoise
3 the other animals
4 lay down and went to sleep
5 He kept on going.
6 the tortoise
7 He didn't think the tortoise would catch up to him.
8 The hare went to sleep, but the tortoise kept on going.
9 proud
10 embarrassed
11 Answers will vary.

### Page 76 Grammar & Punctuation

1 faster, fastest
2 slower, slowest
3 quicker, quickest
4 smarter, smartest
5 stronger, strongest
6 bigger
7 smaller
8 oldest
9 taller
10 best
11 will
12 should
13 would
14 might
15 will/would
16 might/will
17 should/will
18 can

### Page 77 Phonic & Word Knowledge

1 enough, rough, tough. Answers will vary, e.g. buff, cuff, fluff, muff, puff.
2 high, thigh. Answers will vary, e.g. fly, fry, try, my, sigh.
3 cough. Answers will vary, e.g. scoff, trough.
4 laugh. Answers will vary, e.g. scarf, graph, half, laugh.
5 bough. Answers will vary, e.g. now, row, brow, plough, wow.
6 dough, though. Answers will vary, e.g. throw, sew, show, know, flow.
7 hair
8 hare
9 caught
10 court
11 saw
12 sore
13 you're
14 your
15 lie
16 lie
17 bell
18 belt
19 beat
20 cook
21 cork
22 fork

## Unit 18

### Page 79 Reading & Comprehension

1 to make it fun for everyone, to keep everyone safe
2 one
3 to tell people when they are not in the centre of the trampoline
4 nothing
5 It will be slippery.
6 They might be hit by the person on the trampoline.
7 the mat
8 the end of the frame
9 Focus on the trampoline.
10 Answers will vary.

### Page 80 Grammar & Punctuation

1 You should not use a trampoline if it is wet.
2 You should use bare feet when you are on the trampoline.
3 You should face the end of the frame when jumping on the trampoline.
4 Always put your hand up if you want to ask a question.
5 Cover your mouth when you yawn.
6 Cross the road on a pedestrian crossing.
7 only one, should
8 do not
9 must always
10 warning
11 underneath the trampoline
12 on the trampoline
13 off the centre, of the mat

### Page 81 Phonic & Word Knowledge

1 centre S
2 face S
3 focus C
4 control C
5 bounce S
6 choose CH
7 cold C
8 copy C
9 rich CH

| 'ar' vowel sound | 'er' vowel sound | 'or' vowel sound |
|---|---|---|
| 10 partner | 11 person | 13 warn |
| 15 scarf | 12 centre | 14 sure |
| 19 fast | 17 surf | 16 paw |
| 20 glass | 18 girl | 21 hawk |

22 2
23 2
24 3
25 3
26 2
27 3
28 1
29 2
30 3
31 singer
32 teacher
33 jogger
34 writer

## Unit 19

### Page 83 Reading & Comprehension

1 inside Crazy Chicken's fast-food restaurant
2 Answers will vary, e.g. menu board, order stations, tables, chairs, people, servers, cooks.
3 Narrator, Jed, Pirate Jack, Parrot, Captain Pete, Pirate Sal, Server
4 Answers will vary, e.g. Jed: is dressed like a pirate, talks like a pirate, doesn't want to be a real pirate; Captain Pete: likes treasure, thinks Jed is clever, wants Jed to become a pirate.
5 The narrator tells what is happening.
6 treasure
7 chicken nuggets
8 treasure, pieces of eight, nuggets, golden
9 A: Captain Pete: because he has an eye patch, parrot and captain's hat
B: Pirate Sale: because she is a girl and there's only one girl pirate
C: Jed: because he's just a boy and he's dressed up like a pirate
10 Answers will vary.

### Page 84 Grammar & Punctuation

1 "Do you want to place an order?" asked the server.
2 "Aye, that's what we be having. Four serves, me good sir," said Jed.
3 "That be the best treasure we've had for days!" said Pirate Sal.
4 "This be fine treasure, me lad, and you be one fine pirate," said Captain Pete.
5–6 Answers will vary, e.g. They were looking for treasure. Jed paid for the meals with his pocket money.
7–8 Answers will vary, e.g. Do you want to place an order? How would you like to join us on the high seas?
9–10 Answers will vary, e.g. Aye, that's what we be having! That be one fine treasure!
11 Answers will vary, e.g. curious, disgusted, happy, proud.
12 Answers will vary, e.g. surprised, excited.

ANSWERS

# Answers

### Page 85 Phonic & Word Knowledge

1 happy, sad
2 bottom, top
3 hard, easy
4 bad, good
5 scared, safe
6 that, this
7 surprised, bored
8 quick, slow
9 inside, outside
10 ashamed, proud
11 none, all
12 end, start
13 unsure, not sure
14 untidy, not tidy
15 unable, not able
16 unashamed, not ashamed
17 unsafe, not safe
18 unhealthy, not healthy
19 unused, not used
20 unsurprised, not surprised
21 unkind, not kind
22 unfair, not fair
23–28: treasure, gold, nuggets, aye, bounty, that be, this be, high seas
29 pirate

| G | C | H | I | C | K | E | N |
|---|---|---|---|---|---|---|---|
| O | E | I | G | H | T | P | U |
| L | I | G | R | B | A | S | G |
| D | D | H | T | E | B | E | G |
| T | R | E | A | S | U | R | E |
| B | O | U | N | T | Y | V | T |
| E | P | I | R | A | T | E | S |

## Unit 20

### Page 87 Reading & Comprehension

1 exercise
2 strength, flexibility, feeling good, sleep
3 makes you breathe faster, gets your heart pumping
4 skating, swimming, jumping rope
5 flexible
6 strong
7 normal weight
8 1 hour
9 exercise
10 Answers will vary.

### Page 88 Grammar & Punctuation

1 Exercise helps to make you flexible so you can stretch your body.
2 You can do push-ups, and/or you can row a boat.
3 Exercise helps you to sleep so you wake up feeling rested.
4 The best exercise makes you breathe faster, and it gets your heart pumping.
5 You will eat well, and everyday tasks will be easier.
6 good
7 helps, flexible
8 helps, stronger
9 easier, more fun
10 special, rid, bad
11 fitter
12 fittest
13 calmer
14 calmest
15 readier
16 readiest
17 healthier
18 healthiest
19 more flexible
20 most flexible

### Page 89 Phonic & Word Knowledge

1 boxer
2 ox
3 mixer
4 fox
5 six
6 T-Rex
7 taxi
8 text
9 sixty
10 lynx
11 exam
12 excuse
13 exhale
14 exercise
15 extra
16 football
17 daydream
18 weekday
19 gumball
20 everyday
21 daylight
22 basketball
23 meatball
24 eyeball
25 birthday
26 exercised, exercising
27 pumped, pumping
28 stretched, stretching
29 swam, swimming
30 made, making

## Unit 21

### Page 91 Reading & Comprehension

1 Australian reptiles
2 They are both Australian. They are both reptiles. They are both deadly. They both have scales.
3 It is one of the most venomous land snakes in the world.
4 It is the largest living reptile.
5 scales, sand-coloured skin, venom
6 scales, strong claws, sharp teeth
7 to lure prey
8 to swim
9 to warm up
10 to hunt

### Page 92 Grammar & Punctuation

1 full of poison
2 full of mountains
3 full of adventure
4 full of humour
5 full of fame
6 full of joy
7 full of disaster
8 full of hazards
9 Answers may vary, e.g. Crocodiles use their sharp teeth to tear meat.
10 Answers may vary, e.g. Death adders have sand-coloured skin to help them camouflage.
11 Answers may vary, e.g. Both death adders and crocodiles have scales to protect their skin.
12 Answers may vary, e.g. Crocodiles have strong claws for digging.
13 the
14 a
15 an
16 the
17 the
18 the
19 an
20 the

### Page 93 Phonic & Word Knowledge

1 f
2 c
3 h
4 b
5 a
6 d
7 j
8 i
9 e
10 g
11 dessert
12 desert
13 desert
14 dessert
15 desert
16 desert
17 reptile
18 fangs
19 adder
20 prey
21 camouflage
22 lure
23 mottled
24 hooded
25 venomous
26 survival
Word: sandwiches

## Unit 22

### Page 95 Reading & Comprehension

1 the remains of something that lived long ago
2 They decay.
3 to break down or rot
4 They tell us about things that lived in the past.
5 millions of years
6 draw
7 mould: the shape of a plant or animal in a rock
cast: minerals fill a mould in the shape of a plant or animal
trace: the shape of a plant or animal in a rock
8 something found in nature that is not plant or animal
9 soil or sand
10 Answers will vary.

### Page 96 Grammar & Punctuation

1 are
2 is
3 are
4 is
5 is
6 was
7 rots
8 rot
9 leaves
10 leave
11 tells
12 tell
13 Moulds, casts and traces are all types of fossils.
14 A trace fossil is made from things such as footprints, nests, burrows, tracks or trails.
15 Minerals like calcium, potassium, sodium and sulphur occur naturally in nature.
16 Scientists have found fossils of dinosaurs, mastodons and sabre tooth tigers.
17 Fossils have been found in Australia in Winton, Murgon, Canowindra and other places.
18 Fossils can be found almost anywhere in rocks, soil or clay.





TARGETING ENGLISH HOMEWORK YEAR 3 © PASCAL PRESS ISBN 978 1 925726 60 2

# Answers

## Page 97 Phonic & Word Knowledge

1 millions
2 rocks
3 minerals
4 footprints
5 leaves
6 nests
7 scientists
8 teeth
9 kinds
10 moulds
11–30

| | | | | | | | | | | | |
|---|---|---|---|---|---|---|---|---|---|---|---|
| S | E | D | I | M | E | N | T | V | C | M | B |
| C | M | A | L | I | M | A | R | K | A | I | O |
| I | O | U | A | L | A | Y | E | R | S | N | N |
| E | U | B | P | L | A | N | T | L | T | E | E |
| N | L | A | N | I | M | A | L | D | S | R | T |
| T | D | E | R | O | C | K | B | E | H | A | E |
| I | F | R | O | N | S | S | U | C | A | L | E |
| S | F | O | S | S | I | L | R | A | P | I | T |
| T | L | T | R | A | C | E | Y | Y | E | S | H |

31 valuable fossils

## Unit 23

### Page 99 Reading & Comprehension

| | | | | | | | | | | | |
|---|---|---|---|---|---|---|---|---|---|---|---|
| | | [1]V | | | [2]H | | | | | | [3]C |
| [4]B | O | O | S | T | E | R | [5]S | | | | U |
| U | | I | | | A | | I | | [6]Q | | M |
| T | | C | | | D | | D | | U | | M |
| T | | E | | | S | | | | I | | U |
| O | | | [7]A | W | E | S | O | M | E | | N |
| N | | [8]B | | | T | | | | T | | I |
| [9]S | P | E | E | D | | [10]C | | | | | C |
| | | E | | | | [11]I | [12]N | | | | A |
| | | | | | | [13]R | O | C | K | E | T |
| | [14]C | O | N | T | A | C | T | | | | O |
| | | | | | | L | | [15]Y | E | A | R |
| [16]M | A | C | H | I | N | E | | | | | |

### Page 100 Grammar & Punctuation

1 switches, D
2 is, R
3 shouts, S
4 wonders, T
5 enjoys, F
6 worries, F
7 is, R
8 looks, D
9 remembers, T
10 says, S
11 I am glad to hear your voice.
12 Sid is relieved when the rock spins away.
13 Time travel is the best.
14 Sid has an enjoyable ride in the time machine.
15 Bee is glad to talk with Sid on the wave communicator.
16 The machine pushed upward.
17 The rock was spinning away.
18 Sid spoke cheerfully into the headset.
19 Sid left in the time machine yesterday.
20 Sid will be back soon.

### Page 101 Phonic & Word Knowledge

| 'hard g' sound as in **go** | | 'soft g' sound as in **gem** | |
|---|---|---|---|
| 1 glue | 5 mug | 9 gel | 13 bridge |
| 2 gum | 6 game | 10 giant | 14 edge |
| 3 goat | 7 gate | 11 enjoy | 15 large |
| 4 green | 8 gap | 12 fudge | 16 just |

17 gnat
18 gnu
19 stop sign
20 gnome
21 knife
22 knot
23 knitting
24 knight
25 know
26 knew
27 knowledge
28 sign
29 design
30 gnats
31 know
32 sea
33 for
34 knot
35 way

## Unit 24

### Page 102–105 Movie Review

Answers will vary.

## Term 3 Review

### Page 106 Reading & Comprehension

1 keep safe
2 Yes
3 You may be injured.
4 walking, eating, getting dressed, going to school
5 playground
6 wearing appropriate clothing
7 riding a bicycle, swimming, playing cricket
8 skateboarder, footballer, in the snow
9 Answers will vary.
10 Answers will vary.

### Page 107–108 Grammar & Punctuation

1 best
2 stronger
3 fastest
4 safer
5 must
6 can
7 will
8 might
9 Avoid danger zones.
10 Wear the right gear for the activity.
11 Find safer ways to play.
12 important, safe, all times
13 better, avoid
14 matters
15 at the same time
16 to do everyday things
17 by avoiding danger zones
18 in bed for weeks
19 "Do you want to go down to the skatepark?" asked Tan.
20 "Sure! That sounds like fun," said Tema.
21 "Don't forget your safety gear!" said Dad.
22 Where are we going this afternoon?
23 We are going to the skateboard park.
24 This is fun!
25 It is important to have fun, but it is important to stay safe at the same time.
26 You might get sick, or you might be injured.
27 full of danger
28 full of advantages
29 full of poison
30 full of perils
31 full of hazards
32 full of joy
33 the
34 a
35 the
36 an
37 a
38 are
39 is
40 will
41 When you ride roller skates, you need to wear roller skates, knee pads, elbow pads, wrist pads and a helmet.
42 D Tema rode his skateboard safely.
43 S "Awesome," Tan said loudly.
44 R, R, T "I am glad they are safe," Dad thought quietly.
45 local, skatepark
46 busy, skatepark
47 happy, children
48 one, hurt, child

### Page 108–109 Phonic & Word Knowledge

1 enough
2 high
3 cough
4 dough
5 court
6 saw
7 here
8 C activity
9 S centre
10 C school
11 CH chomp
12 CH choose
13 S city

| 'ar' vowel sound | 'er' vowel sound | 'or' vowel sound |
|---|---|---|
| 14 heart<br>15 laugh<br>21 half | 16 pearl<br>17 surf<br>19 bird | 18 warm<br>20 water |

ANSWERS

# Answers

## Page 108–109 Phonic & Word Knowledge (cont.)

22 3
23 1
24 2
25 3
26 3
27 4
28 skater
29 jumper
30 runner
31 unimportant
32 special
33 wrong
34 unadventurous
35 unsafe
36 risk-free
37 worse
38 unhurt
39 unhappy
40 unsafe
41 discomfort
42 incomplete
43 incorrect
44 disapprove
45 six
46 exam
47 mixing
48 extra
49 butterfly
50 football
51 daylight
52 exercising, will exercise
53 swam, swimming
54–56 sheep: need, be, eat
57–59 goat: know, zones, no
60–62 bin: sick, things, if
63–65 sun: some, one, fun
66–68 moon: move, who, school
69–71 kite: time, right, by
72–74 mop: what, so, sock
75–77 egg: bad, help, dressed
78–80 cat: and, have, can
81–83 cake: same, may, safe

## Term 4

## Unit 25

### Page 111 Reading & Comprehension

1 Tessa
2 on a farm
3 They have fun together.
4 They do funny and fun things.
5 Tessa has heard her great-grandparents and thinks they are funny.
6 puzzles and colouring
7 He agrees.
8 She couldn't wait to get there.
9 Sleeping Beauty
10 Answers will vary.

### Page 112 Grammar & Punctuation

1 V, Tessa loved spending school holidays on the farm with her great-grandparents.
2 A, They were fun.
3 A, Tessa was a very lucky girl.
4 A, It was great to be back.
5 A, They had planned so many exciting things to do.
6 V, Dad grinned when he thought about Tessa's great-grandparents.
7 They finally arrived at the farm. (when)
8 The trip from the farm took forever. (when)
9 Tessa spoke excitedly about her holiday. (how)
10 Great Grandpop Alfred joked frequently. (when)
11 Tessa giggled quietly at Great Grandpop Alfred's jokes. (how)
12 Tessa loved going away for the holidays. (where)
13 at/on
14 for
15 from
16 in
17 at/with
18 until
19 between
20 to

### Page 113 Phonic & Word Knowledge

1 holiday
2 finally
3 every
4 funny
5 lucky
6 holidays
7 parties
8 toys
9 monkeys
10 ferries
11 keys
12 families
13 fairies
14 babies
15 jellies
16 funnily
17 sleepily
18 kindly
19 slowly
20 jokingly
21 softly
22 greedily
23 lately
24 boringly
25 excitedly
26 backpack
27 grandparents
28 everyone
29 summertime
30 farmyard

## Unit 26

### Page 115 Reading & Comprehension

1 petroleum jelly
2 sugar
3 cover
4 shells
5 plaster of Paris
6 read the direction on the plaster of Paris packet
7 instructions
8 about 1 cm
9 overnight
10 Answers will vary, e.g. so you can remove them when the paster sets

### Page 116 Grammar & Punctuation

1 coat, set, follow, have, spread, use, press, try, let
2–5 Answers will vary.

| 6 For fossils, you need: | 7 No plaster of Paris, then use: | 8 Scientists study remains of: |
|---|---|---|
| • leaves | • flour and water | • bones |
| • shells | • clay | • teeth |
| • feathers | • plasticine | • footprints |
| • bones | • modelling clay | • feathers |
| • bark | | • fur |
| • flower petals | | • trails |

9 A scientist who studies fossils is called a paleontologist. There are many types of fossils including seashells, footprints, wood, leaf impressions, nests and even burrows.

### Page 117 Phonic & Word Knowledge

1 loaves
2 halves
3 children
4 flies
5 hooves
6 shells
7 branches
8 knives
9 calves
10 sheep
11 B
12 A
13 B
14 A
15 A
16 B

| One syllable | Two syllables | Three syllables | More than three |
|---|---|---|---|
| 17 leaf | 21 plaster | 25 direction | 29 paleontologist |
| 18 shells | 22 cardboard | 26 carefully | 30 television |
| 19 spread | 23 follow | 27 procedure | 31 petroleum |
| 20 bowl | 24 gently | 28 overnight | 32 scientific |

## Unit 27

### Page 118–119 Reading & Comprehension

1 Verse 1 spring, Verse 2 summer, Verse 3 autumn, Verse 4 winter
2 Answers will vary, e.g. early, birds chirrup, wake up; Nature wakes up after winter.
3 Answers will vary, e.g. shimmer, dark clouds, storms; It gets hot and stormy in summer.
4 Answers will vary, e.g. golden leaves, falling, green leaves hold on; Leaves turn different colours and fall off the trees in autumn.
5 Answers will vary, e.g. bare branches, dead leaves, icy winds; It is cold in winter.
6 Answers will vary, e.g. chirp, sing.
7 They are far away.
8 The leaves are golden in the autumn when it starts to get cold.
9 because they are dry
10 Answers will vary.

ANSWERS

# Answers

## Page 120 Grammar & Punctuation

1 Dark clouds gobble up blue skies
2 Bare branches shiver
3 Kites dance in the breeze.
4 The blinking 'open' sign refused to let us pass.
5 The book jumped off the shelf and into my heart.
6 The phone insisted that I answer it straightaway.
7 The tiny boats played hide and seek in the waves.
8 The moon looked down kindly on the lonely travellers.
9–12 Answers will vary.
13 Birds chirruped and told the sleepy head to wake up.
14 The purple hills shimmered in the distance.
15 The green leaves held on tight to the trees.
16 Icy winds blew cold through the valley.
17 The full moon lit the way.
18 The angry wind tossed everything about.
19 The sun shower tiptoed across the playground.
20 Hats and sunscreen promised protection against the harsh sunlight.

## Page 121 Phonic & Word Knowledge

1 sizzle
2 screech
3 moo
4 pop
5 buzz
6 splash
7 creak, creak, creak
8 clatter
9 beep, beep, beep
10 grunt
11 The greedy green goblin gets angry if someone gobbles his gourmet food.
12 Many mighty magicians make mean monsters meek.
13 The sea serpent slides silently through the still waters.
14 Ten tiny turtles try to catch the turning tide before it's too late.
15 Dreadful dragons dreamed up dastardly deeds to destroy and dominate.
16 Answers will vary.

## Unit 28

## Page 123 Reading & Comprehension

1 a hoverboard
2 Bluetooth speaker
3 Zip It Hoverboard
4 order online
5 $50
6 safety approved, safest battery on the market, lifetime guarantee, better than a skateboard
7 It's not harmful to the environment.
8 LED lights, rechargeable battery
9 It's inexpensive.
10 Answers will vary.

## Page 124 Grammar & Punctuation

1 impress, new
2 latest, greatest
3 loves, new
4 more fun
5 best
6 S
7 F
8 F
9 S
10 S
11 F
12 F
13–15 Answers will vary.
16 New safety features!
17 The best hoverboard in the world!
18 You will enjoy riding your hoverboard around the neighbourhood.
19 The first 100 customers to order online will receive a $50 discount. (or !)
20 You won't believe how much fun riding a hoverboard can be.

## Page 125 Phonic & Word Knowledge

1 unsafe
2 unwell
3 incomplete
4 untie
5 inflexible
6 redo
7 reuse
8 return
9 retell
10 remake
11 rerun
12 rejoin
13 reheat
14 reread
15 rebuild
16 skateboard
17 blackboard
18 baseboard
19 sailboard
20 headboard
21 surfboard
22 overboard
23 whiteboard
24 cardboard
25 outboard
26 outboard
27 surfboard
28 blackboard
29 overboard
30 cardboard

## Unit 29

## Page 127 Reading & Comprehension

1 three
2 rocky road
3 igneous
4 tuff
5 basalt
6 igneous
7 sedimentary
8 metamorphic
9 changing
10 Answers will vary.

## Page 128 Grammar & Punctuation

1 are made
2 take
3 form
4 is
5 are
6 cement
7 Hot molten rock forms inside volcanoes.
8 A metamorphic rock is made by heat from the Earth's core.
9 It takes millions of years for sedimentary rocks to form.
10 Hot molten rock inside a volcano is called magma or lava.
11 A metamorphic rock forms under the surface of the Earth.
12 Sandstone is a type of sedimentary rock.
13–14 Answers will vary.

## Page 129 Phonic & Word Knowledge

1 bodies
2 babies
3 donkeys
4 skies
5 libraries
6 stories
7 keys
8 journeys
9 factories
10 days

| | Base verb | Did (past tense) | Doing now (present tense) |
|---|---|---|---|
| 11 | play | played | playing |
| 12 | hurry | hurried | hurrying |
| 13 | try | tried | trying |
| 14 | fly | flew | flying |
| 15 | buy | bought | buying |
| 16 | empty | emptied | emptying |
| 17 | enjoy | enjoyed | enjoying |
| 18 | cry | cried | crying |
| 19 | copy | copied | copying |
| 20 | reply | replied | replying |

| One syllable | Two syllables | Three syllables | More than three |
|---|---|---|---|
| 21 rocks | 24 surface | 27 igneous | 30 sedimentary |
| 22 streams | 25 pressure | 28 sediments | 31 metamorphic |
| 23 Earth | 26 magma | 29 volcano | 32 geologist |

## Unit 30

## Page 131 Reading & Comprehension

1 thousands of years
2 weapons, tools, paint
3 hard and durable
4 ochre
5 grinding stones
6 two
7 a core
8 flaked stone tools
9 timber
10 Answers will vary.

ANSWERS

# Answers

## Page 132 Grammar & Punctuation

1. Rocks and stones have been used for making weapons and tools. (why)
2. The edges of rocks are sharpened to make thin blades or sharp points. (why)
3. First Nations peoples have used rocks and stones for thousands of years. (when)
4. Ochre is mixed with water. (how)
5. Flowers were placed between two stones. (where)
6. Flaked stone tools were made by hitting stones together. (how)
7. The sharp-edged rock could be fastened to timber. (where)
8. First Nations peoples lived in Australia before Europeans arrived in 1788. (when)
9. 
   - axes
   - spearheads
   - other weapons
   - utensils
   - paint
10. 
    - bulbs
    - berries
    - seeds
    - insects
    - flowers
11. The First Nations peoples of Australia eat a wide variety of plant food, including fruit, nuts, seeds, vegetables, roots and grasses.
12. The First Nations peoples of Australia eat a wide variety of meat, including kangaroos, possums, emus, goannas, turtles, fish and shellfish.
13. The First Nations peoples use every part of the wattle tree in different ways, including the leaves, bark, seeds, roots, flowers, sap and wood.

## Page 133 Phonic & Word Knowledge

1. fasten
2. moisten
3. listen
4. fasten
5. soften
6. bridge
7. budgie
8. badge
9. fridge
10. cage
11. judge

| 'ck' sound | 'soft c' sound | 'ch' sound | 'sh' sound |
|---|---|---|---|
| 12 ochre | 15 piece | 18 change | 21 chef |
| 13 school | 16 city | 19 lunch | 22 chute |
| 14 chemist | 17 cent | 20 chess | 23 machine |

## Unit 31

## Page 135 Reading & Comprehension

| | | | | | | | | | | | |
|---|---|---|---|---|---|---|---|---|---|---|---|
| 1 S | O | M | E | W | H | E | R | E | | | |
| I | | | | | | | | | 2 B | | |
| 3 D | R | A | W | 4 B | R | I | D | G | E | | |
| | | | | E | | | | | N | | 5 S |
| | 6 R | E | 7 M | E | M | B | E | R | S | | K |
| | | | A | | | | | | O | | Y |
| 8 C | H | E | C | K | | | 9 P | A | N | E | L |
| O | | | H | | 10 H | | | | | | I |
| N | | 11 T | I | M | E | | | | 12 Z | | G |
| T | | | N | | A | | | | O | | H |
| R | | | E | | D | | | | N | | T |
| 13 O | U | T | | | 14 S | Y | S | T | E | M | S |
| L | | | | | E | | | | | | |
| | | 15 P | O | R | T | H | O | L | E | | |

## Page 136 Grammar & Punctuation

1. R, is
2. D, built
3. T, wishes / D, go
4. D, sits
5. S, says
6. T, remembered / S, told
7. D, stand
8. D, found / S, asks
9. T, thought
10. R, has
11. Sid is lost in his time machine, and Bee and Benson don't know where.
12. Sid is lost in his time machine.
13. Bee and Benson don't know where.
14. Bee wishes she could go, but someone has to stay behind.
15. Bee wishes she could go.
16. Someone has to stay behind.
17. Benson presses the START button so the machine will start.
18. Benson presses the START button.
19. The machine will start.
20. Benson looked everywhere, yet he couldn't see Bee.
21. Benson looked everywhere.
22. He couldn't see Bee.
23. The people wore silver suits, and they rode on solar wave riders.
24. The building looked like a silver bubble, but it had skylights on the top.

## Page 137 Phonic & Word Knowledge

1. distrust
2. dislike
3. disobey
4. disinfect
5. disagreed
6. dishonest
7. unhappy
8. inactive
9. uncomfortable
10. disarm
11. disrespectful
12. incorrect

13–20 somewhere, someone, headset, porthole, glass-topped, skylight, drawbridge, x-ray

21. skylight
22. candlelight
23. moonlight
24. sunlight
25. tail-light
26. headlight
27. searchlight
28. flashlight
29. highlight
30. floodlight

31–40 Side is lost sumwhere in time. Bee and Benson maid a knew time mashine to look for him. Benson went in the machine, but Bee staid beehind. Benson landed in a strange werld wear everythink looked different.
Sid, somewhere, made, new, machine, stayed, behind, world, where, everything

## Unit 32

## Page 138–141 Review

Answers will vary.

## Term 4 Review

## Page 142 Reading & Comprehension

1. She was visiting her great-grandparents.
2. helped make a cake
3. a chocolate cake
4. for dessert
5. She hid under the table.
6. Great Gran didn't want her to see what was going into the cake.
7. magic stuff
8. remove her wrinkles
9. Answers will vary, e.g. nonsense.
10. Answers will vary, e.g. I don't care.

ANSWERS



TARGETING ENGLISH HOMEWORK YEAR 3 © PASCAL PRESS ISBN 978 1 925726 60 2

# Answers

## Page 143–144 Grammar & Punctuation

1 A, super-special
2 A, magic
3 V, snorted
4 They made a chocolate cake first. (when)
5 Tessa stayed quietly under the table. (how)
6 Great Gran sat down on the chair. (where)
7–9 Answers will vary.
10–12 Answers will vary.
13 Answers will vary, e.g. I can see Tessa, Great Gran Em, Great Grandpop, a calendar, a jug, a radio, a table and chairs.
14–15 Answers will vary.
16 Tessa and Great Grandma Em baked a super-special chocolate cake for dessert.
17 Great Grandma Em put the secret ingredients into the huge mixing bowl.
18 The first thing Tessa did was bake a cake.
19 S
20 S
21 F
22 F
23 was
24 told
25 made, hid
26 They baked a super-special chocolate cake for dessert.
27 Everything went into the huge mixing bowl.
28 Great Gran put the cake into the hot oven to bake.
29 S, said
30 T, wondered / R, was
31 F, relaxed
32 D, hid
33 R, is
34 They mixed the ingredients together.
35 Great Gran put the cake in the oven.
36 "You sit under the table while I put in the secret ingredients," said Great Gran
37 "Em thinks the cake will hide all her wrinkles," said Great Grandpop.
38 "This is the best cake ever. I wish I knew what went into it," said Tessa.

## Page 144–145 Phonic & Word Knowledge

1 bowls
2 witches
3 babies
4 recipes
5 halves
6 fish
7 hungrily
8 kindly
9 smoothly
10 carelessly
11 secretly
12 quietly
13 day + light
14 super + special
15 summer + time
16 grand + children
17–18 Answers will vary.

| One syllable | Two syllables | Three syllables | More than three |
|---|---|---|---|
| 19 huge | 22 special | 25 grandparents | 28 everything |
| 20 cake | 23 dessert | 26 chocolate | 29 ingredients |
| 21 bowl | 24 mixture | 27 grandmother | 30 misbehaving |

31 creaked
32 boom
33 splash
34 g
35 t
36 not comfortable
37 not correct
38 not qualified
39 baked, baking
40 hid, hiding
41 saw, seeing
42 popped, popping

| 'ck' sound | 'soft c' sound | 'ch' sound | 'sh' sound |
|---|---|---|---|
| 43 magic | 47 recipe | 51 chuckled | 55 special |
| 44 chuckled | 48 piece | 52 chocolate | 56 chef |
| 45 chocolate | 49 city | 53 lunch | 57 chute |
| 46 secret | 50 cent | 54 witch | 58 machine |

ANSWERS

ANSWERS



TARGETING ENGLISH HOMEWORK YEAR 3 © PASCAL PRESS ISBN 978 1 925726 60 2

ANSWERS

ANSWERS



TARGETING ENGLISH HOMEWORK YEAR 3 © PASCAL PRESS ISBN 978 1 925726 60 2